I0125249

Fortunato Musella
Monocratic Government

De Gruyter Contemporary Social Sciences

—

Volume 8

Fortunato Musella

Monocratic Government

The Impact of Personalisation
on Democratic Regimes

DE GRUYTER

ISBN 978-3-11-072471-4
e-ISBN (PDF) 978-3-11-072172-0
e-ISBN (EPUB) 978-3-11-072183-6
ISSN 2747-5689
e-ISSN 2747-5697

Library of Congress Control Number: 2021951155

Bibliographic information published by the Deutsche Nationalbibliothek
The Deutsche Nationalbibliothek lists this publication in the Deutsche Nationalbibliografie;
detailed bibliographic data are available on the Internet at http://dnb.dnb.de.

© 2024 Walter de Gruyter GmbH, Berlin/Boston
This volume is text- and page-identical with the hardback published in 2022.
Cover image: f11photo / iStock / Getty Images Plus

www.degruyter.com

Contents

1 Introduction. Political leaders at times of the personalisation of the masses

1.1 Political personalisation: macro and micro

On the 6th of January, 2021 people broke into the Capitol building in Washington DC in an attempt to overturn the defeat of Donald Trump. It was the last act of a four-year period when the President had progressively reinforced his position[1] to the point that he had become so strong that he did not want to leave his office[2]. The world remained shocked by the attack against one of the symbols of Western democracy – this iconic sanctuary of representational democracy was under attack by a mass of rioters. Not orchestrated through a complex political organisation, but often connected through social media, they acted on the basis of a one-to-one and emotional linkage to their president who had failed to be re-elected. The core institution in the development of liberal democracy, the Congress, had reached its lowest point in the history of the United States.

American institutions had arrived at this point after the century long establishment of the presidential republic[3]. Although the US Constitution was written

Note: The research leading to this book has been conducted as part of a Relevant Research Project of National Interest (PRIN) 2020 – 2023 "Monocratic Government. The Impact of Personalisation on Contemporary Political Regimes" – Principal Investigator: Prof. Fortunato Musella.

1 A rich strand of literature has looked at the figure of Donald Trump with a comparative and historical perspective, by underlining his exceptional origin as well as his progression on a long-term path of the American presidency, see E.S. Steven, *The Trump presidency: Outsider in the oval office*, Lanham, Rowman, & Littlefield, 2017; J.P. Pfiffner, *The unusual presidency of Donald Trump*, in *Political Insight*, 8, 2, 2017, pp. 9 – 11; J.P. Pfiffner, *The contemporary presidency: Organizing the Trump presidency*, in *Presidential Studies Quarterly*, 48, 1, 2018, pp. 153 – 167; S.N. Siegel, *Political Norms, Constitutional Conventions, and President Donald Trump*, in *Indiana Law Journal*, 93, 2018, pp. 177– 205.

2 The current phase of erosion of the American democracy, 'because of the interactive effects of institutions, identity, and norm-breaking', and the effect of the Trump presidency in such processes, is described in R.C. Lieberman, S. Mettler, T.B Pepinsky, K.M. Roberts, and R. Valelly, *The Trump presidency and American democracy: A historical and comparative analysis*, in *Perspectives on Politics*, 17, 2, 2019, pp. 470 – 479.

3 On the presidential foundation of the American republic, see R.E. Neustadt, *Presidential power: The politics of leadership*, New York, Free Press 1990 [1960]; A.M. Schlesinger, *The Imperial Presidency*, Boston, Houghton Mifflin, 1973; R. Pious, *The American Presidency*, New York, Basic Books, 1979; T.J. Lowi, *The Personal President. Power Invested, Promise Unfulfilled*, Ithaca-New York, Cornell University Press, 1985; J.K. Tulis, *The Rhetorical Presidency*, Princeton,

https://doi.org/10.1515/9783110721720-001

as the first and most accurate application of the doctrine of the separation of powers (Bognetti 2001; Mikuli 2021), and the original Framers were 'mostly concerned – and sometimes obsessed – with the so-called "tyranny of the majority"'[4] (Zeno-Zencovich 2020, 3), American democracy has realised the most impressive trend of concentration of institutional prerogatives on the role of the president since the beginning of the nineteenth century. Today, many commentators have recognised the fall of the Founding Fathers in circumstances where the 'American constitutional system still relies on brinksmanship to control the plebiscitarian presidency' (Ackerman 2010, 2017, 245 – 246). While the country has bet on strong presidents to realise fast decision-making and to bolster international vitality, democracy has survived only by balancing their overflowing power through a well-defined institutional setting. And now, as in Lowi's prophecy, the future of democratic institutions rests upon the resolution of the urgent problem of the rise of the presidency as an increasingly dominant office that communicates directly with a mass constituency, thus bypassing mediating institutions such as parliament and political parties[5] (Lowi 1985).

Democracy is under pressure in other areas of the world as well. The strengthening of political leaders in a direct connection with individualistic masses is not part of American exceptionalism[6], but a diffuse phenomenon in the international scenario. In several contemporary democracies the general thesis remains confirmed, calling for greater attention from political scientists, in that 'the century that has just started will be the age of personalisation, just as the previous one was the century of mass collective actors' (Musella and Webb 2015, 226). On the one hand, after the decline of the structural and ideo-

---

Princeton University Press, 1987; S. Fabbrini, *Il presidenzialismo Americano. Governare gli Stati Uniti*, Roma-Bari, Laterza, 1993; F. Musella, *Il Premier diviso. Italia tra presidentialismo e parlamentarismo*, Bocconi, Milano, 2012.

4 Initially, the main risks of concentration of power were associated with the strengthening of political parties: 'in James Madison's most famous essay, he leaves no doubt that he has party in mind when he expresses grave fear of "factions" which can become majorities (Federalist #10)', see M. Calise and T.J. Lowi, *Party*, in *Hyperpolitics. An Interactive Dictionary of Political Science Concepts*, Chicago, Chicago University Press, 2010, p. 171–177, p. 171.

5 On the affirmation of the plebiscitary conception of the American Presidents see R.A. Dahl, *Myth of the Presidential Mandate*, in *Political Science Quarterly*, 105, 3, 1990, pp. 335 – 372; B.D. Wood, *The Myth of Presidential Representation*, Cambridge, Cambridge University Press, 2009; R. Tatalovich, S.E. Schiern (eds.), *The Presidency and Political Science. Paradigms of presidential power from the founding fathers to the present*, London, Routledge, 2014.

6 The theory of Americanism is supported by a very long cultural tradition, that may include exponents such de Tocqueville and Stalin, and which is discussed in M.S. Lipset, *The first new nation: The United States in historical and comparative perspective*, New York, Basic Books, 1963.

logical foundations of Western democracies, a radical shift from collective to individual actors and institutions has occurred in several political systems. On the other, individualism, which had represented the dominant Western culture since the 1970s (Lash 1979), and which is now fed by the widespread diffusion of new technologies, may largely flourish with the progressive disaggregation of the main vehicles of collective identities. Through the general collapse of collective, contemporary society, it is now made up by a swarm, rather than a mass unified by a single spirit, which marches in one direction (Byung-Chul Ha 2017, 12).

Consequently, as an increasing number of scholars have underlined, as a result of the prevalence of the personalisation in the changing traits of representative regimes in the last years, most of them look at the process with preoccupation, as the new course poses unknown challenges (Mair 2013; Cross, Katz and Pruysers 2018; Rahat and Kenig 2018; Garzia 2019; Levy 2021).

While political leaders have gained centrality on the democratic scene, a process of fragmentation has occurred at the mass level where political parties play their traditional role with difficulty. This book analyses the consequences of both the personalisation of political leaders and the masses on democratic government, by asking whether it is possible to keep together *demos* and *kratos* in a post-particratic context.

1.2 Personalisation of government

While personal politics has been strongly associated with a pre-democratic or undemocratic realm of politics, it has also proved to be compatible with the routines, discourse, and boundaries of liberal regimes (Calise 2011, 1860). The laboratory for this combination – which is quite unnatural according to traditional political theory[7] – was in the United States, paving the way for the rise of strong

---

7 Three decades on from Giovanni Sartori's statement, his judgment is still valid: 'the vital role of leadership is frequently acknowledged; nonetheless it obtains only a negligible status within the theory of democracy' (G. Sartori, *Democracy Theory Revisited*, Chatham, Chatham House, 1987). Political science has often tended to underline the tension between democracy as a system of government centred on the *demos* and the word *leadership* referring to a concentration of power on a single person, so that the 'fear of leadership is the basic justification of democracy' (K.P. Ruscio, *The Leadership Dilemma in Modern Democracy*, London, Edward Elgar Publishing, 2004, ix; J. Kane and H. Patapan, *The Democratic Leader: How Democracy Defines, Empowers and Limits Its Leaders*, Oxford, Oxford University Press, 2012). This point has been developed in Chapter 1: *Leader and party: still an Oxymoron*, in F. Musella, *Political Leaders beyond Party Politics*, Cham, Palgrave, 2018, pp. 1–30.

presidents in a context of free elections. The choice of a prominent figure at the top of the American institutions was at first opposed because of its similarity with the British monarchy, which had been felt to be a symbol of political oppression. The American Framers remained quite suspicious of concentrations of power, so that their debates presented ambivalent feelings about executive power – and it is very significant that the American government was never defined as the 'executive' (Pious 2007, 66; Fisher 1971; Best 1987). Yet a few years after US independence, the presidency was introduced at both the federal and state level, as it needed to have a large and ambitious national potency. The Founding Fathers perceived the advantage in having a unique symbol and agent for so large a territory as the United States, the largest democracy in the world. They agreed with Hamilton's statement in the 70th Federalist, 'energy in the Executive is a leading character in the definition of good government'. The idea of a 'personalised state' appeared as a promising and challenging innovation in the landscape of Western states, which was also open to adoption by other contemporary democracies[8], although this was not always easy.

Coming as a necessary compromise, the precise definition of an institutional framework acting as a check and balance system derived from the perceived peril that one branch would be able to control too much power. The institutional model of a president-centred constitutional asset, as represented by the American Republic, has been made possible through the precise application of the doctrine of separation of powers formulated in Montesquieu's *Spirit of Laws* (1748). Indeed, the US architecture of power was strongly based on this French philosopher's discovery 'that liberty might be the result not of superior civic morality but of a correct organisation of the State' (Sabine 1961). The concentration of power in a single leader had to be avoided through balanced institutions. The following words that Hamilton pronounced just after the foundation of the Republic may be underlined, so intense was the fear that the presidency would turn into despotism: 'in framing a government which is to be administered by men over men, the great difficulty lies in this: you must first enable the government to control the governed; and the next place, oblige it to control itself' (James Hamilton, The Federalist No. 51). The system of separation of powers was the way to reconcile personal powers with democratic ideals.

Nevertheless, the aspirations of the Framers became increasingly difficult to realise during the nineteenth century, as the US executive branch of the govern-

---

8 In particular, the widespread application of this concept in Latin American countries tends to show the fragility of the presidential system when combined with multi-party systems, as in the main thesis of the volume A. Valenzuela and J. Linz (eds.), *The Failure of Presidential Democracy*, Baltimore, Johns Hopkins University Press, 1994.

ment seemed to acquire disproportionate power. According to some scholars, in the Convention of Philadelphia in the summer of 1787, the Founding Fathers anticipated all the perplexities of the American future, as well 'because their original intent can be supposed to decide constitutional questions in perpetuity' (Schlesinger 1973). Indeed, while it was clear from the beginning that the presidential system would require accurate institutional arrangements to keep at bay its natural tendency towards autocracy, this idea was reinforced when American political theory had to forge the idea of a 'plebiscitary democracy', with the rise of an 'imperial presidency' after World War II. This was a notion that had been previously associated with the 'personal dictatorship conferred by the people in accordance with constitutional norms' (Michels 1962 [1911], 212).

It started with President Woodrow Wilson, during his classic Constitutional Government of the United States (1908), when he proved to be one of the first voices to state that 'there is but one national voice in the country, and that is the voice of the President'[6]. Indeed, although he wrote a book in 1885 entitled *Congressional Government in the United States*, by stating that the Congressional branch represented the central nervous system of the American living constitution, in a couple of decades he had retraced his steps, noting the evolution of the American Republic towards presidential centrality. Passing from support to the open critique of the previous constitutional systems, Wilson paved the way for the ascendancy of the role of the main interpreter of popular will[9].

In the following decades, the institutional strengthening of the presidency passed though the setting up of the 'presidential branch'[10], with a sharp increase of executive offices and agencies, and their progression with regard to autonomy and complexity which so 'profoundly changed the nature of the presidency and its occupants' ability to act in politics, policy, and imagery' (Ragsdale and Theis 1997, 1316; Dickinson and Lebo 2007). In this direction, a turning point is represented by Roosevelt's reorganisation of the presidency, which was 'hit by a firestorm denunciation of plugging a dagger into the very heart of democracy', as 'the first act arising the fears of dictatorship from Washington to the populace at large' (Lowi 1985, 3). Two cornerstones of the US government approach were

---

9 Indeed, Wilson appeared 'as the repudiator of original understandings of the president's role and the seminal advocate of changes we now associate with modern modes of leadership', see T. Bimes and S. Skowronek, *Woodrow Wilson's Critique of Popular Leadership: Reassessing the Modern-Traditional Divide in Presidential History*, in *Polity*, 29, 1, pp. 27–63, p. 27.
10 This expression was introduced in N. Polsby, *Some Landmarks in Modern Presidential-Congressional Relations*, in A. King (ed.), *Both Ends of the Avenue*, Washington, American Enterprise Institute, 1983, pp. 1–25, p. 20, and it was popularised by J. Hart in *The Presidential Branch. From Washington to Clinton*, New York, Chatham House, 1995.

subjected to discussion under Roosevelt's administration (Musella 2012a). If until then, in line with the doctrine of dual federalism, the states had retained exclusive competence for all that concerned them, there was instead a clear expansion of federal legislation at the expense of member states; second, the intervention of the federal government in the field of economics and social legislation seemed to contradict the principle of laissez faire typical of American public philosophy. Indeed, in this 'new American State', national government grew, especially in the area of welfare and redistributive policies (Lowi 2009, 116). This model of government continued to expand in the next decades (Comba 2007). Under the Reagan presidency, such process continued so that one may speak of the spread of a Second Republic as an institutionally, constitutionally, and ideologically distinct epoch in American history[11]. When the imperial pesidency was affirmed in the second part of the nineteenth century, most of 'the resistance to giving a "single man", even if he were President of the United States, the unilateral authority to decide' was surpassed (Schlesinger 1973, 5).

Building on such processes, the growth of the American presidency may be observed – and measured – in the legislative arena. The presidents started to use – or to abuse – several legislative decision-making instruments to strengthen their position: for instance, the escalation of executive orders was associated with changes in their nature, so that from being an administrative tool they acted as a way of allowing the president to enter the field of legislation. As considered by Branum (2002, 9), 'presidential orders have not merely impacted government employees, but they have also impacted individuals outside the government'. At the same time, while an increasingly frequent legislative delegation from the Congress to the presidency occurred with the complicity of the Supreme Court[12], the American president tended to use the legislative instruments at his disposal in a more autonomous and extensive way. It is worth noting the fundamental role of veto power in the rise of the presidency, which lost the revisionary vocation as the Framers had understood it in the constitutional convention, to become a tool to directly intervene in national legislation (Spitzer 1988).

Thus, with reference to Congress–Presidency relationships, Theodore J. Lowi (1969) concludes that the word 'legicide' is the best one to define the more and more extensive legislative prerogatives of personal presidents. As the Founding

---

11 Changes in the constitutional culture of the country have been also visible in the sentences of the Supreme Court, progressively more open to recognize a more active role of the executive in the legislative field, see G.W. Howell, *Unilateral Powers: A Brief Overview*, in *Presidential Studies Quarterly*, 35, 3, 2005, pp. 417–439.
12 See J.A. Segal, H.J. Spaeth and S.C. Benesh, *The Supreme Court in the American legal system*, Cambridge, Cambridge University Press, 2005, particularly pp. 41–70.

Fathers made a deliberate effort to divide control of the powers, 'this division was inherently unstable' as the presidency had exceeded its constitutional limits. This is the reason why a long list of contributions on American institutions have concentrated attention on the presidential expansion 'during the Depression, the Second World War, the Cold War', and 'thereafter reacted, often with protestations at what they believed to be excesses of power' (Pious 2009, 458).

1.3 Monocratic government as an emerging trend

Today this process has been continuing to a visible and clear point. Democratic presidents meet the constraint of re-election, which shapes and limits the horizon of presidential decision-making. Nevertheless, after such a long historical process of institutional strengthening, presidents may experiment with an increasing autonomy during the mandate. This has stimulated the debate among scholars on the consequences of an executive-centred government, which has sustained and justified, 'the persistence of this tyrannophobia through American history' (Posner and Vermeule 2009, 14). Especially during periods of crisis, as after the Twin Towers attacks, some observers have noticed that the US executive has become 'unbound'. The necessity for rapid action made the powers of presidency so broad as to 'leave rational legislators and judges no real choice but to hand the reins to the executive and hope for the best'[13] (Posner and Vermeule 2009, 1652). As we will see in this volume, this trend took a step forward during the pandemic, as several chief executives interpreted it as a way to extend their prerogatives under the use of emergency decrees (Ginsburg and Versteeg 2020a; 2020b).

Thus it has become increasingly clear that personalisation of politics has produced a shift from collective to individual actors and institutions in contemporary democracies, and from voting behaviour to governmental steering (Poguntke and Webb 2005; Karvonen 2010; Costa Lobo and Curtice 2014; Musella 2018; Rahat and Kenig 2018; Cross et al. 2018). Indeed, although noting national differences in terms of institutional and political assets, scholars tend to put emphasis 'on the general trend rather than on the variance they identified' (Cross et al. 2018, 24): the balance between leader and parties has been moving towards monocratic actors in the last years, all over the world, from the US to Europe. Many scholars started to note that parliamentary governments have become

---

13 For a critical discussion of the theory of the 'unbound executive' see J. Waldron, *Separation of Powers or Division of Power?* in *NYU School of Law, Public Law Research Paper* 12, 20, 2012.

more similar to the American model of government, by assuming, however, a quite reassuring position in stating that current institutional transformation remains within the perimeter of classical models of government. When the concept of presidentialisation attracted attention everywhere (Elgie and Passarelli 2020), and some authors considered it to be synonymous with 'Americanisation' (Helms 2015), it has seemed to express a significant move completely enclosed in traditional constitutional models, although it suggests looking at them in a more flexible way. Yet institutional transformations have proved to be even more radical: we are moving today in a *terra incognita*, where the growth of leaders' power goes hand in hand with the high fragmentation of democratic electorates, resulting in uncertain consequences for the democratic order.

With special reference to the latest and more incisive steps of such a path, the *monocratic government* may be defined as a result of three interrelated processes:

a) the development of a direct – not mediated by parties and often emotional – relationship with the individualistic masses, so that the leader assumes the role of a political representative 'above the party';

b) the affirmation of a monocratic principle of political action, so that the leader tends to become the true dominus of party organisation and controls governmental activities as well. A corollary of this statement is the use of unilateral and often emergency legislative powers on the part of the political leaders, as clearly appeared during the pandemic phase;

c) a process of increasing fragmentation of collective actors traditionally deputed to control and counterbalance the power of political leaders, such as parliament and political parties.

Monocratic government represents an unexpected result in contemporary democracies, especially with regards to the first Framers' prescriptions, though its progression has taken place over several decades. Sometimes the personalisation of government has been introduced by formal constitutional changes. The most relevant example in Europe is represented by constitutional reforms leading to presidential or prime-ministerial pre-eminence, such as in the passage from the French Fourth Republic to the Fifth Republic, or with the introduction of direct elections for the prime minister in Israel in 1996. Maurice Duverger noticed the novelty of the marriage between personal power and liberal institutions after de Gaulle's constitutional reforms, when he said that the French President has become a 'monarque republicain' (Duverger 1974). And with recent French presidencies combining mediatic popularity and international visibility, other scholars have preferred to speak of French hyper-presidencies such as in the case of Nicholas Sarkozy (Ventura 2009; Bréchon 2010, 116).

The strengthening of monocratic figures in France, such as in the United States, was regulated by law, and inserted in a system of the cautious separation of powers. Significantly, de Gaulle himself defined the principle of separation of powers as the prohibition of concentrating all powers in the hands of one body. He paved the way for a central role of the president of the Republic in stating that the separation of power had to avoid powerful leadership and, perhaps more importantly in his view, was designed 'to limit the destructive influence of the Parliament of the Third Republic whose perilous inability to carry out state policies led to the weakening of governmental power, anarchy and the collapse of the Republic in the Second World War' (de Gaulle 1970; Kostadinov 2016). Thus, while de Gaulle's interpretation of power was based on his 'Bonapartist' relationship between the presidency and the French citizenry[14], he made a clear choice of the institutionalisation of personal power, resulting in an unprecedented model of a 'dual executive' subsequently followed by a good number of countries inside and outside Europe (Elgie and Moestrup 2008; Clift 2008; Elgie 2011).

More recently, while increasing favour towards strong presidents has been registered in democratic systems, this has not often paved the way for formal changes to constitutions. An increase in the level of presidentialism in different continents may be noticed, so that the direct legitimation of the head of government is becoming the rule for a large number of 'presidential republics' (Blondel 2015). In addition to this, scholars have added that several parliamentary regimes have produced rules and practices similar to presidential systems, even without any modification of the formal constitutions (Poguntke and Webb 2005; Musella and Webb 2015). Indeed, where formal changes did not occur, transformations of political parties, in interaction with the institutional asset (Samuel and Shugart 2010), made the leaders the centre of party organisation, and consequently the dominus of governmental activities. Very often structural changes in the executive administration have provided more means of government at the disposal of the heads of government. This was exemplified by the way Tony Blair transformed the hearth of Whitehall by recruiting more than 2,000 staff to his 'own' office. Furthermore, the German chancellor's office under Angela Merkel, is made up of 600 civil servants who were mostly nominated by the chancellor herself.

---

14 On this point see also J. Gaffney (*France in the Hollande presidency: The unhappy republic*, Basingstoke, Palgrave, 2015, pp. 36–68) who stresses the constitutive 'elements' of presidential character and how they affected the performance and evolution of the French Fifth Republic.

Among parliamentary democracies, Italy is one of the countries which has showed an evident strengthening of the figure of the head of government, so turning its long established 'integral parliamentarism'[15] into a front-runner in the age of presidentialisation. The rise of the Italian Second Republic, a contested expression for the lack of a formal constitutional change, progressively endowed the *Presidente del Consiglio* with new prerogatives and powers[16]. The march of administrative reforms has reinforced the executive since the 1980s, and this has been accompanied by the transformations of the role and functions of the prime minister. No less relevant are changes affecting the electoral system during the 1990s, when the party system's polarisation, the formation of pre-electoral instead of post-electoral coalitions, and the indication of the names of leaders within the symbols shown in each ballot, brought about a kind of informal direct election of the prime minister[17]. As far as the legislative process is concerned, many scholars have noticed a relevant shift of prerogatives from the parliament to the governmental branch in the last three decades (Ferrajoli 2018): emergency bills have become more and more numerous, thus representing a predominant part of the total of legislative bills, while delegated legislation has largely expanded, especially to respond to necessities imposed by EU regulatory activities and other important structural reforms.

Some countries have chipped away at the foundations of democracy, as has happened in Hungary where Prime Minister Orbán has replaced it with an authoritarian regime: 'since taking power, Orbán and Fidesz lawmakers have systematically dismantled the institutions of liberal democracy – an independent judiciary, civil service, non-governmental organisations, and the free press

---

15 This is the expression used by one of the major analysts of the Italian political phase during the First Republic, Gianfranco Miglio, to emphasise the relevance of the proportional rule and consensus making in a 'fully parliamentary' regime, see G. Miglio, *Le contraddizioni interne del sistema parlamentare-integrale*, in *Italian Political Science Review/Rivista Italiana di Scienza Politica*, 14, 2, 1984, pp. 209 – 222.

16 P. Calandra, *Il governo della Repubblica*, Bologna, Il Mulino, 1986; M. Calise, *Il governo*, in F. Barbagallo (eds.), *Storia dell'Italia repubblicana*, Torino, Einaudi, 1997; pp. 347 – 397; A. Criscitiello, *Il cuore dei governi. Le politiche di riforma degli esecutivi in prospettiva comparata*, Napoli, Edizioni Scientifiche, 2004; A. Maccanico, *Il tramonto della repubblica dei partiti. Diari 1985 – 1989*, Bologna, Il Mulino, 2018.

17 The idea of an institutional 'transition' is at the centre of many Italian political science contributions, which have taken seriously the passage from the First to Second Republic, although no constitutional reforms have been passed, see R. D'Alimonte and S. Bartolini (eds.), *Maggioritario finalmente? La transizione elettorale 1994 – 2001*, Il Bologna, Il Mulino, 2002; S. Ceccanti and S. Vassallo, *Come chiudere la transizione*, Bologna, Il Mulino, Bologna, 2004; G. Pasquino, *Teorie della transizione e analisi del sistema politico: il caso italiano*, in *Italian Political Science Review/Rivista Italiana di Scienza Politica*, 31, 2, 2001, pp. 313 – 327.

– rewritten the constitution, and changed electoral laws to ensure that Fidesz stays in power' (Johnson 2018, 19). Very often democratic institutions do not die, but they are openly treated as having done so by the leader's accumulation of power and lack of forbearance against political and institutional opposition, in a context of increasing polarisation (Levitsky and Ziblatt 2018). Although the gradual degradation of a constitutional regime poses clear difficulties of diagnosis (Uitz 2015), Hungary's departure from liberal standards has been acknowledged by global scholarship.

Yet the high level of personalisation of politics has led to doubt about the balance of power in several consolidated democracies as well, as classical democratic institutions, such as parliaments, are being weakened with regard to their traditional role. As has been stated, such 'decline is marked less by constitutional democracies being overthrown than by an increase in regimes that retain the formal institutional trappings while flouting the norms and values on which constitutional democracies are based'[18] (Loughlin 2019, 435). Along these lines, Levinson and Balkin (2010) prefer to talk of 'constitutional rot' instead of using the abused term 'constitutional crisis', by proposing the idea that there is a progressive fading of constitutional norms and a slow decay in the features of our system of government that may operate over long periods of time[19]. This is a process, however, that may be more evident in contingent phases when the crisis takes place: although the debate is still open as to whether degradation may lead democracy to an effective end, there is no doubt that the form of 'democratic' government is changing its nature and borders. Especially during the pandemic, such dynamics resulted in the vertiginous institutional rise of executive power as the participation of parliaments in decision-making was reduced to little more than ratifying executive proposals. Contemporary democracies have

---

18 A theory of constitutional degradation is taking form, see M.A. Graber, S. Levinson and M. Tushnet (eds.), *Constitutional Democracy in Crisis?*, Oxford, Oxford University Press, 2018; T. Ginsburg and A.Z. Huq, *How to Save a Constitutional Democracy*, Chicago, University of Chicago Press, 2018.

19 'Constitutional rot, in other words, can eventually cause a democratic constitution to fail both as a *democratic* constitution – because the system degenerates into an oligarchy or autocracy; and as a democratic *constitution* – because the constitution no longer can keep political disagreement within the bounds of law and peaceful political dispute', J.M. Balkin, *Constitutional Crisis and Constitutional Rot*, in *Maryland Law Review*, 77, 1, 2017, pp. 147–160, p. 155. It is quite impressive that such a strong thesis has started to be applied to the US case, see C. Sunstein, *Can It Happen Here? Authoritarianism in America*, New York, HarperCollins, 2008. With reference to the Trump presidency, see D. Frum, *How to build an autocracy*, in *The Atlantic, March*, March 2017, https://www.theatlantic.com/magazine/archive/2017/03/how-to-build-an-autocracy/513872/.

been experiencing a transitory suspension of the general rules which, together with restrictions on the constitutional freedoms of citizens, end up attributing to governments the extraordinary competence to exercise legislative functions[20]. During the emergency phase, chief executives have dominated national decision-making, whereby the gross of the legislative production has been transferred from the parliamentary body to the executive and the decrees were used as an ordinary instrument of government. Furthermore, the direct methods of political communication have often emphasised their institutional position, thanks to an innovative and intensive use of old and new media. Indeed, they were in charge of the task to 'make meaning' around the COVID-19 crisis during the year that will be forever impressed on the collective memory as the 'annus horribilis'[21] (Boin et al. 2021), in a spiral of concentration of power and visibility that has led to doubt on the stability of the most consolidated democracies. Thus, the coronavirus phase has tended to make even clearer the long-term spread of monocratic government.

1.4 The personalisation of the masses

With the coming of the masses at the beginning of the nineteenth century, the period of crisis due to the incapacity of people to self-organise was resolved by the rise of the organisation of political parties. As in the contribution by Ortega y Gasset, the revolt of the masses derives from the fact that 'the individuals who made up these multitudes existed, but not qua multitude' (1960, 13), but

---

20 Indeed, as it has been observed, the virus has put much of humanity at risk, while at the same time posing a grave challenge to governance systems everywhere, see T. Ginsburg, *Foreword for Special Issue on Legislatures in the Time of COVID-19*, in *The Theory and Practice of Legislation*, 8, 2020, pp. 1–2. On the theme whether a parliament should work during the COVID crisis see E. Rayment and J. Vanden Beukel, *Pandemic Parliaments: Canadian Legislatures in a Time of Crisis*, in *Canadian Journal of Political Science/Revue Canadienne de Science Politique*, 53, 2, 2020, pp. 379–384; P. Thomas, *Parliament Under Pressure: Evaluating Parliament's Performance in Response to COVID-19*, in *The Samara Centre for Democracy*, 2 April 2020, https://www. samaracanada.com/democracy-monitor/parliament-under-pressure
21 Government communication research has been, however, an emerging field in the last decade, thus giving rise to the progressive idea of chief executives communicating with people, especially during crisis management, see M.J. Canel and K.B. Sanders, *Government communication: An emerging field in political communication research*, in *The Sage Handbook of Political Communication*, 2, 2012, pp. 85–96; M.J. Canel and K.B. Sanders, *Government communication*, in G. Mazzoleni, K.G., Barnhurst, K.I. Ikeda, R.C., Maia and H. Wessler (eds.), *The International Encyclopaedia of Political Communication*, New York, John Wiley & Sons, 2015, pp. 1–8.

they became a political body through a political party's actions. This brought about many cultural and political consequences, with a process of homogenisation of society which destroyed many traditional relationships, and the masses presented themselves as the great subject of history. In Heinrich Triepel's precious lesson (1927), the masses were incorporated through this way into the State. Although 'atomistic individualism overwhelmed development of modern democracy' (Triepel 1967, 126–127), political parties allowed individualistically formed masses to participate in government. Consequently, democracy was considered possible only when individuals were connected in collective organisations which 'summarize targeted individuals' will' (Kelsen 1967), and resulted in a completed party-State (Leibholtz 1958; Mortati 1940).

In the second part of the last century, with the progressive decline of political parties and their grasp over society, the political leader acted as a substitute point of reference for the masses. Again, the leader realised the incorporation of the masses, in a plebiscitary relationship stimulating the identification of citizens with the leader's physical and institutional body. The concept of a leader's democracy synthesises the capacity of single top politicians to shape the preferences of voters, so as to give meaning to political processes and to act as the individual responsible for the performance of the government (Pakulski and Körösényi 2012; Calise 2016). Moreover, as far as the leader appears fully responsible for governmental action, permanent electoral campaigns have centred on this figure. The US presidents have provided an important starting point for this process when the rise of personal presidents during the second part of the nineteenth century led to the combination of increasing presidential visibility and the consequent escalation of public expectation (Lowi 1985).

Once again it is difficult to overestimate the innovations of Franklin D. Roosevelt who used the radio to connect the apex of American institutions to people: his famous 'little fireside chats' allowed the president to enter in citizens' homes by creating an intimate and direct contact. Presidents before him had their messages filtered by newspapers controlled by political parties, while Roosevelt, in contrast, was able to speak to people in real time. During the same years, polling techniques saw rapid and widespread developments, so that the presidency acquired the ability to understand popular orientations as well: the institution of the presidency tended to include a 'public opinion apparatus' to be more reactive to citizens' preferences (Jacobs and Shapiro 1995; Eisinger 2003). After him, with the development of mass media such as television, the president became the centre of public life by establishing 'political constituencies for themselves, independent of party organisations, and thereby strengthened their own power relative to that of Congress' (Ginsberg et al. 2017, 276). According to Robert Dahl, when a direct relationship between the president and electors occurs, it realises a pseudo-democratic mystique of presidential mandate, with the president exploiting all the resources of his office to overcome any resistance to a particular policy in Congress, perhaps even by appealing to the public (Dahl 1990). Obviously, these trends concern chief executives in contemporary democracies, who have developed a direct and intimate relationship with citizens. However, this also applies to political systems with no direct elections for the president: the leader has tried to incorporate the masses as a vehicle for public identification and political action.

More recently, political leaders have had to face the latest chapter of the process of personalisation. The social body, which the leader should represent, has been more and more affected by a spiral of fragmentation. Thus, the president now has to channel more individualistic and fluctuating publics[22], as an effect of both social and political drivers.

High degrees of fragmentation occur at both electoral and institutional levels. From the first point of view, the disintegration of the electorate is becoming evident, thus resulting in a high level of electoral mobility. Changes in voting behaviour between elections has largely increased in later years, in line with a strong party system dealignment: in countries such as Italy, the Netherlands, and France we register that the value of the electorate's mobility exceeds a quarter of the electorate. In the same way, one may also recall the 2015 and 2017 British general elections that according to Fieldhouse et al. (2019, 1) represented 'electoral shocks' underlying how 'the electorate has become increasingly volatile at the individual level'. Indeed, while in 2015 the share of votes obtained by parties other than Labour, Conservative, and LibDem reached its highest in the British electoral history, in 2017 the Labour–Conservative two-party share obtained the highest result since 1970 (Hobolt 2016; Baines et al. 2020). As other cases may be added, there is plenty of evidence that shows rapid changes of the electorate among electoral consultations, with the consequence that most contemporary democracies seem to be in constant upheaval. Looking at the

---

22 Since the early 1990s, citizenship has appeared as being fragmented into a variety of distinct publics, each focussing on specific issues of immediate importance (J. Thomassen, *The European voter: a comparative study of modern democracies*, Oxford, Oxford University Press, 2005). R.J. Dalton (*Comparative Politics: Micro-behavioral Perspectives*, in R. Goodin and H.D. Klingemann [eds.], *A New Handbook of Political Science*, Oxford, Oxford University Press, 1996, 346) has observed 'a shift away from a style of electoral decision-making based on social group and/or party cues toward a more individualized and inwardly oriented style of political choice. Instead of depending upon party élites and reference groups, more citizens now try to deal with the complexities of politics and make their own political decisions. What is developing is an eclectic and egocentric pattern of citizen decision-making'.

US, Brady notes that 'in the years between 1992 and 2014, the United States saw a level of instability or flip-flopping of electoral results comparable to the 1874 – 1894 period'[23], and the electorate appears restless around the globe.

At other times the growth of fragmentation can be ascertained with respect to the change of opinion of citizens on specific themes. Very often electors' preferences rapidly change positions on policy issues: for instance, the word 'regrexit' was coined in 2016 with reference to the behaviour of those people regretting the decision to vote for Britain leaving the EU just after voting for it. It was quite unexpected that a relevant percentage of British electors, as documented in postvote polling, changed their mind on the UK's exit from the European Union. Yet the phenomenon is only one of the latest manifestations of the instability which has characterised Western electorates, who are consequently easy prey for political leaders able to ride public opinion on crucial public issues.

In the dynamic of mass personalisation, the leaders may carry out aggregative processes through the intensive use of new technologies and tools of algorithmic persuasion as well. The diffusion of digital technologies has acted as a strong driver for such transformations, with a large majority of the world's inhabitants connected to the web resulting in a new form of individualism. Indeed, personalisation is the main process that digital innovation has fostered: never before has more emphasis been placed on citizens' participation. Individualism is the psychological and behavioural basis of the democratic experiments that have accompanied the spread of the new technologies. Since the 1990s, experiments in virtual democracy have promised to create a digital polis by allowing for public deliberation by rational citizens. In addition to this, political parties have benefitted from digital innovation by facilitating information exchanges and communication among activists, members, and elected representatives, and also by creating new opportunities for mobilisation (Norris 2001; Margetts 2006; Gibson and Ward 2009). The advent of social media has relaunched such processes by mobilising citizens through digital platforms. Nevertheless, although new forms of political parties have started to emerge, the creation of collective bodies is becoming more and more difficult (Gerbaudo 2019a). Digital leaders have become the only actors able to communicate with large publics, yet at the cost of remaining dependent on the social media corporations they rely on for their electoral success.

As far as institutional splintering and disintegration are concerned, fragmentation is implicated in the origin of the weakening of parliamentary institu-

---

23 D.W. Brady, *Globalization and Political instability. How the transformation of the world economy shook up Western politics*, in *The American Interest*, 11, 6, 8 March 2016.

tions. An increase in the average effective number of electoral parties from 4.8 to 5.4, and in the average effective number of parliamentary parties from 3.9 to 4.2 has been transversally noted in contemporary democracies over the last twenty years (Katz and Mair 2018, 153; Rahat and Kenig 2018, 60). For instance, in Spain the number of effective parties has gone from 2.7 to 4.7 in the last twenty years, so determining the end of the Iberic post-Transition two-party system. The same is true for the British party system which reached a value of 4.3 in 2020 in terms of effective number of parties. In addition to this, fragmentation is very often associated with the legislative party switching on members of parliament who change party affiliation during the course of a parliamentary term (Ceron and Volpi 2019; Klein 2018). In Italy, the number of MPs that have decided to switch parties, or coalitions, between elections has increased significantly: 'the average number of MPs switching party increased from 21 in the decade 1983–1994, to 80 in the period 1994–2006 and then to 116 during 2006–2017, while the average number switching from one parliamentary group to another increased from 93, to 200, to 212' (Regalia 2018, 93). These factors have increased the marginalisation of parliaments in legislative processes, with clear consequences for the whole political system.

The weakening of the legislative capacity of parliaments depends on party polarisation as well – that is in many ways the other face of fragmentation. Indeed, looking at the American Congress, Abramowitz (2018, 187) points out that until the recent past 'it was much easier to build bipartisan coalitions to pass legislation. There were enough moderate-to-liberal Republicans and moderate-to-conservative Democrats to enable cross-party coalitions on some major issues. Today, however, there are almost no members in the middle in either chamber, and divided party control almost inevitably leads to confrontation and gridlock'. In other words, 'recent conditions of divided party government and relatively narrow partisan majorities in Congress have provided a political context within which increased polarisation has had strongly negative effects on the quality and quantity of public policy' (Carmines and Fowler 2017, 379). Thus, with control of both chambers at stake, party polarisation has been altering the legislatures just as it has been transforming the role of presidential leadership. When presidents encounter growing difficulties in reaching agreements, this process may represent the main asset for – and obstacle to – legislative expansion of contemporary political leaders (Musella 2018).

When the leaders are unable to govern, they may be tempted to take more power by changing the institutional setting where they operate. Indeed, an increasingly polarised and fragmented politics leads to political stalemate and policy gridlock in parliament which, in turn, may contribute to a change in the balance of power between the executive and legislative branches (Barber and McCarty 2015). While political parties still have the duty of building bipartisan agreement in national policy-making, where hyper-fragmentation occurs, they prefer gridlock and stalemate to compromise (Curry et al. 2020; Tuttnauer 2020; Zucco and Power 2020). At this point a strong leader may try to go down the road of reinforcing his power even more. And the idea of abandoning democracy can spring to mind.

1.5 An autocratic tendency?

The number of democratic constitutions increased after the Second World War in the Western world, and remained limited to Europe for several decades. In the middle 1980s, when Arendt Lijphart wrote his seminal book on democratic regime types, which introduced the classical distinction between majoritarian and consensual ones, his classification only included 21 countries[24]. The second edition of this volume, published after 15 years, could enthusiastically refer to almost 36 democracies[25]. Yet the path of democracy has not been so triumphant.

Conversely, while in the last quarter of a century the passage from authoritarian rule to democracy was expected on the global scale, today the regression of democratic regimes is suspected (Erdmann and Kneuer 2011; Mounk 2018; Schenkaan and Repucci 2019; Haggard and Kaufman 2021). There is plenty of proof showing that contemporary democracies have been put under pressure[26]. The Freedom House, the authoritative institute devoted to systematically evaluating democracies on a yearly basis, titled one of its most recent reports in a way that does not allow any room for doubt: 'Democracies in Retreat'[27]. Even

---

24 A. Lijphart, *Democracies: Patterns of Majoritarian and Consensus Government in Twenty-One Countries*, New Haven, Yale University Press, 1984.

25 A. Lijphart, *Patterns of Democracy: Government Forms and Performance in Thirty-Six Countries*, New Haven, Yale University Press, 1999.

26 See: D. Acemoglu and J.A. Robinson, *Why Nations Fail: The Origins of Power, Prosperity and Poverty*, London, Profile Books, 2012; S. Levitsky and D. Ziblatt, *How Democracies Die*, Broadway, 2018; M.A. Graber, S. Levinson and M. Tushnet (eds.), *Constitutional Democracy in Crisis?*, Oxford, Oxford University Press, 2018; T. Ginsburg and A.Z. Huq, *How to Save a Constitutional Democracy*, Chicago, Chicago University Press, 2018.

27 Freedom House, *Freedom in the World 2019. Democracy in Retreat*, Washington, 2019. The thesis of the decline of the democracy, or at least of its quality, is documented in a very long list of publications, looking at single case studies (A. Ágh, *The Decline of Democracy in East-Central Europe. Hungary as the Worst-Case Scenario*, in *Problems of Post-Communism*, 63, 5–6, 2016, pp. 277–287; J.G. Andersen, *Political power and democracy in Denmark: decline of democracy or change in democracy?*, in *Journal of European Public Policy*, 13, 4, 2006, pp. 569–586), or in a

in long-standing democracies, several political forces question basic principles like the separation of powers, and target minorities for discriminatory treatment.

These authoritarian tendencies emerge from both within and outside the existing structures and become even more dangerous if we consider that 'citizens in a number of supposedly consolidated democracies in North America and Western Europe have become more cynical about the values of democracy and more willing to express support for authoritarian alternatives' (Foa and Mounk, 2016, 7; Harms et al. 2018). Thus, anger at political elites and political dissatisfaction have fuelled substantial discontent in many democratic countries, as documented in relevant research on public opinion changes and as demonstrated by the emergence of anti-establishment leaders, parties, and movements on both the right and left of the political spectrum[28]. More recently, while alternatives to democracy have become more attractive, and the phase of the pandemic has added new elements of doubt on the capacity of democratic leaders to face extreme challenges, it appears to be progressively clear that democracy is changing its nature and practice.

In this book, we will focus attention on two interrelated processes of monocratic government that have challenged democracy as it developed throughout the nineteenth century: the rise of a stronger leader, and that of the individualistic masses.

After the decline of mass parties occurred in the nineteenth century, and a new personalistic model of political organisation was affirmed, the leader has become the only channel through which to incorporate and involve the masses into politics today: or, more clearly stated, the leader is the only figure who can embody the people (Urbinati 2019). As leaders become more powerful, there is also a tendency to see this as a consequence of a direct electoral mandate, stressing personal responsibility and autonomy versus other institutional actors. Nevertheless, this sense of autonomy cuts both ways: while the leader has become more independent of party, they often lack the adequate support of their own majority in parliament (Webb, Poguntke and Kolodny 2012).

The classic theory of presidentialism has already shown how presidential government may be problematic, with highly fragmented multiparty systems and electorates (Valenzuela and Linz 1994). Indeed, in such a context, presidents

comparative perspective (G. Erdmann, *Decline of democracy: loss of quality, hybridisation and breakdown of democracy*, in *Zeitschrift für Vergleichende Politikwissenschaft/Comparative Governance and Politics*, 1, pp. 21–58, 2011; T. Smolka, *Decline of democracy – the European Union at a crossroad*, in *Zeitschrift für Vergleichende Politikwissenschaft*, 1, 25, 2021, pp. 81–105).
28 See inter alia Pew Research Center, *Many Across the Globe Are Dissatisfied With How Democracy Is Working*, 29 April 2019.

tend to become reluctant to assume the institutional limitation posed by a system of division of powers, which at the same time does not find adequate support in the legislative branch. The temptation may arise to establish an autocratic regime, or simply to affirm the rule of a single leader in an apparent respect for the rules of democracy.

2 Personal governments

2.1 Introduction

Government is one of the key concepts in the tradition of political thought. It refers to a 'political system' in the broad sense of the term, namely the political actors responsible for the authoritative allocation of values in a society, and the system of relations that develops among them (Easton 1953). From this point of view, the concept of government appears as a standard feature of politics. Indeed, one or more organs providing political directions to citizens – from tribes to state, and up to international and supranational organisations – have played a central role in the social group, since the beginning of recorded time (Finer 1997; Blondel 2001). Furthermore, the concept of government suggests activities and functions crucial for the scope of politics itself, for instance, defence: the protection of the territory against all enemies and the unity of the political community.

In a narrow sense, the concept of government refers to the functioning of the executive branch and takes on a more historically oriented meaning. In this respect, the rise and consolidation of the government follow the process of the formation of the modern state. Whilst it was an auxiliary body subordinate to the monarch during the Middle Ages, it became one of the pillars of the separation of powers regimes during the constitutionalisation of monarchies which followed both revolutionary and evolutionary pathways in different national contexts (Milewicz 2020). Therefore, the term government means the 'executive', a body which engages in various relations with the other institutions of the State. Governments have different terms of office and compositions according to each national context. This demonstrates their peculiar traits in being devoted to the execution of policies, while leaving the definition of general rules to the parliament.

Nevertheless, the role of the executive in established democracies has bypassed these constraints in recent years, since it has increasingly played a central role in areas that constitutional theory would seem to take away from it. The executive's characteristics differ greatly according to certain features: constitutional provisions, conventions, regulations, customs, and routines of the national contexts (Rhodes 2006). Yet, despite different constitutional frameworks, one of the most crucial trends in recent years relates to the role of the prime minister within the governmental structure, based on the general rule that when parties are strong the executive leader is a *primus inter pares* (Von Beyme 2011). Conversely, he strenghtens his role during times of crisis or when parties are

https://doi.org/10.1515/9783110721720-002

weak. As it was noticed early in the 1990s, in countries with a solid tradition of party government, a mix of circumstances and rule-setting leads to the affirmation of the figure of political leader. For instance, Foley (1993, 283) tends to conclude that the British premier has converged with the American president. On comparatively similar ground, Poguntke and Webb (2005) provide insight on the process of de facto presidentialisation which has been the effect of three processes, or rather three faces of presidentialisation: direct access to the electoral constituency through various forms of media populism, a monocratic as well as charismatic grip upon the party organisation, and – last but not least – the strengthening of the cabinet office and governmental control over the legislative process[29]. Seventeen years on their research project, presidents and prime ministers have become – despite their different institutional positions due to regime type[30] – the predominant figures in several contemporary democracies. After a secular and quite linear trend of limitation of the executive prerogative though constitutional constraints, there has been a recent and very rapid process of re-empowerment which has tended to coincide with the autocratic turn in old and new democracies[31]. Today we could ask if the process of the strengthening of political leaders is changing the nature of our democracy *itself,* by putting it under pressure when it combines with intense processes of the individualisation of the masses. The premise of any division of power, indeed, is that the leader may meet a limitation to their expansion in vigilant and well-organised society.

As the twofold meaning of government shows that this concept may differ from both these perspectives, the conceptual matrix provided in this chapter results as an attempt to incorporate – and merge – both approaches within democratic political regimes. As a result, starting from classical definitions of government types, it will present the 'monocratic government' as a process of the

---

29 A substantial debate has been occurring in the political science discipline on the utility, and opportunity of such a category, see L. Helms, *The Presidentialisation of Political Leadership: British Notions and German Observations*, in *Political Quarterly*, 76, 3, 2005, pp. 430 – 438; R. Heffernan, *There's No Need for the '-isation': The Prime Minister is Merely Prime Ministerial*, in *Parliamentary Affairs*, 66, 3, 2013, pp. 636 – 645; P. Webb, T. Poguntke, *The presidentialisation of politics thesis defended*, in *Parliamentary Affairs*, 66, 3, 2013, pp. 646 – 654.
30 The distinction between presidents and prime ministers, rightly repeated by Keith Dowding (*The prime ministerialisation of the British prime minister*, in *Parliamentary Affairs*, 66, 3, 2013, pp. 617 – 635), should not lead to the expunging of the presidentialisation thesis from the political science vocabulary, which has the merit of opening a fertile scientific debate.
31 It starts from the thesis of the empowerment of political executives, by indicating their 'rediscovery' in a new and promising field of political science research R.B. Andeweg, R. Elgie, L. Helms, J. Kaarbo, F. Müller-Rommel, *The Political Executive Returns*, in *The Oxford Handbook of Political Executives*, Oxford, Oxford University Press, 2020, pp. 1 – 22.

strengthening of the political leader in both decision-making and in a direct relationship with an increasingly individualised society.

2.2 Forms and dynamics of government

According to traditional constitutional models, a few defining criteria are enough to establish the differences between the forms of government. They are strongly anchored to the dichotomy that contrasts presidentialism and parliamentarism, with the direct election of the presidents providing the crucial element for dividing the political realm into two parts. Riggs (1997, 253) sharply concludes that 'two main forms of democratic governance exist on the basis of Western examples: the presidentialist design illustrated by the United States, and parliamentarist forms developed in Western Europe'.

The classification of the institutional world focussed on these two forms of government may have been only enriched by the interest in semi-presidentialism starting from its French foundation[32], and then developed with a rapid diffusion in several emerging democracies. Yet, although some scholars tried to introduce more accurate classifications of regime types (Shugart and Carey 1992), constitutional families were supposed to encompass the political reality of every democracy on the basis of a very simple – and crucial – set of institutional factors[33]. A rich political science literature, however, has shown that each regime type may differ along with several political variables; first of all, the impact of parties

---

32 Semi-presidentialism is also the object of a fruitful strand of research, often providing large comparative analyses. Cf. R. Elgie, *Semi-presidentialism in Europe*, Oxford, Oxford University Press, 1999; R. Elgie and S. Moestrup (eds.), *Semi-presidentialism in Central and Eastern Europe*, Manchester, Manchester University Press, 2008. Yet debate is open as to whether semi-presidentialism may be considered a third form of government beyond the parliamentary and presidential ones, or as an intermediate case between them. On this point see G. Pasquino, *Semipresidentialism. A Political Model at Work*, in *European Journal of Political Research*, 31, 1, 1997, pp. 128–137.

33 According to a very parsimonious definition, presidentialism means 'a regime in which (1) the president is always the chief executive and is elected by popular vote or, as in the US, by an electoral college with little autonomy with respect to popular preferences; and (2) the terms of office for the president and the assembly are fixed' (Mainwaring and Shugart 1997, 449). Moreover, according to historical and empirical analysis on written constitutions, Cheibub et al. (2014) show how real forms of government represent a veritable hybrid, because they show no resemblance to the classic types in relation to a long list of constitutional provisions concerning the power of executives and legislatures. See also more recently S. Ganghof, *Beyond Presidentialism and Parliamentarism. Democratic Design and the Separation of Powers*, Oxford, Oxford University Press, 2021.

and the party system on the classification or functioning of forms of government (Sartori 1976; Elia 1970; Volpi 1997).

In this chapter, the attempt at an articulated definition of the concept of government aims to grasp the dynamic dimension based on the assumption that both presidentialism and parliamentarism may change over time. The principle dimensions of government are the main axes in our matrix-based conceptualisation, which follows a consolidated methodology of theory-making[34].

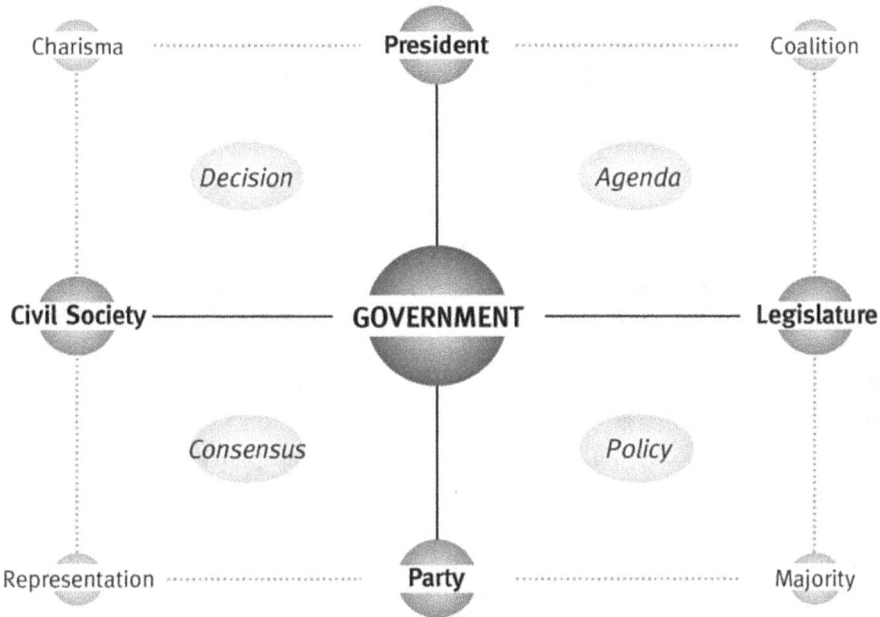

Charisma .... **President** .... Coalition

Decision *Agenda*

Civil Society ─────── **GOVERNMENT** ─────── **Legislature**

Consensus *Policy*

Representation .... **Party** .... Majority

Figure 1: The matrix of government. *Source:* Hyperpolitics.net, https://www.hyperpolitics.net/hyperdictionary/quadrants.php?entry=government

The vertical axis describes the competition for governmental control, with political parties and presidents as the two main actors in the struggle for power. Although from an institutionalist point of view they must cooperate – or at least

---

34 The reference here is to the methodology of Hyperpolitics, which constructs each matrix the same way, with an identical configuration of twelve concepts, thus offering 'a system for controlling the logical consistency of conceptual links toward theoretical argument' (M. Calise and T. Lowi, *Hyperpolitics. An Interactive Dictionary of Political Concepts*, Chicago, Chicago University Press, 2010, p. 17).

find areas of agreement – their true natures put them in open conflict. As Calise observes (2006, 81) they embody two different principles of authority, monocratic versus collegial, and they also differ in relation to the principle of legitimacy: 'direct and personal in the case of presidents, individual and collective in the case of parties'.

From an historical point of view, the political party has been a machine for elite formation and consolidation. According to Robert Michel's iron law of oligarchy, every complex organisation, regardless of how democratic it was when it started with basic principles, eventually centralises power to a restricted group of people. He outlined this law after extensively observing the German Socialist Party at the beginning of the last century (Michels 1962 [1911]), where the 'organisational imperatives necessarily gave rise to a caste of leaders whose superior knowledge, skills, and status, when combined with their hierarchical control of key organisational resources such as internal communication and training, would allow them to dominate the broader membership and to domesticate dissenting groups'[35]. Although recent trends of personalisation of political parties, however, confirm the general rule of a centralised hierarchy over mass organisations, they also substitute the figure of a single leader to that of a few elite individuals[36]. On the one hand, new types of personal parties have been forged, through the prototype (subsequently widely imitated) of Silvio Berlusconi's Forza Italia, 'an artificial party designed on paper on the basis of a sophisticated analysis of the political market, and an extraordinary capacity for managerial organisation' (Calise 2000 [2010], 75, translated in Newell 2018, 76), which founded its rationale on leadership dominance over a docile organisation. On the other hand, personalisation has also strongly influenced larger and well-established organisations with processes of organisational change tending to emphasise the role of the apex figures, by often introducing new methods of direct nomination of the leader though popular involvement. More recently, the digital-

---

35 J. Sluyter-Beltrão, *Iron law of oligarchy*, in *Enclyclopaedia Britannica*, https://www.britannica.com/topic/iron-law-of-oligarchy
36 The concept of 'personal party' has been coined by Italian political science, see M. Calise, *Il partito personale*, Roma-Bari, Laterza, 2000. The phenomenon has then been analysed from a comparative perspective: R. Gunther and L. Diamond, *Species of political parties: A new typology*, in *Party Politics*, 9, 2, 2003, pp. 167–199; F. Musella and P. Webb (eds.), *The Personal Leader in Contemporary Party Politics*, in *Italian Political Science Review / Rivista Italiana di Scienza Politica*, 45, 3, 2015; T. Kostadinova and B. Levitt, *Toward a theory of personalist parties: Concept formation and theory building*, in *Politics & Policy*, 42, 4, 2014, pp. 490–512, which also contains the article of G. Pasquino that has a very eloquent title, *Italy: The Triumph of Personalist Parties*, in *Politics & Policy*, 42, 4, 2014, pp. 548–566.

isation of political parties has also added a 'new act' to developing parties by creating a direct relationship between party leaders and the electorate where charisma plays a significant role. As it has been observed, 'in contrast to the representative model of democracy where politicians were figureheads and parties were the true repositories of power, the hyperleader may have a far larger social media base than their organization. They float above the party, lifting it into the air through their personal visibility' (Gerbaudo 2019b). The result is that Michels' "iron law of oligarchy" finds a partial re-formulation, with the passage – also intuited by Max Weber (1947 [1922], 105–106) – from the centralisation of all powers in the hands of the few to one person who stood at the top of the party[37]. Although the process of personalisation may be considered a general and cross-national phenomenon in the contemporary world, the contrast between the rule of the few and the rule of the leader will remain constant in every political organisation.

The systems of government in contemporary democracies are characterised by a particular equilibrium between the power of parties and the power of the presidents. One key feature of presidential systems is the autonomy presidents enjoy with respect to both majority and opposition parties. On the other pole, party government relates to the leading role of political parties in forming cabinets and setting the governmental agenda. Furthermore, the presidentialisation of politics involves a shift of the decision-making powers away from parties to presidents in areas such as governmental activities, party organisation, and electoral processes (Poguntke and Webb 2005). This process does not necessarily involve formal changes to the constitution. In any case, parties pose an obstacle to the rise of presidents, and their prerogatives remains stronger in parliamentary regimes based on the expression of a vote of confidence on the part of the parliament.

The horizontal axis (legislature–civil society) refers to the basis of governmental legitimacy, that can be realised through the legislature or directly by civil society. Looking at the experience of parliamentarism, party governments may find support within the majority party in parliament or in coalition agreements between social elites, particularly when the latter are characterised by ethnic-cultural divisions. In the former case, changes in consensus and in parliamentary groups may have consequences on the life cycle of political executives; in the latter case, an agreement to share power finds its basis in the need to ensure political stability, along with the rules and institutions of consensus democ-

---

37 I called this passage the 'iron law of leadership' in the volume F. Musella, *Political Leaders beyond Party Politics*, Cham, Palgrave, 2018.

racy aiming at broad participation in government. With regard to presidential regimes, an elected president may be strongly conditioned by the compromises carried out in parliament, or they should become the main driving governmental force by creating a direct relationship with citizens during both the electoral campaigning and their term in office. The emphasis on the formal mechanisms of the election of the president does not allow for a good understanding of different stages of development of presidentialism, as one may clearly notice in the case of the United States, which has passed from the classic model of the separation of powers to more recent trends of presidential government.

Four property spaces result from the intersection of the two axes (see Table 1), concerning two types of party government in the lower part of the matrix, and to two forms of presidential government in the upper one. The weakening of party systems in the lower sections derives the increasing weight of the quadrant which depicts democratic presidents searching for power on the edge of their formal prerogatives.

2.3 The Westminster model

The lower right quadrant represents the party government *par excellence*, the ideal type, which is called 'Westminster' whose original and fullest realisation was in England. It is one the most admired and difficult-to-imitate models of government in the world, and based on three necessary conditions: (a) elections with a simple majority; (b) bipartism; (c) strongly disciplined parties (Sartori 1994, 118). The corollary of bipartism is the one-dimensional and moderate contrast between parties that usually takes place on the left–right axis. While in many European democracies parties have fostered collective action drawing upon divisions, in England the proximity between the main parties' position was the result of the high degree of social homogeneity (Lijphart 1999). Therefore, despite the fact that a series of constitutional reforms have tried to introduce the Westminster model in several contemporary democracies, its 'export' usually results in failure. Thus, as is very common in the academic literature and with frequent risks of conceptual stretching, the idealised Westminster model has become an imperfect descriptor of political systems which 'developed significant ability to "mislead"' (Mackintosh 1970, 4; Russell and Serban 2020).

The ideological attractiveness of this model of government is linked to the clarity and linearity of its concrete functioning: a rationalist conception clearly showing the link between parties and democracy (Katz 1986; Calise 2010). The 'efficient secret' of the English parliamentary form of government – as Bagehot pointed out a century and a half ago (1867) – is the almost complete 'fusion of powers' between the executive and the legislature. The common element is the majority party that on the one hand displays full control over the legislative agenda/activity thanks to its organisational cohesion, and on the other, it elects the government as 'commission of the legislative body' (according to Bagehot's famous definition). Once the electorate is presented with a wide-ranging policy programme and once voters provide a party with a mandate for action, the government has the full ability to define and implement policies. This is the reason why we find *policy* in the middle of the quadrant. Then the electorate will reward or sanction the government for its actions.

Yet it is the British model that has been waning in the last years, because of the transformation of its party system and the subsequent strengthening of the figure of the prime minister. In his introduction to the reprint of *The English Constitution*, Crossman indicates the distance which separated the current British political system from the classical period of parliamentary government, as the postwar epoch has seen the final transformation of cabinet government into prime ministerial government. While 'even in Bagehot's time it was probably a misnomer to describe the premier as chairman, and primus inter pares', in more recent times 'his powers have been steadily increased, first by the centralisation of the party machine under his personal rule, and secondly by the growth of a centralised bureaucracy, so vast that it could no longer be managed by a cabinet behaving like the board of directors of an old-fashioned company' (Crossman 1963, 51). During the last half century, the reinforcement of the prime minister's position has been noticed in many contributions within the British political system, which has started to denounce the emergence of an absolute power at the centre of the old, admired institutions (Hinton 1960; Jones 1985; Heffernan 2005), and has been questioning whether the prime minister was becoming more similar to the American president (Foley 1993; Poguntke and Webb 2005; Heffernan 2013, Dowding 2013). While institutional differences still matter in radically distinguishing regime types (Dowding 2013), with reference to our conceptual matrix such scholars would notice how the British case has been climbing the vertical axis towards more centrality of political leaders.

This is the consequence, indeed, of a second and often overlooked tendency of the British political system: the creeping decline of the party system, empirically detectable in the weakening of the two-party system and decreasing party discipline on the part of MPs. The number of people who strongly identify with a political party has declined significantly. Greater volatility in electoral support has led to the fragmentation of the party system, so that traditional overall majorities are harder to achieve (Green and Posser 2016; Duffy et al. 2019). Looking at the legislative activities Marco Valbruzzi notes that 'the frequency of "rebel votes" was minimal until the end of the 1970s, when the executive could count on cohesive majorities, then it grew significantly in the following decades, topping the peak with the coalition government between 2010 and 2015' (Valbruzzi 2020, 229). The crisis of the traditional Bristish bipartism has raised doubts about the efficient secrecy which has featured as part of the Westminster model, based on the capacity of the majority party to connect legislature with the cabinet by acting as the main player in the making of policy.

2.4 The consensual government

A different regime of party government is depicted in the low left quadrant, where the search for a consensus becomes the main objective in order to reach political stability. The politics of compromise represents the operational code of a divided society, where social 'blocs live side by side as distinctly separate subcultural communities, each with its own political and social institutions and with interaction and communication across bloc boundaries kept to a minimum' (Lijphart 1968, 58).

More particularly, a PR electoral system protects minorities' representation and then forces the main political parties to reach agreement on the basis of compromise in the formation of coalition cabinets (Lijphart 1977; Pennings 1997). Thus, the executive becomes a clearing house of the different interests of the parties in government, which retain high levels of autonomy and mutual veto power. In this case, the building of political consensus within society is an essential part of the scope of government, even at the expense of governmental efficiency, thus responding to the need for an institutional mechanism 'that includes rather than excludes, and that tries to maximize the size of the ruling majority instead of being satisfied with a bare majority' (Lijphart 1999, 32). Consequently, the chief executive assumes a mediating role among ministers, in a complex system of power (Fischer 2014; Linder and Mueller 2021).

We may, for instance, think of political systems crossed by specific linguistic, ethnic, religious, or ideological divisions. This is the case with a 'consensus' democracy such as the Netherlands, which is the true prototype of this model of democracy, where 'leaders overcome the distances between mutually isolated social blocs and resolve disputes typical of non-consensual contexts' (ibid. 1968, 104). In this respect, we can also mention countries that aim to create new institutions through broad party coalitions in their democratic transition. This group includes post-war Italy, where strong ideological conflicts do not allow for the adoption of the British majoritarian formula in a nascent democracy. As authoritatively pointed out by Constantino Mortati in the *Constituent Assembly*, one should create technical devices to achieve a greater stability, by taking into account the political–social elements that are necessary to give this stability an effective realisation (Mortati 1973).

Seen retrospectively, this statement seems to be a viaticum to the realisation of 'integral parliamentarism', with 'the total control of parties over parliament and executive activities through groups "temporarily" majoritarian legitimized to govern through delegations of their "representatives", although they were bounded to seek, daily, the consensus of the assembly' (Miglio 1984, 210).

2.5 The limits of presidentialism

The upper right quadrant describes the classical US system of the separation of power. In the prototype of presidentialism, the leader is at the centre of the political arena because of three fundamental aspects. First, the president is elected though a popular vote, thus gaining an independent electoral consensus. Second, based on the popular vote, the president's term is fixed and does not depend on parliamentary confidence. Finally, the president embraces in a single figure the role of both the prime minister and the president of the republic. Their role concentrates many prerogatives: they are asked to give political direction to the nation, symbolically represent the state, act as the apex of public administration, intervene in legislation with presidential vetoes or autonomous presidential decrees, sign international treaties, and intervene as commander-in-chief of the armed forces (De Luca 2011; Milkis 2011; Ginsberg 2016). As the most used handbooks in American politics have repeated to generations of students, the power of the president is rooted in the Constitution which clearly asserts that 'the executive power shall be vested in a President of the United States of America' (Article II). Yet, although this may appear to be the profile of a plenipotentiary leader, the system of separation of power does not give the president adequate control over the legislative processes, and in this may disclosure a source for failure of such a system of government.

Indeed, despite their direct electoral mandate, the president may become a 'general without army' because they depend on congressional support to carry out their programme (Shugart and Carey 1992; Sartori 1994). And this is even more true when the president's party has no majority in either chamber, with the balance of power resulting in a 'divided government' (Fiorina 1992; Edward et al. 1997; Conley 2002; Cox and Kernell 2019). At other times, the majority party is unable to direct and regulate the behaviour of parliamentarians because of the lack of party discipline which characterises the US political system. Therefore, the governmental agenda often results from the aggregation of different political interests, through a process of legislative logrolling. In both cases, the president lives a clear contradiction between the surplus of personal legitimacy they gained and their capacity for implementing public policies, as described in the eloquent formula 'power invested, promises unfulfilled' in the famous subtitle of the volume "The Personal President" (Lowi 1985). The combination of an increasingly presidential visibility and the consequent escalation of political expectations makes it extremely difficult for the president to fulfil promises made during the election period.

Presidentialism is one of the more criticised forms of government in the world because of its institutional features. On the one hand, the perils of presidentialism in established democracies relate to political impasse as well as decision-making slowdowns[38]. In the better cases, micro-sectional pieces of legislation derive from the lack of agreement on major issues (Jones 1995, 38; Cheibub et al. 2004). On the other hand, and more dangerously, the limits of presidentialism in unconsolidated democracies stand with their formalised and rigid arrangements. It becomes difficult facing political crises as the president cannot be replaced because of the fixed and independent term of office (Linz and Valenzuela 1994). This is the reason why comparative politics has tended to emphasise more the attitude of parliamentary forms of government to produce stable democracies[39], with presidentialism always in a grey zone which risk the nightmare of introducing authoritarian regimes.

2.6 The wave of presidentialisation

In the upper left quadrant presidential government becomes fully presidentialised. By reviving the popular mandate through permanent campaigning, presi-

---

38 See also the study of K. Maeda (*Two modes of democratic breakdown: A competing risks analysis of democratic durability*, in *The Journal of Politics*, 72, 4, 2010, pp. 1129–1143, p. 1141) which finds statistical evidence of the fact that 'presidents in presidential systems are more likely to become authoritarian than prime ministers in parliamentary systems ... Conflicts with other governmental institutions that may arise due to separation of powers may tempt presidents into seeking unconstitutional measures to achieve their goals'.

39 In this respect empirical analysis showed that 'constitutions that prescribe government responsibility are more popular than presidential constitutions. Between 1974 and 2008, there have been 80 transitions to democracy; 37 of these were in countries that were experiencing democracy for the first time. Of the countries where democracy was first implanted in 1974 or after, 62% chose a parliamentary constitution. Thus, the tendency among recent democratising countries has been to choose a constitution that requires governments to maintain the support of a majority in parliament' (J.A. Cheibub and B.E. Rasch, *Constitutional parliamentarism in Europe, 1800–2019*, in *West European Politics*, 2021, pp. 1–32, p. 2).

dents take full advantage of their direct relationship with the electorate asserting their leadership in the decision-making process. Starting from the 1930s, the United States evolved towards an entirely new regime, the so-called Second Republic, which was founded on presidential powers. State interventionism, the increase of control over federal administrations, and the early diffusion of radio as a means of communication all contributed to the transformation of the president into the chief of the nation (Pious 1979). With regards to modes of legislation, a new interpretation of decree powers and legislative decrees can be observed that, according to several authors, represented the clearest trend of the executive expansion of constitutional powers (Ackerman 2010).

More generally, the strengthening of the presidency was based on a new ideological device, adapted by the old Max Weber's lesson (1922) on the legitimate power: plebiscitary democracy. Indeed, a quite different democratic theory was forged: the presidency was the genuine voice of the people being the only institution elected by the entire electorate. The main task of the president – as observed by Wilson – 'is to understand our time and the needs of our people, to be his voice and interpret' (Tulis 1987, 135–136). The President is supposed to be completely able to respond to citizens' demands with no intermediaries such as political parties.

The logic of plebiscitary government applies to both Latin American and post-communist areas as well, where the president usually deals with a multiparty and fragmented system (Rhodes-Purdy and Madrid 2020). Populism is the nucleus of a presidentialism that very often opens up some risks of autocratic involution (De la Torre and Peruzzotti 2018). Nevertheless, these trends are not exclusive to presidential regimes. Indeed, this quadrant is also the space for the creation of France's Fifth Republic in 1958 which produced an authoritative political leadership by introducing a new form of government: semi-presidentialism. Also in parliamentary systems, the possibility to create direct and personal links with civil society enables chief executives to shape issues in a way that will attract media attention[40]. In the age of mass communication, this may lead to an emphasis on themes with a wide and dramatising impact, whether in the national or international arenas, with the consequence of setting presidents' actions free from constitutional constraints (Lowi 1985).

---

40 On this point J. Gaffney (*France in the Hollande presidency: The unhappy republic*, Basingstoke, Palgrave, 2015, p. 38) underlined how de Gaulle's communication 'was in great part maintained throughout his presidency by his own Soviet-style control of the national TV and radio media. His "unmediated" relationship was not only mediated, it was this to the exclusion of other mediations'.

This quadrant also allows for further and unpredictable developments. Indeed, it is worth underlining that today the strengthening of political leaders is occurring in a context of fragmentation of the electorates, and this is putting democracy under pressure[41]. This is the reason why so many scholars have started to fear that monocratic government can also slide into autocracy in more consolidated regimes. The myth of the 'end of history' with the complete affirmation of the liberal order and its capacity to divide power is being replaced by theories of autocratic revival, first linked to the 'fallacy' of electoralism in emerging democracies (Schedler 2006; Staffan 2009; Levistky and Way 2010), and then to more consolidated ones. Although such theories have to be confirmed by a process which is still taking place, they point to the decline of the main indicators of a healthy democracy[42]. We cannot say the last words while noting, however, that political leaders are very often using 'their democratic mandates to launch legal reforms that remove the checks on executive power, limit the challenges to their rule, and undermine the crucial accountability institutions of a democratic state' (Scheppele 2018, 547). In our terms, however, this is the point where monocratic government begins, by combining high levels of leadership and mass personalisation.

2.7 Conclusion

The traditional constitutional models define government in a quite static way, according to the simple distinction between presidentialism and parliamentarism. Although they portray complex and mutable relationships among constitutional bodies, regime types appear as strongly determined by basic and lasting elements such as the direct election of the head of government or the fixed or

---

41 Additionally, deepening polarisation can also become a danger to democracy because polarised voters become more willing to pass over democratic backsliding as long as it helps their own side (A. Prezorwski, *Crises of Democracy*, Cambridge, Cambridge University Press, 2019; M. Graham, M. W. Svolik, *Democracy in America? Partisanship, Polarisation, and the Robustness of Support for Democracy in the United States*, in *American Political Science Review*, 114, 2, 2020, pp. 392–409).

42 K.L. Scheppele (*Autocratic legalism*, in *The University of Chicago Law Review*, 85, 2, 2018, pp. 545–584, p. 546) notes that 'Every Freedom House democracy indicator has declined since 2006, and 105 countries suffered net declines in democracy indicators during the decade from 2006 to 2016', see A. Puddington, *Breaking Down Democracy: Goals, Strategies, and Methods of Modern Authoritarians*, (Freedom House, June 2017), archived at http://perma.cc/DCK4-VVLL. A more recent Freedom House report also confirmed such trends, with very explicit titles: *Democracy under siege*. The document can be retrieved here: https://freedomhouse.org/sites/default/files/2021-03/FIW2021_Abridged_03112021_FINAL.pdf

variable duration of the executive. Nevertheless, two considerations indicate a more accurate understanding of the dynamics related to political institutions. First, the role of the state changes over time, according to the dominant public philosophy and necessity of its intervention. For instance, after the development of welfare programmes, the state is supposed to be responsible for ensuring the safety of the members of society, or at least a large part of it; furthermore, after a financial crisis, or a pandemic emergency, the state is called on to act as a form of providence (Cassese 2014). Second, an element supporting a dynamic view of forms of government concerns decisional power attributed to top political actors. As we observed in this chapter, during the second half of the twentieth century, the vast majority of governing has drawn upon the capacity of parties to act as intermediate structures between society and government. In a parliamentary regime, parties formed and controlled the executive branch of government though votes of confidence; at the same time, also in presidential regimes, despite their direct election, political leaders strongly depended on political parties to define and implement their political programme. Today, with the crisis of the traditional political parties, it is instead very evident when we look at their relationship with members of parties (Dalton and Wattenberg 2002), that chief executives have been endowed with relevant legislative instruments to govern, which they have used in a progressively more extensive and innovative way, until they have come to dominate the democratic political systems.

The matrix presented in this chapter is an attempt to incorporate and merge formal and dynamic approaches to government from a perspective that goes beyond formal constitutional charters, and with a particular reference to the impact of personalisation on contemporary politics and the direct relationship between the president and citizenry. While presidents and prime ministers strengthen their positions within the democratic scenario, they also become the main legislative actor, despite the prerogatives given to parliaments by national constitutions. In this way some authors have considered the boundaries between forms of government more labile, despite their evident differences in terms of institutional traits. And other scholars start to fear that a similar lability may be relevant to the borders between a democratic and an autocratic regime. When single political figures become so essential to the functioning of democracy, an old question is again raised: is it possible to have a democracy without parties?

3 Fragmented Electorates and Parliaments

3.1 Beyond party politics

In several ways, the death of political parties remains one of the most prolific fake news stories of our days. Indeed, as anticipated by those authors noticing the decline of American political parties during the 1970s (Broder 1972; Wattenberg 1984), which was then documented in other European countries (Daalder 1992; Dalton and Wattenberg 2002; Whiteley 2011), the party crisis thesis has become a recurrent statement in political analysis. Yet it has also become a main source of misunderstanding in the next decades, when instead political parties have demonstrated themselves to be one of the most adaptive political actors in democratic systems of government[43]. Political parties have continued to play a crucial role in the functioning of the state machinery, while also evolving new organisational models to react to the main societal transformations (Katz and Crotty 2005; Green and Coffey 2010), such as personalisation and digitalisation of politics[44] (Calise and Musella 2019; Gerbaudo 2019a; Musella 2020d; Deseriis 2020). Thus, even if mutated and almost unrecognisable, political parties remain so necessary for democratic processes and institutions, from electoral competitions to the legislature and executive activities, that one could not imagine a democratic state without them[45].

---

43 Mauro Calise (2015) has noted that, compared to other political institutions, political parties have been proved to be able to cross different political and constitutional stages with a remarkable flexibility. Indeed, while 'the three pillars of the liberal regime – parliament, government, and the judiciary – have undergone relatively small changes in the past century' it is the political party that 'has evolved through quite different forms and roles ... as a Protean transmission belt of all sorts of societal pressures' (M. Calise, *The personal party: an analytic framework*, in *Italian Political Science Review / Rivista Italiana di Scienza Politica*, 45, 3, 2015, pp. 301–315, p. 301).
44 A very clear example of the vitality of political parties is their quick response to the digitalisation of politics. Organisations like the Pirate Parties that have emerged in many Northern European countries, such as the Five Star Movement in Italy, Podemos in Spain, and France Insoumise in France, have utilised the disruptive effect of technological change to search for a new organisational model: 'digital assets, virtually accessible by any device, become a substitute for physical infrastructure [such] as offices, circles and sections that characterise the traditional parties' (P. Gerbaudo, *The digital party. Political organisation and online democracy*, London, Pluto Press, 2019, p. 15).
45 This is the famous Schattschneider's position who, in *The Semi-Sovereign People* (Chicago, Holt, Rinehart, and Winston, p. 1), stated that democracy without parties was unthinkable, putting them at the centre of any modern government. In this line of thinking, classical contributions have highlighted how the role of parties is necessary for representative democracies, see

https://doi.org/10.1515/9783110721720-003

On the other hand, there is a kernel of truth in the narrative that states the end of parties. Indeed, they have been progressively weaker in the way they interact and stay in society: there are those who think that the age of party democracy has passed, referring essentially to the weakening of political parties as an 'active intermediary' between the citizens and government (Mair 1984, 171), which is related to both 'structural-organisational factors on one side, and factors involving the functions performed by the party on the other side' (Ignazi 1996, 550). From this point of view, by excluding the fact that there will be a possibility for the party to reinvigorate their organisational presence, as 'for the foreseeable future, this option seems unavailable at least across the European democracies', scholars have been stated that 'the mass party is dead'[46] (Katz and Mair 2009, 760). The comatose state of political parties refers precisely to what an important tradition of related research has called 'party on the ground'[47], and concerns several variables affecting party life. The distance from the golden age of mass party politics has been revealed by membership numbers, with the absolute numbers of party members nearly halving since the 1980s (Van Biezen, Mair, and Poguntke 2012). With the spread of 'parties without partisans' (Dalton and Wattenberg 2002), it also has been noticed that membership ratios have continued to decrease in most democratic countries during the last decades (Van Haute 2011; Van Haute, Paulis and Sierens 2018), with a direct impact on many aspects of party organisations (Kölln 2015). The sharp reduction in party membership goes hand in hand with the declining proportion of voters claiming strong partisan affinities (Poguntke 2002; Webb 2005). As there are various causes for declining party membership (Dahl and Tufte 1973; Bartolini and Mair 1990; Morlino 1998), strong evidence has been collected on the 'discolored' party identity (Webb 2005), a process of 'disenchantment of the citizenry and inability of parties to shape not only the attitudes of citizens but also the agenda of the media'

Bryce (*Modern Democracies*, New York, Macmillan, 1921) and Sartori (*Representational Systems*, in D.L. Sills [ed.], *International Encyclopaedia of the Social Sciences*, 13, 1968, pp. 470–475.).
46 This is the conclusion reached by Katz and Mair by examining the use of the cartel party category in a twenty-year-old research tradition, see R.S. Katz and P. Mair, *The Cartel Party Thesis: A Restatement*, in *Perspectives on Politics*, 7, 4, 2009, pp. 753–766.
47 The reference here is to the famous Katz and Mair's three faces of party organisation: 'The first is the party in public office, e.g., in parliament or government. The second is the party on the ground, that is the members, activists, and so on. The third is the party central office, that is, the national leadership of the party organization which, at least in theory, is organizationally distinct from the party in public office, and which, at the same time, organizes and is usually representative of the party on the ground' (R. Katz and P. Mair, *The evolution of party organizations in Europe: the three faces of party organization*, in *American Political Science Review*, 14, 1993, pp. 593–617, p. 594).

(Enyedi 2014, 194). We are witnessing, indeed, a growing departure from the main pillars that have characterised conventional engagement in mass organisations such as political parties and trade unions.

The consequences of such trends may be very radical. A long political theory tradition tends to consider party stability as essential for democracy itself: 'partisanship has been postulated in the political science literature as functioning as a preserving or stabilizing influence on public opinion, and consequently on the political system as well' (Wattenberg 2009, 10). Thus, the end of partisanship corresponds to the decline of one of the main columns of contemporary representative regimes. Consequently, many scholars have started to fear the crisis of democracy as we know it. For some of them, political leaders in the new context may take the role of the unique point of public identification and claim full responsibility to govern. As parties have changed, and as the mass party model has passed away (Mair 2005, 2013), this may pave the way for monocratic regimes.

3.2 The era of fragmentation

From an historical point of view, political parties have enabled modern politics through an intense action of mass mobilisation, by offering a long-term, affective attachment to one's preferred political identity (Dalton 2016). Starting from the first American national election surveys in the 1950s, electoral research has shown the concept of 'party identification' as the most important one to study and with which to predict party behaviour: a long-term, affective, psychological identification with one's preferred political party was the basis of the choices of the American voters, and the same was discovered for other Western countries[48] (Campbell et al. 1960). Political parties acted as collective actors because they incorporated and represented relevant and compact blocs of society, by confirming strong and enduring linkages to voters (Dalton, Farrell and McAllister 2011). This was also confirmed by European studies which clearly showed that political parties were able to incorporate and stabilise the masses on the basis of social divisions concerning ethnicity, religion, and territoriality (Lipset and Rokkan 1967). A basic observation on – and proof of – how electoral choices were

---

48 The American Voter produced by Campbell and colleagues emerged as a '"paradigmatic" work, setting the boundaries and standards for subsequent research' (G.M. Pomper, *The impact of the America voter on political science*, in *Political Science Quarterly*, 93, 4, 1978, pp. 617–628, p. 617) and was the most representative book in asserting that voters followed a stable psychological attachment to a preferred party.

based on a sense of identification and loyalty was that 'the party alternatives, and in remarkably many cases the party organisations, were older than the majorities of the national electorates' (Mair 1997).

This assumption has been challenged by recent democratic processes, as even more consolidated representative regimes have to live with a high level of party instability. While in post-war democracies electoral patterns indicated that voters' choices could be predicted on social variables, such as the basis socioeconomic status, religious belief, and place of residence, in the last decades 'long-term election studies for most affluent democracies generally show a shrinking number of partisans or a weakening of the strength of party identities over time' (Dalton 2016; Clarke and Stewart 1998; Fiorina 2002; Hajnal and Lee 2011; Schmitt 2014; Klar and Krupnikov 2016). This follows the process of 'de-freezing' the divisions that were the origin of the stabilisation of the democratic electorate. In the last years the erosion of traditional alignments has left behind an ideologically confused and volatile electorate, that puts emphasis on short term factors for electoral choices, by concentrating attention more on single issues rather than on long-term factors of affiliation. This is accompanied by a sharp increase in the probability of the electorate changing positions between elections (Crewe and Denver 1985).

This electorate may be more easily 'captured' by an appeal of the political leaders. In the absence of party cues, voters will rely more heavily on the appeal of the candidates' personalities to decide their vote (Carey and Shugart 1995; Marsh 2007). Indeed, the electoral market is now open for all political entrepreneurs who want to try a new enterprise as 'an ever more volatile electorate appears to have relinquished any stable linkage to the original cleavages where most major parties had found, for over a century, their source of ideology, authority, and consent'[49] (Calise 2015, 313; Costa Lobo 2014; Rahat and Kenig 2018). As McAllister (2007, 582) confirms: 'with weaker partisan loyalties, and in the absence of strong social links to specific parties, such as class or religion, voters are more likely to switch their vote between elections, or to abstain. In these circumstances, weaker voter attachments to parties should enhance the role of the leader in both the mobilization and conversion of the vote'. Yet there is nothing that says that the capacity of personal leaders in attracting vot-

---

[49] The analogy between the electoral and economic market was anticipated by the formulation of the market-based economic model of democracy, first outlined by Joseph Schumpeter (*Capitalism, Socialism and Democracy*, New York, Harper, 1942) and popularised by Anthony Downs (*An Economic Theory of Democracy*, New York, Harper & Row, 1957).

ers may contribute to stabilising the electorate over time[50]. Instead, it seems that instability has entered the political world[51] with party dealignment.

Focussing attention on the last two decades, which is in the scope of this volume, two processes appear as particularly relevant in the dynamics of mass dealignment.

First, the lack of stable party ties may be observed by analysing the high level of political volatility in contemporary democracies (Drummond 2006; Mainwaring and Zoco 2007; Dassonneville and Hooghe 2011)[52]. In Figure 1, the Pedersen index of volatility[53] (discounting the fact that the measure may lead to some misinterpretations [Casal Bértoa, Deegan-Krause and Haughton 2017]), is one of the most useful tools to evidence the general trend towards the increase in volatility and electoral instability. France, Italy, and Hungary are the countries which show the highest values in our set of democracies, where an average of 20% of the electorate change their preference between two elections. Despite the differences in electoral law and in institutional assets, the growth of volatility appears to be a cross-national trend.

Moreover, the number of political parties has grown in such countries even if we adopt a restrictive definition of what is a 'new party'[54] (Figure 2). Indeed, in

---

50 The emergence of new political parties, in turn, brings to us to the highest level of fragmentation and we can imagine that the higher the degree of fragmentation, the smaller the interparty ideological space and, therefore, the higher the probability that voters shift their preferences.

51 A. André, S. Depauw and S. Beyens, *Party loyalty and electoral dealignment*, in *Party Politics*, 21, 6, 2015, pp. 970–981, underline that party loyalty is lowest where partisan dealignment is strongest by analysing 15 advanced industrial democracies.

52 Recent studies have also revealed a process of convergence in the levels of electoral volatility between Western European party systems and Central and Eastern European ones. See V. Emanuele, A. Chiaramonte and S. Soare, *Does the Iron Curtain Still Exist? The Convergence in Electoral Volatility between Eastern and Western Europe*, in *Government and Opposition*, 55, 2, 2020, pp. 308–326.

53 The classic measure for electoral volatility is the Pedersen Index: $TEV=\Sigma|Vi,t\text{-}1\text{-}Vi,t|/2$, in which Vi,t is the vote share for a party at a given election (t) and $Vi,t\text{-}1$ is the vote share of the same party at the previous elections (t-1) (see M.N. Pedersen, *The dynamics of European party systems: changing patterns of electoral volatility*, in *European journal of political research*, 7,1, 1979, pp. 1–26).

54 Defining a 'new' political party is not a simple task. Some scholars consider new parties both those which have roots in other party formations – therefore resulting from mergers, splits or reorganisations – and those which are formed as completely new actors in party politics (R. Harmel and J.D. Robertson, *Formation and success of new parties: A cross-national analysis*, in *International Political Science Review*, 6, 4, 1985, pp. 501–523; N. Bolleyer, *New parties in old party systems: persistence and decline in seventeen democracies*, Oxford, Oxford University Press, 2013). On the contrary according to S. Bartolini and P. Mair (*Policy competition, spatial distance*

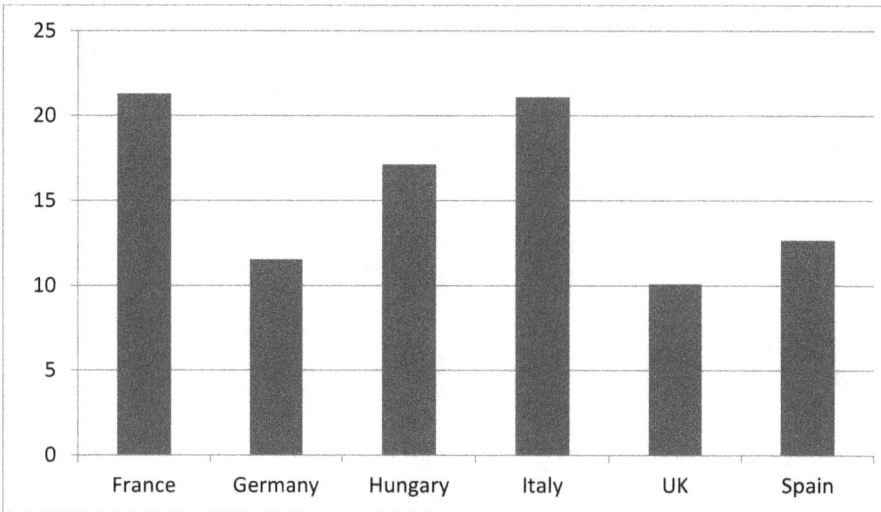

Figure 1: Electoral volatility on average in our six countries (2000 – 2020). *Source:* own elaboration based on F. Casal Bértoa, *Database of WHO GOVERNS in Europe and beyond*, PSGo, 2021, available at: whogoverns.eu

our set of democracies, 24 new parties have emerged in the span of time which we considered. Italy shows the highest number of new parties per parliamentary term, thus appearing as the most unstable country in our set of democracies. Spain, Hungary, and France display a clear trend towards the increase of number of parties, as well (see Figure 2). The emergence of new parties is affected by social, political, and structural factors (Harmel and Robertson 1985), leading to the crisis of the established parties[55] (Ignazi 1996) and with the capacity for 'party system innovation' (Chiaramonte and Emanuele 2017).

---

and electoral instability, in *West European Politics*, 13, 4, 1990, pp. 1– 16) a party is considered as new when it does not derive from the structure of an existing party. In following this approach, we consider new parties to be those that are 'not successors to any previous parties, have a novel name and structure' (*How unstable? Volatility and the genuinely new parties in Eastern Europe*, in *European Journal of Political Research*, 44, 3, 2005, pp. 391– 412, p. 399). Mergers, electoral coalitions, and splits of pre-existing political parties are not considered to be new parties. Yet even with such a restricted definition, the trend of an increase in the number of parties in our set of democracies is very clear.

55 More generally speaking it is associated with the emergence and the electoral success of new parties which relies on, among other factors, a new political opportunity structure for political parties, see P. Lucardie, *Prophets, purifiers and prolocutors: Towards a theory on the emergence of new parties*, in *Party Politics*, 6, 2, 2000, pp. 175 – 185. Moreover, the new political offer remains

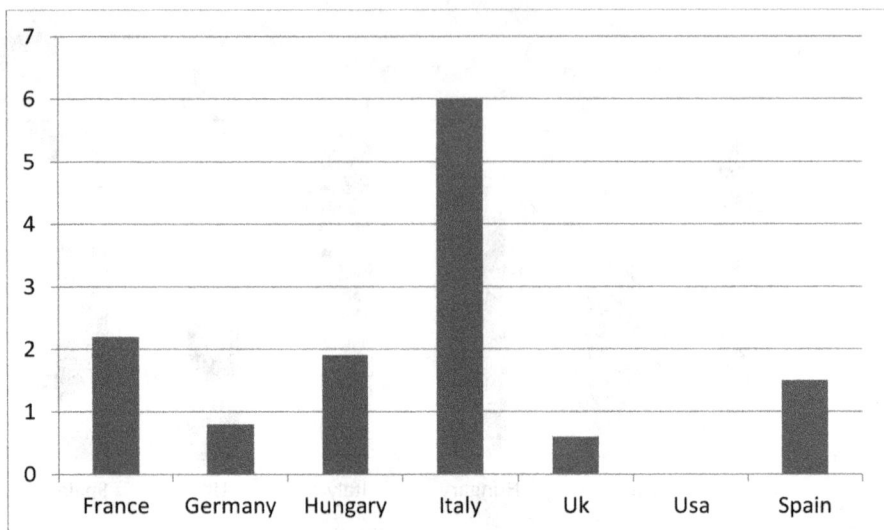

Figure 2: Number of new parties per term. *Source:* own elaboration based on F. Casal Bértoa, *The database is WHO GOVERNS in Europe and beyond*, PSGo, 2021, available at: whogover-ns.eu.
* The general period taken into consideration is 2000–2020. The timespan for each country is slightly different as it is based on data already available, but it covers about twenty years for each country.
** Only new parties with more than 0.5 per cent of the vote are included. Independents are also excluded.

Due to the birth of new political parties, the effective number of parties[56] in our set of democracies has tended to increase in the last twenty years, as 'voters

---

associated with the spread of anti-establishment sentiments that pave the way for the emergence of 'anti-party parties'. On this point and with particular reference to the relationship between anti-party sentiment and votes for extreme parties see R.J. Dalton and S.A. Weldon (*Public images of political parties: A necessary evil?*, in *West European Politics*, 28, 5, 2005, pp. 931–951), and especially for the Italian case L. Bardi, *Anti-Party Sentiment and Party System Change in Italy*, in *European Journal for Political Research*, 29, 3, 1996, pp. 345–363.

56 According to G.B. Powell (*Contemporary Democracies: Participation, Stability, and Violence*, Cambridge, Harvard University Press, 1982), party fragmentation is the degree to which the electoral support – and so parliamentary representation – is divided among different political parties. The effective number of parties (see M. Laakso and R. Taagepera, *Effective Number of Parties: A Measure with Application to West Europe*, in *Comparative Political Studies*, 12, 1, 1979, pp. 3–27) measures the fragmentation of a political system: the more parties there are, the more fragmented the system, and vice versa. Rather than take the total number of all existing

spread their votes over time among a growing number of parties (most likely also genuinely new ones) and that parties tend to split' (Rahat and Kenig 2018, 60). In France the effective number of parties goes from five to seven in the two decades considered, in Germany from four to six, and in Spain it doubles from three to seven.

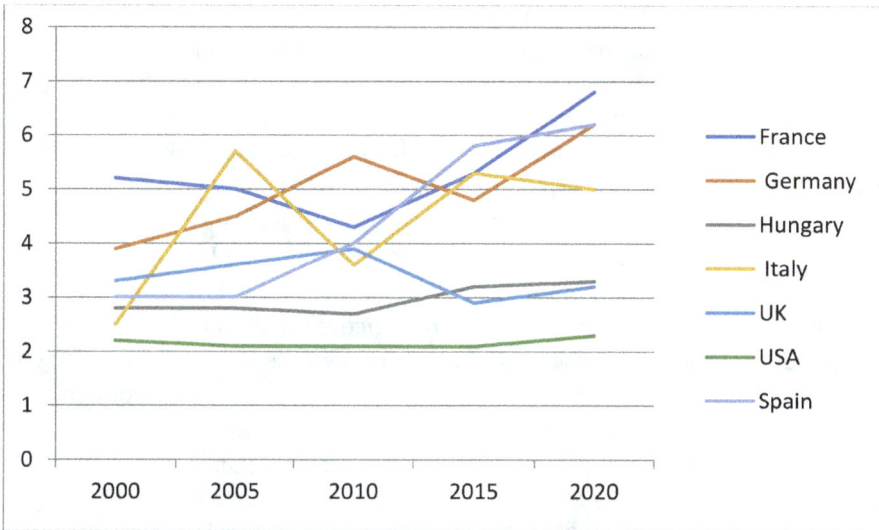

Figure 3: Effective number of electoral parties. *Source:* own elaboration based on F. Casal Bértoa, *The database is WHO GOVERNS in Europe and beyond*, PSGo, 2021, available at: whogoverns.eu.
* The general period taken into consideration is 2000 – 2020. The timespan for each country is slightly different as it is based on the data already available, but it covers about 20 years for each country.
** Only new parties with more than 0.5 per cent of the vote are included. Independents are also excluded.

Western party systems appeared unrecognisable even when compared with a recent past. Classical bipartisanships, such as British and Spanish ones, have been challenged by the emergence of third poles (Rodon and Hierro 2016; Hutter and Kriesi 2019). From the weakening of the main divisions structuring the tradition-al party systems and unprecedented levels of party volatility, derives a 'wave of party system de-istitutionalisation' (Chiaramonte and Emanuele 2017) that will

---

parties, the index takes into consideration the significant/relevant parties and their relative size, going further than the numerical 'format'.

have inevitable consequences on systems of government in terms of (monocratic) leading actor.

3.3 The spread of polarisation

Political scientists converge on a point concerning democratic political systems: clearly fragmented, they have tended to be more polarised. Polarisation has been negatively related with the efficiency and stability of democracy and with the functioning and the dynamic of party system, thus appearing as a typical trait of democratic systems that are not completely consolidated (Körösényi 2013; Wang 2014). 'Polarised pluralism' is Giovanni Sartori's (1966) label to qualify the party system where anti-system political parties[57] realise centrifugal dynamics, with an explicit historical reference to the delays of the Italian party system in comparative perspective. Indeed, the Florentine scholar has pointed to ideological polarisation as a true peril for the functioning of party systems and as a particular element of those regimes crossed by excessive radicalism. Today, although polarisation is still usually considered a serious problem for democracy, linking to different undesirable effects such as 'legislative gridlock, elite incivility, income inequality, and mass disengagement' (Lupu 2015, 331), it is also spreading as a diffuse feature of contemporary democracies in different geographical contexts (Dalton 2008; Powell 2010). Many contributions have taken American politics as an example of polarisation, with the separation of the two major political parties 'that implies an intense disagreement in the preferred policy solutions and preferences of political actors', as it may reveal behaviour at the level of American political elites, as well as at the level of the masses[58], and

---

57 In Giovanni Sartori's theory of 'polarised pluralism', the concept of anti-system parties is crucial. Sartori defines an anti-system party as one which 'erodes the legitimacy of the regime it opposes'. Furthermore, he argues that the presence of anti-system parties reveals a strong ideological distance, and the ideological distance results in pro-system parties. In the so called 'First Italian Republic', Sartori calls attention to MSI (*Movimento Sociale Italiano*) and PCI (*Partito Comunista Italiano*) as examples of anti-system parties on the extreme poles of party competition. For a more in-depth understanding see: G. Sartori, *European Political Parties: The Case of Polarized Pluralism*, in J. LaPalombara and M. Weiner (eds.), *Political Parties and Political Development*, Princeton, Princeton University Press, 1966, pp. 137–176.

58 For a review of polarisation in the American politics, see M.J. Hetherington, *Putting Polarisation in Perspective*, in the *British Journal of Political Science*, 39, 2, 2009, pp. 413–448, and with reference to an empirical analysis of polarisation in the US Senate: A. Abramowitz and J. McCoy, *United States: Racial Resentment, Negative Partisanship, and Polarisation in Trump's America*, in *The Annals of the American Academy of Political and Social Science*, 681, 1, 2019, pp. 137–156. The

which is explored in both the national and subnational political arena (Jordan and Bowling 2016, 220). Here the negative relationship between polarisation and volatility is particularly evident[59]. Yet in a few years polarisation emerged as an established fact in different countries (McCoy, Rahman and Somer 2018).

Scholars who focused attention on polarisation, following a Downsonian perspective based on spatial models, have generally used two methods for measuring it: the first one, concerning the study of elite polarisation, calculates the distance between the medians (or means) of the distribution of political parties over a policy issue or along the ideological continuum in an institution such as a parliament or a constitutional court (Ditslear and Baum 2001; Abramowitz and Saunders 2008). The second method looks at the distributions of opinions by using surveys or other means of opinion gathering (Clark 2009, 147). The two methods reveal, however, high levels of interconnection because of the relationship between the electorate and representatives[60].

As a way of combining both the approaches, one of the most used operationalisations of polarisation has been proposed by Dalton, for whom polarisation 'reflects the degree of ideological differentiation among political parties in a system' (Dalton 2008, 900). The Dalton index of polarisation takes into account the range of party positions on policy issues/Left–Right scale and their electoral size. Indeed, as Dalton argues (2008, 906): 'conceptual measure of party polarisation should include two elements: (a) the relative position of each party along the Left–Right scale and (b) the party's position weighted by party size (because a large party at the extreme would signify greater polarization than a splinter party in the same position)'.

---

rise of affective polarisation is largely observable in American public opinion polarisation as well, with Democrats and Republicans strongly divided: S. Iyengar and S.J. Westwood, *Fear and loathing across party lines. New evidence on group polarisation*, in *American Journal of Political Science*, 59, 3, 2015, pp. 690–707) confirm that the polarisation of the American electorate has dramatically increased in the latter years.

59 See: R.J. Dalton, *Modeling ideological polarization in democratic party systems*, in *Electoral Studies*, vol. 72, available online 30 May 2021.

60 The relationship between mass and elite polarisation remains open, however. According to the well-known literature on public opinion, a certain degree of correspondence is measured between the two processes, see J.M. Lee, *Assessing Mass Opinion Polarization in the US Using Relative Distribution Method*, in *Social Indicators Research*, 124, 2, 2015, pp. 571–598. Adopting a contrary position, Fiorina and Abrams (2009) examine the widening electoral disconnect between polarised elected officials and common citizens, see P.M. Fiorina and S.J. Abrams, *Political polarization in the American public*, in the *Annual Review of Political Science*, 11, 2008, pp. 563–588.

Thanks to the available data of the Comparative Study of Electoral Systems (CSES), we can observe the on-going polarisation trend in four of the seven countries considered, with Spain and France displaying the highest level of the measure (Figure 4).

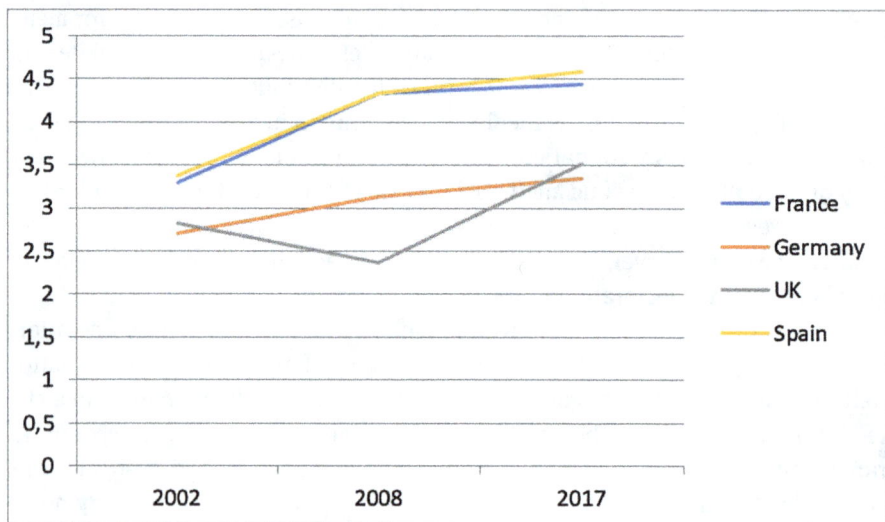

Figure 4: Polarisation trend (Dalton Index) in four countries. *Source:* own elaboration based on the CSES data (Comparative study of electoral systems, cses.org).

This is an important trend as an increased polarisation may lead to the expansion of executive authority at the expense of a diminished legislature. As noted in the United States 'perhaps one of the most important long-term consequences of the decline in legislative capacity caused by polarisation is that Congress's power is declining relative to the other branches of government' (Barber and McCarty 2015). Also this tendency can fuel the space for monocratic governments.

3.4 Consequences for policy making

Legislative activities provide us with an additional perspective with which to look at the phenomenon of party fragmentation. As a long-standing debate on the relationship between party dealignment in the electorate and the behaviour of parties' representatives in the legislative arena has been initiated (Bowler 2000; Thies 2000; Hazan 2003), most evidence confirms that the combination of electoral volatility and polarisation results in a more undisciplined legislative assembly. Indeed, from the weakening of stable party identification derives more individualistic behaviour on the part of representatives, which very often tends to undermine majority cohesion and discipline.

As one of the most significant indicators showing this trend, party switching – or *transfuguismo* – has been observed in many other European democracies[61]. Frequent changes in the party affiliation of representatives usually appear in times of democratic consolidation or rapid institutional transformations, when instability produces uncertainty in political relations and affiliations. However, if defections become continuous and assume the characteristics of personal be-trayals, they can be considered a clear indicator of the crisis in political parties, even in most consolidated democracies (Verzichelli 1996a, 1996b; Musella and Vercesi 2019). And this tends to feature the overall party system, whose stability appears as challenged by an excessive quantity of intra-party movements.

This is what is occurring in an increasing number of democracies. In the following figure, while a lesser number of party switchers may be counted in 'Westminster democracies', high values are registered in France and Italy, with more than one hundred MPs changing their affiliations in each parliamentary term.

As the growth of party indiscipline is a transversal trend for contemporary democracies, one may focus on Italy as one of the clearest examples of increased parliamentary fluidity. Indeed, despite the expected reduction in the number of political parties and simplification of the overall party system that accompanied the advent of the so-called Second Republic in Italy, empirical evidence concern-ing parliamentary groups has confirmed a high level of assembly fragmentation, along with a frequent increase in the number of parliamentary groups in the phase between two elections (Musella 2014).

Data on parliamentary defections show a declining party and coalition loy-alty which has occurred quite regardless of adopted electoral rules. A growing number of MPs decide to change parliamentary group during the legislature.

---

61 It is not the case that party switching has become a fashionable concept in Western coun-tries. It is also the origin of several proposals of constitutional reforms to avoid excessive MP mobility, emerging as a cross-national phenomenon (W. Heller and C. Mershon (eds.), *Political parties and legislative party switching*, New York, Springer, 2009; E. Klein, *Explaining legislative party switching in advanced and new democracies*, in *Party Politics*, 27, 2, 2021, pp. 329–340). Anti-defection legislation has also been investigated in the last two decades, and 'many nations enshrine anti-defection provisions in their constitutions, which are not depositories for tempo-rary legislation' (K. Janda, *Laws against Party Switching, Defecting, or Floor-Crossing in National Parliaments: The Legal Regulation of Political Parties*, Working Paper 2, 2009 August, p. 1).

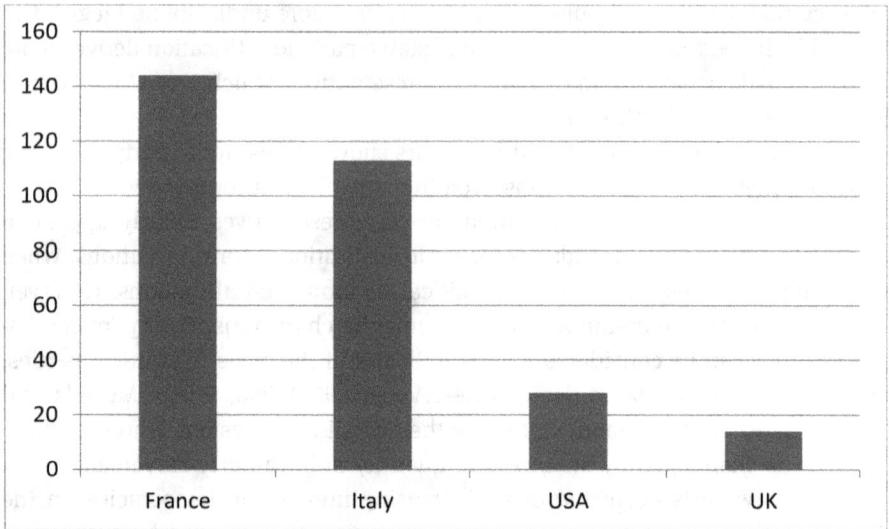

Figure 5: Party switching per term. *Source:* own elaboration based on parliamentary archives. Switchers are counted once per legislature.

At the beginning of the 1990s, the majoritarian electoral system constituted a decisive factor in stimulating a more direct relationship between representatives and citizens, and consequently, in fostering individualistic behaviour in the legislature. It was surprising that 261 deputies and 129 senators changed groups during the thirteenth legislature, and 50 per cent of these moves were from one coalition to another: 'the *gruppo misto*, initially composed of 26 members, has become the third group in the *Camera dei Deputati* with a composition of one hundred members' (Caretti 2001). Yet after the introduction of the proportional electoral law in 2005, the so-called *Porcellum* was not able to reinforce the relationship between political parties and their affiliates. If it attributed more power in nominating candidates to the party elite, this was not sufficient to control party members, who were often ready to offer themselves to the highest bidder between elections. Thus, the new electoral system was incapable of producing an effective reduction in parliamentary indiscipline (Fusaro 2007; Di Virgilio et al. 2012). The rise in party switching has continued in more recent times: concentrating attention on the trend that followed in the period 2000–2020, we noted that an increasing number of deputies changed groups in the Chamber of Deputies especially in the sixteenth and seventeenth terms (Figure 6).

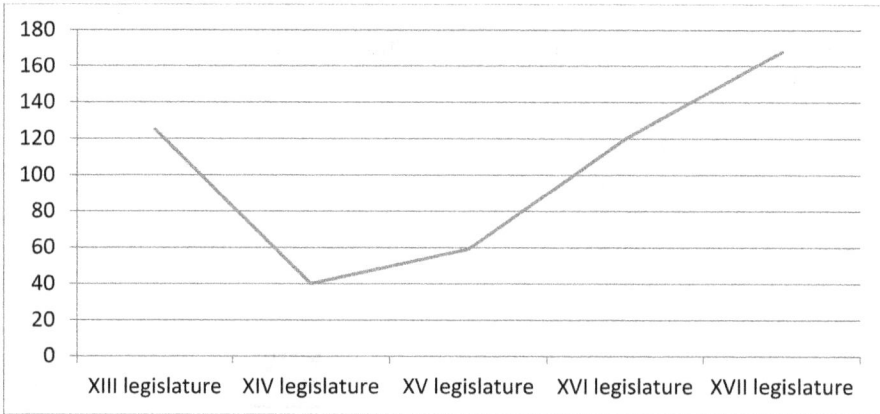

Figure 6: Party switching in Italy 2000 – 2020. *Source:* own elaboration based on parliamentary archives. Switchers are counting once per legislature.

Italy shows also how fragmentation in its Parliament is strongly associated with low legislative performance as well. As part of the broader phenomenon of the personalisation of politics, MPs' individualism is also very evident 'in the use of individual parliamentary instruments, an increase in single-authored initiatives for activities that could also be conducted collectively, a larger concentration of visible parliamentary activities' (Wauters, Bouteca and de Vet 2019, 246), and finds its confirmation in the devaluation of the law as the main channel for political direction.

Still focussing attention on the Italian case, in a context marked by parties in crisis and the personalisation of politics, there has been growing competition between individual members of the Parliament, leading to a parallel increase in the number of bills presented. In the thirteenth legislature, because of the particular political turbulence due to Tangentopoli scandals[62], a genuine anomaly occurred: parliamentary initiative bills reached a record of 10,000 (Musella 2012a, 139). Yet such a trend was also repeated in the following legislatures, with more than 7,000 bills initiated under the Berlusconi and Monti governments. Between the thirteenth and the sixteenth legislatures, MPs were responsible for more than 90 % of the proposals put forward, peaking at 95.7 % during

---

[62] The Tangentopoli scandals uncovered the most extensive networks of political corruption ever to come to light in post-war Italy in the early Nineties. The traditional parties collapsed, and it paved the way for Berlusconi's decision "to take the field" in 1994 and for the establishment of the so-called Second Italian Republic.

the fourth Berlusconi government. In fact, the monthly average of draft proposals has increased, doubling in number from the 1980s to the 1990s and reaching over 250 per month over the last 10 years (De Micheli and Verzichelli 2004). Most of these proposals do not become law, rather serving a more propagandistic or symbolic function. Indeed, after Tangentopoli, only a small percentage of MPs' proposals actually passed, with the figure remaining below 1% for some legislatures (Table 1).

Table 1: Success of legislative proposals coming from government or parliament.

Term	Executive proposals	approved (%)	Parliament proposals	approved (%)	Total	Monthly average
I	2547	80.6	1375	18.9	3922	63
II	1667	84.4	2514	19.1	4181	72
III	1569	82.8	3688	13.0	5257	87
IV	1569	75.4	4414	17.5	5983	100
V	977	64.2	4189	5.1	5166	103
VI	1255	67.7	4597	5.9	5852	122
VII	1022	55.5	2646	3.7	3668	102
VIII	1358	55.6	3980	7.2	5338	116
IX	1287	44.1	4642	4.7	5929	124
X	1471	50.3	6920	4.6	8391	150
XI	862	27.9	4269	5.3	5131	221
XII	1143	23.0	5020	0.9	6163	257
XIII	1453	49.1	10479	2.3	11932	199
XIV	707	53.9	8637	1.7	9344	158
XV	285	32.3	5062	0.3	5347	223
XVI	482	63.1	8399	0.1	8881	128
XVII	412	68.7	6896	0.1	7308	119
XVIII	282(2020)		4471		4753	86.4

Source: own elaboration on data from the Italian Senate, senato.it

A more personalised legislative assembly has been formed as a consequence of a more individualised society. The Italian Parliament has become a chaotic environment for law-making, that stimulates political leaders to find alternative and autonomous channels for legislation. Several studies that investigate the executive–parliament relationship have emphasised that high parliamentary fragmentation drastically reduces ordinary legislation in favour of the government's decrees and legislation protected through votes of confidence or other similar tools (De Micheli 2020)[63].

3.5 Political leaders facing individualised societies

Fragmented and polarised electorates are the joy and torment of every political leader. On the one hand, leaders acquire more power and develop more capacity to communicate with people without intermediation, by proposing themselves as an alternative to rule 'the void' of representative regimes once occupied by political parties (Mair 2013)[64]. Yet, on the other hand, as intuited by one of the more lucid analysts of the rise of US presidential powers, while leaders have been vested with more powers in contemporary democracies, it is very likely that their electoral promises will remain unfulfilled (Lowi 1985). Indeed, once in government, leaders discover insufficient support on the part of divided legislative assemblies: in recent decades, political party systems across the Western world have fragmented and have seen their support base collapse, with clear consequences for parliamentary activities. In the United States this is true at the point that 'the understandable concern that many have today is whether in times of divided government – but not only then, given the Senate filibuster rule, which remains in place on policy matters – the absence of a "majority government" will make it too difficult to generate the kind of concerted political action required for legislation' (Pildes 2014, 805; Lee 2015a).

This has also been proposed as the origin of the 'temptation' of presidents to extend their powers in order to overcome legislative impasse or slowdowns (Carmines and Fowler 2017). Indeed, when the Congress did not acquiesce to the president's legislative agenda, the president 'vastly expanded his authority, and the authority of his successors, to regulate – that is, to make policy decisions' (Posner 2005, 4). For European parliamentary systems, which have affirmed the crucial role of the legislative assembly as the core of the political system, the gap with the past may be even greater, with the chief executive extending their powers outside the constitutional provisions regulating their role. Consequently, the principle of division of power has been challenged by

---

63 A more in-depth analysis of executive–legislative and presidential relationships is provided by Bolton and Thrower (2015), in their framework for a theory of 'presidential unilateralism'.
64 On the new role assumed by political leaders in a post-particratic context see also K. Aarts, A. Blais and H. Schmitt, *Political Leaders and Democratic Elections*, Oxford, Oxford University Press, 2011; F. Musella, *Political Leaders beyond Party Politics*, Cham, Palgrave, 2018.

an acknowledged shift of prerogatives and functions from parliament to government (Blanco Valdés 2012; López Guerra et al. 2000).

It comes as no surprise that the move toward greater personalisation in democracy has been happening slowly over the course of the last several decades, and such processes have largely showed that personal politics is not directly associated with authoritarian regimes (Kane and Patapan 2012; Musella 2018)[65]. Yet the spread of the personalisation of the masses and the definite erosion of mass parties represents a further challenge for democracy. The overarching process of personalisation is starting to raise some doubts on whether our democracies can cope with such a high level of political destructuring, and many contributions have pointed to how democratically elected governments have been undermining independent institutions, thus entering a period of 'democracy without guardrails'[66]. What happens when individualism becomes an established fact? As the process of personalisation of politics has been going on – at both leader and base level – the more crucial and worrying question is posed by those scholars interested in regime change: what is the level of political fragmentation that a democratic political system may endure?

---

65 The global rise of personalised politics has already been observed as a process of diffusion of authoritarian regimes: 'In 1988, personalist regimes comprised just 23 percent of all dictatorships. Today, this percentage has almost doubled, with personalist dictators ruling 40 percent of all authoritarian regimes', cf. B. Geddes, J. Wright and E. Frantz, *Autocratic Breakdown and Regime Transitions: A New Data Set*, in *Perspectives on Politics* 12, 2, 2014. Yet the question here is whether more consolidated democracies may combine their structures and internal mechanism with a progressively higher level of leader and mass personalisation, see A. Kendall-Taylor, E. Frantz and J. Wright, *The global rise of personalized politics: It's not just dictators anymore*, in *The Washington Quarterly*, 40, 1, 2017, pp. 7–19.
66 It is the book already cited by S. Levitsky and D. Ziblatt, *How Democracies Die*, New York, Crown Publishers, 2018. For a discussion see the book review by L. Johnson, *Democracy Dies a Slow Death*, in *Yale Journal of International Affairs*, 13, 2018, pp. 19–24.

4 The expansion of governmental decrees

4.1 An under-evaluated field of analysis

The growth of government is one of the clearest tendencies of modern politics, as reported by a rich abundance of research analysis concerning the different variables of its activities. By conventional budget and gross national product measures, government's role and functions have increased over the course of the nineteenth century, especially with the birth and extension of welfare programmes: 'as a result, governments everywhere in developed world have moved from a sometimes trivial to a now uniformly considerable role in shaping national expenditures'[67] (Peltzman 1980, 209). 'Big government' has constituted a truly remarkable and irreversible phenomenon[68], that would encounter a partial rethinking only starting in the 1990s with the spread of neoliberal ideas, to move on again with the financial, terrorist, and pandemic crises that would follow in the next years[69]. This is also supported by an increasing demand for government from individual citizens or groups of citizens 'with each party having a desire for some form of a publicly provided good, externality reduction, or redistribution of income' (McCormick and Tollison 1981; Garrett and Rhine 2006, 17), as well as by the perennial – we can say innate – search of bureaucrats them-

---

67 An important body of research focusses on salient features of the growth of government from a political and historical perspective, by considering factors explaining changes in the demand for – and supply of – government, in specific countries; see A. Suphan and J. Veverka, *The growth of government expenditure in Germany since the unification*, in *FinanzArchiv/Public Finance Analysis*, 23, 2, 1963, pp. 169–278; D.C. North, *The growth of government in the United States: an economic historian's perspective*, in *Journal of Public Economics*, 28, 3, 1985, pp. 383–399; G.K. Fry, *Growth of Government*, New York, Routledge, 2019. For a discussion see P.D. Larkey, S. Chandler and M. Winer, *Theorizing about the growth of government: A research assessment*, in *Journal of Public Policy*, 1, 2, 1981, pp. 157–220.
68 Most scholars agree that 'taking all factors into account, the best forecast for the twenty-first century may be for stabilized government, but not shrinking government', see R.G. Holcombe, *Government Growth in the Twenty-First Century*, in *Public Choice*, 124, 1/2, 2005, pp. 95–114, p. 111.
69 The call for more intensive state action will be considered in Chapter 6 of this volume, which is dedicated to the pandemic emergency. It is no coincidence that the theme of the 'return of the state' has returned to political science studies following the statist response to the financial crisis registered in the last years, see J.D. Levy, *The return of the state? France's response to the financial and economic crisis*, in *Comparative European Politics*, 15, 4, 2017, pp. 604–627; H. Kundnani, *Europe after the Coronavirus: A 'Return of the State'?* in *IAI Papers*, 20, 32, 2020. With reference to the pandemic times, when societies are forced to turn inward in search of State protection, see the recent volume by P. Gerbaudo, *The Great Recoil: Politics After Populism and Pandemic*, London, Verso Books, 2021.

https://doi.org/10.1515/9783110721720-004

selves to maximise the size of their agencies' budgets and volume of activities (Niskanen 1971).

Other scholars prefer concentrating attention on the escalation in the number and professionalisation of staff in executive structures, arriving at a similar conclusion on their rapid development: the transition from a few secretaries serving the executive branch at the beginning of the nineteenth century to the complex and articulated offices of today's administrations in a few decades has also concerned vast countries such as the United States (Polsby 1978; Dickinson 1999). The development of executive offices is part of the more general escalation of public bureaucracies over the last century. Furthermore, the progress in terms of staff and an advisory system was seen as a sign of the 'presidentialization of premiership' in several European countries (Pryce 1997).

Yet the key variable for understanding the strengthening of government in the last decades refers to legislative patterns pointing to a shift of power to the executive body. Legislative powers still represent an under-evaluated topic in the field of executive politics, with different strands of literature that struggle to reach unity. Indeed, the study of how executives affect public policies tends to be anecdotal although it responds to one of the main questions of comparative politics (Doyle 2020). Indeed, apart from some attempts to consider the strength of political executives along with their formal prerogatives (Carey and Shugart 1998; Sartori 1997; Metcalf 2000; Cheibub 2007), a few contributions have focused on legislative powers as a mirror of an effective form of government for a country. Conversely, the analysis of legislation has become a crucial part of investigating government change in the last few years. In sharp contrast to the doctrine of separation of power that would attribute to parliament the last word in general rules produced for society, the executives have been progressively provided with relevant channels to intervene in law-making while assuming the classical prerogatives of parliamentary bodies, which especially but not exclusively – in presidential countries such as United States – 'has often failed to defend its constitutional powers' (Fisher 2011, 2406).

In this chapter we will focus on three different arenas of executive expansion to look at how the executives 'legislate' in our set of democracies.

4.2 Delegative democracy?

Guillermo O'Donnell's (1999) depiction of delegation democracy was used to analyse the Latin American countries characterised by low economic and political development. Indeed, the Argentine author found it very difficult to refer to the classical category of representative democracy for unconsolidated democracies in this part of the globe. Thus, in his famous essay, O'Donnell explains that in a delegative democracy 'whoever wins election to the presidency is thereby entitled to govern as he or she sees fit, constrained only by the hard facts of existing power relations and by a constitutionally limited term of office' (1999, 164). In this subtype of democracy, a strong leader has a free rein to act and justify his or her acts in the name of the people (Collier 1997). A very low horizontal accountability is assured, on the basis of the assumption of a greater vertical accountability toward people. In particular, the most controversial point is that presidential powers tend to remain unchecked by legislatures, courts, or other mechanisms, as a consequence of the weakness of an immature state of law. Consequently, although such democracies seem to meet formal democratic prerequisites such as free elections, they do not comply with the basic principle, that is division of power: from a different angle this also reminds us of the 'failure of presidential democracy' identified by Linz and Valenzuela (1994) when they analysed such system of government far from the United States.

Since the 1990s the O'Donnell's subtype was considered useful to understand the reality of both the 'new players in town' of third wave democracies as well as new trends in more consolidated ones. On the one hand, the emergence of a 'grey' area between consolidated representative democracies and authoritarian regimes has led to the adaptation of the O'Donnell thesis to countries such as Central American ones, the Philippines and North Korea, or Russia and Ukraine[70]. On the other hand, the old representative democracies may seem to regress into delegative ones, or at least become more similar to them, when some conditions are fulfilled[71]: '1) presidents who present themselves as being "above" the party; 2) institutions such as congress and the judiciary that are

---

[70] On specific countries see L.E. Anderson, *The Authoritarian Executive? Horizontal and Vertical Accountability in Nicaragua*, in *Latin American Politics and Society*, 48, 2, 2006, pp. 141–169; A. Croissant, *Legislative Powers, Veto Players, and the Emergence of Delegative Democracy: A Comparison of Presidentialism in the Philippines and South Korea*, in *Democratization*, 10, 3, 2003, pp. 68–98; N. Robinson, *The Politics of Russia's Partial Democracy*, in *Political Studies Review*, 1, 2003, pp. 149–166; L. Shevtsova, *The Problem of Executive Power in Russia*, in *Journal of Democracy*, 11, 1, 2000, pp. 32–39; P. Kubiček, *Delegative Democracy in Russia and Ukraine*, in *Communist and Post-Communist Studies*, 27, 4, 1994, pp. 423–441.

[71] Other similar approaches have been expressed by those authors speaking of '*decisionismo*' (see H. Quiroga, *Parecidos de Familia. La Democracia Delegativa y el Decisionismo Democrático*, in G. O'Donnell, O. Iazzetta and H. Quiroga (eds.), *Democracia Delegativa*, Buenos Aires, Prometeo, 2011, pp. 35–52), or the strengthening of presidential leadership M.M. Ollier, *Centralidad Presidencial y Debilidad Institucional en las Democracias Delegativas*, in G. O'Donnell, O. Iazzetta and H. Quiroga (eds.), *Democracia Delegativa*, cit.

viewed as "a nuisance", with accountability to them considered as unnecessary impediment; 3) a president and his staff who are the alpha and omega of politics; 4) a president who insulates himself from most existing political institutions and organized interactions and becomes the sole person responsible for "his" policies' (Stepan and Skatch 1993, 19 – 20). Linz and Valenzuela were right in saying that this may happen more easily in presidential countries: the direct election of the president is, indeed, an important requisite allowing for the spread of a plebiscitary system of government, so that the pure parliamentary system appears 'a more supportive evolutionary framework for consolidating democracy than pure presidentialism' (1994, 22). Nevertheless, party change results in the crucial element in determining the leader's dominance in parliamentary systems too, so that centralised party organisations have been producing the strengthening of single leaders. As an effect of such processes, although according to some authors the concept of 'delegative democracy' may not fit completely those democracies which followed a long-term path of institutionalisation of power[72], an increasing number of observers have been agreeing that they are getting closer to it. Thus, this leads us to consider that the so-called 'transition paradigm', that would expect a general diffusion of democracy around the world, expressed hopes that were overly optimistic, as most countries have tried to enter a more uncertain terrain between democratic and non-democratic types of government[73] (Carothers 2002).

An important way to evaluate and measure delegation of power is focussing on the way chief executives take control of legislative means[74]. In a classic analysis, Carey and Shugart (1998) have shown how delegation toward the executive

---

72 See the index proposed in Lucas González, *Unpacking delegative democracy: digging into the empirical content of a rich theoretical concept*, paper presented at the conference *Guillermo O'Donnell and the Study of Democracy*, 2013.

73 As for the attempts to catch this grey zone we find a lot of new 'hybrid' categories such as the concept of 'electoral authoritarianism' by S. Levitsky and L.A. Way (2002). In the author's words ' recent academic writings have produced a variety of labels for mixed cases, including not only "hybrid regime" but also "semidemocracy", "virtual democracy", "electoral democracy", "pseudodemocracy", "illiberal democracy", "semi-authoritarianism", "soft authoritarianism", "electoral authoritarianism", and Freedom House's "Partly Free"' (p. 51).

74 Since the end of 1990s in a good number of contributions, such as that of Shugart and Carey, 'the terms of the debate over parliamentarism and presidentialism have broadened to include a more explicit concern for policy', but this move has remained quite unpursued in the following years, see K. Eaton, *Parliamentarism versus Presidentialism in the Policy Arena, Reviewed Work(s): Executive Decree Authority by John M. Carey and Matthew Soberg Shugart: Structure and Policy in Japan and the United States by Peter F. Cowhey and Mathew D. McCubbins: Do Institutions Matter? Government Capabilities in the United States and Abroad by Bert A. Rockman and R. Kent Weaver*, in *Comparative Politics*, 2000, 32, 3 2000, pp. 355 – 376, p. 355.

has happened though the increasing authority of presidents to act without concurrent legislative action in widely different political environments. Conventional
wisdom considers that policy making by decrees is a pernicious and rare usur-
pation of power, as a way of circumventing a hostile parliament by stepping
on its more consolidated prerogatives at the same time. Yet, although single leaders dominate law making especially in particular geographical areas such as the
post-Soviet world (Protsyk 2004) or Latin America (Ferreira Rubio and Goretti
1998), this is also becoming an increasingly diffuse phenomenon in more stable
democracies. For a quarter of a century since the Shugart and Carey edited book,
the 'executive decree authority' has continued to develop, such that it now leads
us to suspect relevant consequences for the future of representative democracies.

Before entering into the comparative analysis of this trend, it is worth focussing on the clearer example in this field represented by the use of American presidents of executive orders to accomplish policy goals, along with the increasing
difficulty of legislation to pass laws in the Congress (Deering and Maltzman
1999). Presidential decrees have been interpreted as 'inherent power' and they
are neither specified in the Constitution nor delegated by congressional statute
or resolution. As was claimed by Theodore J. Lowi et al. (2019, 172): 'in modern
times, executive orders have not been "merely administrative" but rather have
had the broader effects of legislation – rules with actual policy content – despite
avoiding the formal legislative process'. Indeed, over the years, presidential
power has grown to represent a real law-making function (Olson and Woll
1999), contravening the principle of separation of powers that the Founding Fathers established.

Executive orders have shown a very significant increase in the last decades,
as documented by an abundant literature[75]. Branum (2002) notes that while 'the

---

75 The political science literature dedicated to the executive orders has grown quantitatively
and qualitatively in the last years. Cf. K.R. Mayer, *Executive Orders and Presidential Power*, in
The Journal of Politics, 61, 1999, pp. 445 – 466; K.R. Mayer, *With the Stroke of a Pen: Executive Orders and Presidential Power*, Princeton, Princeton University Press, 2001; R.K. Mayer and
K. Price, *Unilateral Presidential Powers: Significant Executive Orders, 1949 – 1999*, in *Presidential
Studies Quarterly*, 32, 2002, pp. 367 – 386; W. Howell, *Power without Persuasion: The Politics of Direct Presidential Action*, Princeton, Princeton University Press, 2003; A.L. Warber, *Executive Orders and the Modern Presidency: Legislating from the Oval Office*, Boulder, Lynne Rienner Publishers, 2006; J.A. Fine and A.L. Warber, *Circumventing Adversity: Executive Orders and
Divided Government*, in *Presidential Studies Quarterly*, 42, 2012, 256 – 274; A.L. Warber, *Public Outreach, Executive Orders, and the Unilateral Presidency*, in *Congress & the Presidency*, 41, 2014,
269 – 288; Y. Ouyang and R.W. Waterman, *How Legislative (In)Activity Impacts Executive Unilateralism: A Supply and Demand Theory of Presidential Unilateralism*, in *Congress & the Presidency*,
42, 2015, 317 – 341; B. Rottinghaus, A.L. Warber, *Unilateral Orders as Constituency Outreach: Ex-

first twenty-four Presidents issued 1262 executive orders', the following 'seventeen issued 11,855 orders'. Consequently, many scholars fear 'that this practice has gotten out of control over the past 80 years or so, resulting in an inappropriate usurping of Congress' legislative power by the executive branch' (McCoy 2018; Warber 2006). It was, however, in the last years that this claim appeared as particularly valid for the combination of powerful presidencies and less capacity of judiciary and other constitutional bodies to provide robust guidelines to its political action.

Indeed, focussing on the last twenty years, the use of executive decrees has reached very high levels. As we can observe in the following figure, the number of executive orders issued by presidents of the United States is currently growing. After a period of decline between 2005 and 2017, the number of executive orders has started growing again. We can therefore assert that the red line in the figure below represents the 'direct presidential governance' (Lowi et al. 2019, 182), with an impact so immediate on the administration that it also presents a variety of conflicts with existing principles of administrative law (Cooper 1986).

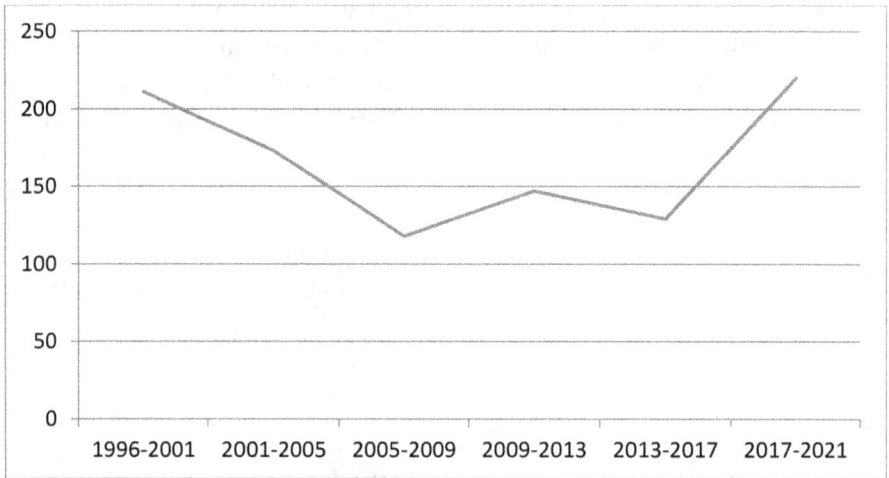

Figure 1: Evolution over time of the presidential executive orders in the USA.

ecutive Orders, Proclamations, and the Public Presidency, in *Presidential Studies Quarterly*, 45, 2015, 289–309; S. Thrower, *Calling the Shots: The President, Executive Orders, and Public Policy*, in *Political Science Quarterly*, 133, 4, 2018, pp. 781–784.

Thus, although the presidential use of executive orders has been conditioned on different types of causal factors, and not solely attributable to the 'institutionalized presidency' (Krause and Cohen 1997), contributions on the way they are issued tend to emphasise them as a way that allows the president to govern alone. Indeed, the dominant model to explain the use of executive decrees underlines strategic elements so that when 'a president's legislative success rate declines (rises) in each chamber, they will be more (less) inclined to issue executive orders as a mean to circumvent the legislative process' (Krause and Cohen 1997, 462; Deering and Maltzman 1999). This is confirmed also by the studies, not so numerous when compared to the analysis of congressional legislation, devoted to understanding the substance of executive orders, which tend to give them 'the same legal standing as a law passed by Congress' (Warber, Ouyang and Waterman 2018). This is the case with areas such as stem cell research, climate change, and immigration, all issues on which there have been many executive orders (Carmines and Fowler 2017).

Executive orders have also been provided as an important part of the presidential political programme, by revealing 'a vehicle for important substantive change – as with Obama's expansion of protections for the employees of federal contractors, seeking to restrict government procurement dollars to companies who agreed to pay a higher minimum wage, ban discrimination on the basis of sexual orientation and identity, provide paid sick leave, and tighten compliance with laws mandating "integrity and business ethics"' (Rudalevige 2016, 870). The same has been the case with President Trump, whose overall volume of executive orders has been remarkably similar to that of other presidents, but with a relevant amount of them dedicated to the theme, crucial for his political line, of immigration, so that 'of the 56 immigration-related EOs and 64 proclamations issued since 1945, Trump has issued 10 and nine, respectively' (Waslin 2020). Presidential decrees have been strongly conflicted with the fact that legislation on individual rights is a typical prerogative of democratic parliaments in the history of every constitutional state. More recently, after the passing of the torch to Joe Biden, the trend continued along the same lines: the current president has made an aggressive use of decree powers since he entered in the White House as well, with 17 orders signed after his inauguration in relevant areas such as immigration, the economy, and climate change.

Moreover, executive powers may be put in the more general framework of presidential prerogatives. Indeed, their increase in quantity has been associated with the rise of veto powers as an alternative way for the president to have a voice in legislative bargaining. Presidents have been endowed with the prerogative to refuse a bill that has been passed by the legislature and thus can prevent its enactment in law through veto powers. Yet this has become a way for presidents to legislate with the assemblies, with the tendency of producing a so-called line-item veto that allows a president to partially object to a bill while allowing other parts of the bill to be signed into law. Veto powers were designed by the Framers 'to establish a government of limited powers. Even so, they fretted about the potential for the abuse of power. They feared a tyrannical national legislature, but also the elevation of an autocratic monarch' (Spitzer 1988, 303). However, in the end, the veto became a major tool of presidency-building. As Cameron (2009) argues: 'some of the most important legislation of the past three-quarters of a century was killed, postponed, or substantially shaped through veto'. Especially when the majority in Congress is held by a party other than that of the president, through the veto, or its threat, the president can enable legislation or negotiate with his/her counterpart.

However, one may find an exception to this trend in latter years, as it can be noticed that the use of presidential veto power has clearly fallen, since President Clinton and President Trump, who prefer to 'legislate' through direct forms of decree. Indeed, it seems that unilateral action has privileged channels such as executive orders, as they 'combine the highest level of substance, discretion, and direct presidential involvement' (Mayer 2001, 35; Rudalevige 2012).

4.3 The politics of executive policymaking: a comparative overview

The new centrality of political leaders in the governmental arena has modified the way in which legislation is enacted. Indeed, as leaders become more powerful, there has also been a tendency to give them full responsibility to govern. The consequent phenomenon is the emergence of the so-called 'executive laws', that are governmental acts that turn into legislative tools (Musella 2018, 107). Thus, when a leader gains a large degree of popularity and visibility, 'a vicious cycle could occur where presidents break legislative impasses by "solving" pressing problems with unilateral decrees that often go well beyond their formal constitutional authority' (Ackerman 2000a, 646–647). The passage of prerogatives from the parliament to the executive is, in the first place, documented by a sharp increase in governmental activities, as has been shown in an extensive piece of empirical research on national legislation in the second part of nineteenth century (Escobar et al. 2020). As scholars have noted a more general tendency towards the government's growing influence over the agenda-setting process (Tsebelis and Rasch 2011), the analysis of executive decrees is the most immediate way to evaluate it.

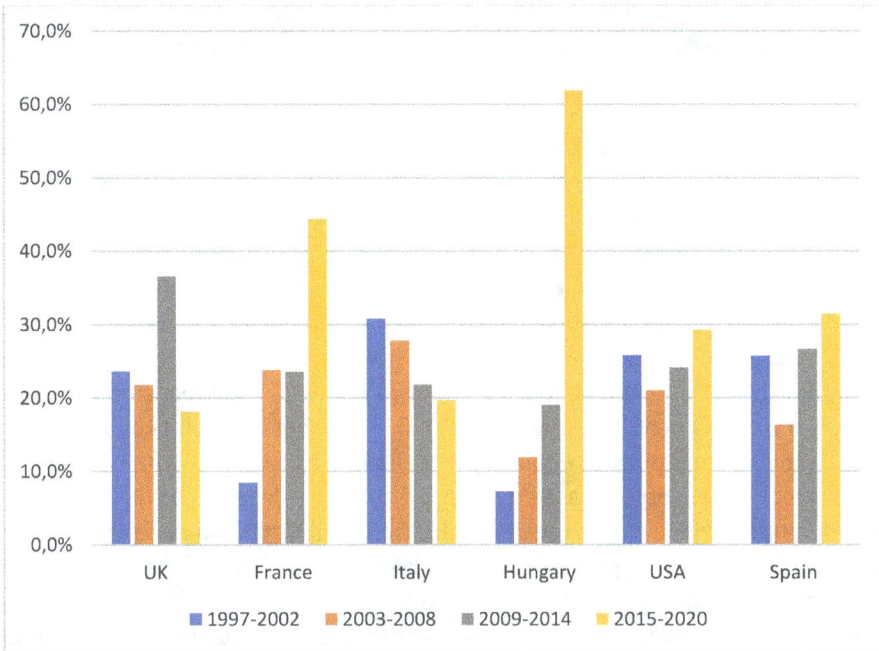

Figure 2: Executive decrees on national legislation in selected countries. *Source:* own elaboration, see Appendix B.

Table 1: Executive decrees in selected countries

	1997–2002		2003–2008		2009–2014		2015–2020	
UK	11744	23,6%	10815	21,7%	18204	36,6%	9004	18,1%
France	80	8,4%	227	23,7%	225	23,5%	424	44,4%
Italy	202	30,8%	182	27,7%	143	21,8%	129	19,7%
Hungary	340	7,2%	558	11,9%	894	19,0%	2907	61,9%
USA	248	25,7%	202	21,0%	232	24,1%	282	29,3%
Spain	107	25,7%	68	16,3%	111	26,6%	131	31,4%

Source: own elaboration, see Appendix B.

Firstly, we begin our analysis of the executive decree authority by looking at its use in six countries: the United Kingdom, the United States, France, Italy, Spain, and Hungary from 1997 to 2020. We aim to show whether we can identify the expansion of executive normative powers over the last two decades. In France we examined the '*ordonnance*', in Spain the '*decreto ley*', in Italy the '*decreto-legge*', in Hungary the government decree (primary or based on powers delegated to the executive by acts), in the US we examined the 'executive orders', and in the UK the statutory instruments. Then, we calculated the average rate on four equally distant cluster periods (1997–2002; 2003–2008; 2009–2014; 2015–2020). Although such instruments are not comparable, as they are regulated by national constitutions in a different way, they may be portrayed in a common picture in order to show how democratic executives pursue the same purposes through diversified channels. Indeed, different kinds of decrees, though incomparable from a formal legal perspective, are put in the same class – according to a classical tradition of comparative studies (Sartori 1991) – *with respect* to a specific research question concerning the government's expansion in contemporary political systems.

Indeed, we observe that over the last two decades, the expansion of executive authority has been emerging as an established fact in several countries (Figure 2). The most significant trends may be discovered in two countries, Hungary and France, where an increased number of executive decrees highlights the political reinforcement of the executive. In France, the '*ordonnances*' rapidly increased from the first period under analysis (1997–2002) to the most recent years, when the figure goes from 8.4% to 44.4%. While expressing a more general tendency, this data is consistent with a process of personalisation of government imprinted by the French president, especially during Macron's elevation to power (Vittoria 2021). Indeed, since the 1990s, and even more so after the 2002 constitutional reform which reduced the presidential mandate to five years like the Assembly's one, '*ordonnances*' became an important part of 'the institutional ascendency of the French President' in governmental activities[76] (Cole 2019, 20).

In Hungary, the strengthening of the executive has gone along with the presidentialisation of politics in this and other such countries[77], and – for an increas-

---

[76] A. Vittoria notes the significant use of ordinances under Macron's presidency, who used such a tool 210 times in the period from 14 May 2017 to 7 August 2020: 'by considering the daily incidence of ordinances – the ratio of the absolute number of approved ordinances and total days in the presidential term – as a measure of the intensity of presidential recourse to ordinary standardization, it is interesting noting that Macron's presidency is precisely that one to be more characterized by a strong recourse to the power of executive decrees, with 0.178 ordinances per day, followed by Hollande (0.165), Chirac in his second term (0.118), and then Sarkozy (0.099)' (A. Vittoria, *La presidenza Macron. Tra populismo e tecnocrazia*, Milano, Mimesis, 2021, p. 124–1125, my translation).

[77] On the Hungarian presidentialisation see A. Körösényi, *Parlamentáris vagy elnöki kormányzás? Az Orbàn kormány összehasonlító perspektívából*, in *Századvég*, 20, 2001, 3–38. See also G. Ilonszki, *Az elnöki parlamentarizmus és a parlament*, in *Századvég*, 2, 2002, 109–133; F. Mandák, *Signs of Presidentialization in Hungarian Government Reforms – Changes After the New Fundamental Law*, in S. Zoltán, F. Mandák and Z. Fejes (eds.), *Challenges and Pitfalls in the Recent*

ing number of scholars – its democratic backsliding (Ágh 2016; Buzogány 2017; Bogaards 2018; Sata and Karolewski 2020). In this respect, we may notice that the figure increases from an average value of 11.4% between 2003 and 2008 to a value of 61.9% between 2015 and 2020. Very significantly, the rise to power of Viktor Orbán and the several constitutional reforms enacted since 2010 have brought about effective instruments to expand the role of the executive.

Moving elsewhere in Europe, the Spanish case underlines the rise of *decreto ley* from 25.7% during the first span of time to 31.4% in the latter one. The first Aznar government, with the People's Party holding only a relative majority of the *Congreso*, signalled the first expansion of the use of this instrument in recent Spanish democratic history (Rodríguez-Teruel 2020). The lowest percentage falls between 2003 and 2008, a period of time that showed the crucial role of the *Tribunal Constitucional* in limiting and specifying the 'nature' of the decree law. Nevertheless, a constant increase over the last years and a peak during 2016–2020 may be noticed, when 131 decree laws were issued leading several scholars to put the question of whether the use – or abuse – of decree laws 'has broken the balance between the executive and the legislative organ' (Pérez Sola 2020).

In the United Kingdom, the rise of statutory instruments has been particularly evident starting in the mid-2000s. According to Loft (2017, 8) 'in comparison to the slow decline in Acts, the number of SIs have grown slowly during the second half of the twentieth century, before rapidly rising in the 1990s, peaking in the 2000s [...]. An average of 2,100 UK SIs was issued annually from the 1950s to around 1990. This then rose to an annual average of 3,200 in the 1990s, 4,200 in the 2000s, and fell to around 3,000 a year on average during the 2010s'. Moreover, the rise of executive powers took place without efficient parliamentary scrutiny (Valbruzzi 2020) and increasingly showed the difficulties of the UK Parliament that have appeared in recent times because of Brexit and the COVID-19 outbreak.

Moving to the other side of the Atlantic, the delegation of power to the executive in the United States is slightly different and has historically led to major troubles in comparison to European countries. Indeed, 'the delegation doctrine is situated in a constitutional power struggle between Congress and the President, with both actors having independent democratic legitimation and not infrequently conflicting goals. It is not surprising that the delegation

---

Hungarian Constitutional Development. Discussing the New Fundamental Law of Hungary, Paris, Éditions L'Harmattan, 2015, pp. 148–168. On recent constitutional reforms in such country see F. Musella, *Constitutional Change in Presidentialised Regimes. Paths of Reform in Hungary and Italy*, in *DPCE Online*, 39, 2, 2019.

of legislative power, to institutions whose constitutional legitimacy is considered so doubtful, poses major problems' (Pünder 2009, 256–257). Our data show an increase of the executive orders over the last years. In particular, the Bush presidency has intensified the expansion of power by the office of the president, leading some authors to warn that under this presidency the 'Madison's nightmare' became a reality (Shane 2009). This trend was prolonged during the Obama Presidency and more recently we observed a peak during the last period of time, during the Trump Presidency[78]. Moreover, a high number of executive orders have been accompanied by other means that reinforce presidential power, such as a memoranda, proclamations, and other forms of unilateral action. Indeed, according to Lowi et al. (2019, 288) 'relatively few memoranda were issued in the 1950s, 1960s, and early 1980s, when the annual number of executive orders was fairly high, but in the 1970s, late 1980s, and 1990s, memoranda generally outnumbered executive orders. Presidents have also made greater use of proclamations, as their number has increased rather steadily from 52 in 1945 to 168 in 2016'.

Looking at Italy, if we consider the number of decree laws, we may observe that the number of governmental decrees is very similar to laws enacted by the Parliament (Figure 2). In addition, during the unstable political majority led by Romano Prodi (2006–2008), the number of decree laws exceeded the ones enacted by the Parliament. This trend is observable also looking at the current legislature. After the financial and economic crisis, the 2018 'political earthquake' with the rise of the Five Star Movement and Lega, and the highly polarised M5S-PD government has generated fertile humus for the rise of executive power, and this has been further enhanced because of the current pandemic. More recently, the tendency towards the expansion of executive decree authority has been largely accelerated in the time of the pandemic, when Conte advanced the way executive decrees are issued by referring to acts directly produced by the Italian *Presidente del Consiglio*. This is the reason why executive decrees, framed by the Constitution as exceptional measures, became a very diffuse instrument, transcending the emergency (Simoncini 2006; Ronga 2020), to realise the political programmes of increasingly personalised Italian governments.

---

78 The risks that the use – and abuse – of executive power may have on contemporary American and international politics have been clear under the Trump Presidency and its attempts to reduce the flow of immigrants. We may think for instance of the executive order that instituted the highly controversial 'Muslim ban' restricting travel and immigration to a large list of countries in order to protect national security, or to the declaration of a national emergency concerning the southern border of the United States (Proclamation 9844).

4.4 The government in parliament

The growth of normative powers of governments is an evident trend in contemporary democracies. It is a tendency, however, that goes hand in hand with the ampler space that the government has carved out in ordinary legislative activities. Although legislation is one of the most ancient and traditional tasks for legislative assemblies, executives have been increasingly able to produce legislation with a very high success rate. The central purpose of this section is to document the role of government in parliament by looking at its impact on the policy making process. Specifically, it analyses this phenomenon from a comparative perspective, looking at the average number of government sponsored bills over the last two decades.

In France, the measures of constitutional engineering at the basis of the Fifth Republic were designed to give the government 'a commanding role in the legislative process' (Keeler 1993, 521). Indeed, the Constitution empowered the executive in the law-making arena by instituting specific mechanisms of agenda-setting (Kerrouche 2006). This has resulted in a strong presence in parliamentary processes. As Figure 3 shows, government-sponsored bills (*projets de loi*) have exceeded those initiated by parliament (*propositions de loi*) over the last twenty years.

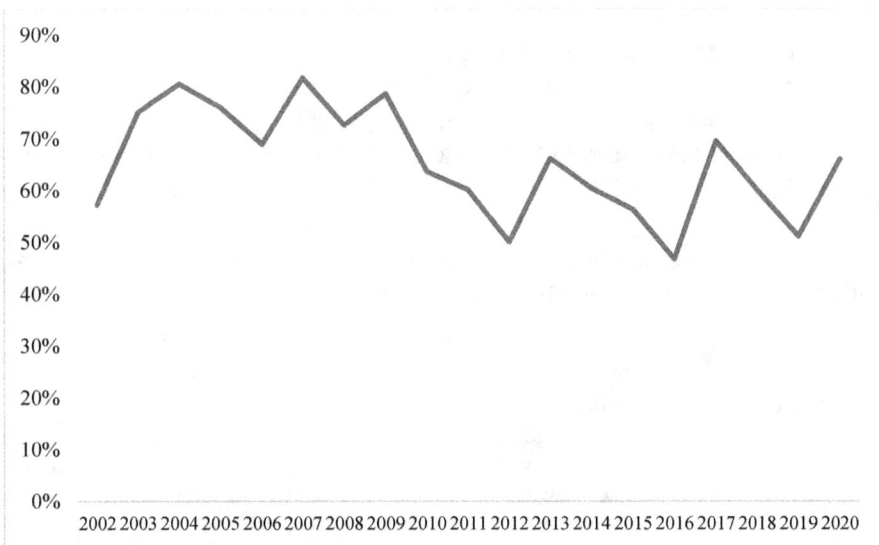

Figure 3: Evolution over time of projets de loi (%) in France. *Source:* own elaboration on data from Legifrance.gouv.fr.

The volume of French legislative output confirms that the French government represents a powerful law-making actor. First, the Fifth Republic governments have dominated the parliament legislative proposals by producing 65% of the *projets de loi* from 2002 to 2020. Second, some differences among governments may be underlined in the timespan considered: for instance, during the Hollande presidency (2012–2017), the government pushed a more limited number of *projets de loi* per year through parliament: indeed, the latter reached the same percentage of parliamentary initiatives in 2016. Conversely, this percentage was very high under the Chirac and Sarkozy presidencies, when legislative proposals coming from the executive reached a peak of 82%. This trend also seems to be confirmed under the Macron presidency. Executive dominance was particularly clear during 2020, when over 40% of the *projets de loi* were related to coping with the COVID-19 pandemic crisis. Additionally, other constitutional instruments, such as the provision that allows the government to force the passage of a bill, have been used by governments to accelerate the legislative process and to overcome the risks of an unstable majority. A point of great concern relates to how French governments have increasingly resorted to Article 49.3 of the French Constitution over the last twenty years[79]. The so-called 'guillotine' article allows bills to bypass the parliamentary vote and/or to overcome a period of weak and fragmented majorities. In particular, under the Socialist government led by Manuel Valls (2014–2016), this instrument was used six times, with three of them being to approve the controversial labour reforms strongly supported by the Hollande presidency. More recently, the former Prime Minister Eduard Philippe invoked this article to pass a reform of the French pension system.

The centrality of government in law making may be registered also in Germany, whose Constitution (article 36 Grundgesetz) allows the executive to propose a law. As Figure 4 shows, the legislative initiatives of the Bundesregierung have been emerging as a consolidated reality of German politics over the last two decades. The growing number of government initiatives appears sharply evident, with the figure rising from 70% of the overall number of laws under the first

---

79 Before the 2008 constitutional reform this article was forcefully used under the Michel Rocard government (1989–1991). After 2008, the government could only use it on one bill per parliamentary session and in specific areas of policy. According to the French Constitution (Art. 49.3): 'The Prime Minister may, after deliberation by the Council of Ministers, make the passing of a Finance Bill or Social Security Financing Bill an issue of a vote of confidence before the National Assembly. In that event, the Bill shall be considered passed unless a resolution of no-confidence, tabled within the subsequent twenty- four hours, is carried as provided for in the foregoing paragraph. In addition, the Prime Minister may use the said procedure for one other Government or Private Members' Bill per session'.

Schröder government (in the period 1998–2002) to 88% during the third Merkel government (2013–2017). Indeed, during the executives led by Angela Merkel, it became clear that 'by virtue of its superior access to information and its influence on the dominant political parties, the Cabinet effectively determines legislative policy' (Currie 2008, 2147; Dalton 2008).

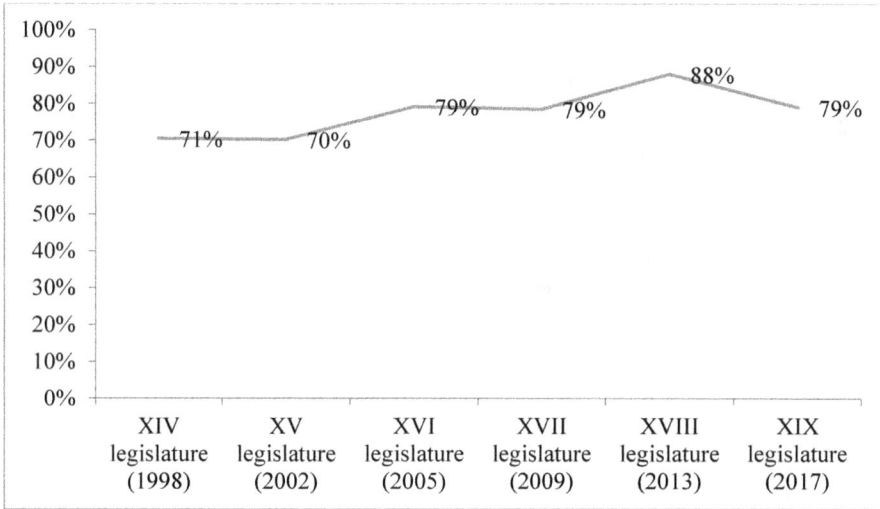

Figure 4: Evolution over time of government legislative initiatives (%) in Germany. *Source: Statistik der Gesetzgebung* for the time period 1998–2013, Vercesi (2020) for the XIX legislature until December 2020.

Looking at the absolute values of government sponsored bills, it is worth noting that they increased from 274 during the second Schröder government (2002–2005) to 487 during the first Merkel government (2005–2009), a value that has become more or less stable until today. From then on, 'decision-making was mainly processed within the executive, incorporating legislative actors at a rather late stage' (Fleischer and Parrado 2010, 369). Therefore, the management of a large coalition, a peculiar trait of contemporary German politics, seems not to have a great impact on limiting executive dominance over the legislative process, with Merkel's leadership acting as the main 'antidote' against paralysis (Mushaben 2016).

Moving elsewhere in Europe, we can observe similar patterns in terms of governmental bills in Hungary, where the strengthening of the executive in the legislative arena may be read as a consequence of the rise of the regime of Viktor Orbán. As Figure 5 shows, the number of executive bills has an average value of

78.6% from 1998 to 2018. Starting from the first Orbán government (1998 – 2002), the strengthening of the Hungarian executive has easily translated into its predominance over the deliberative processes (Kopecký, 2004). This process has been further enhanced in the aftermath of the 2010 'ballot box revolution' and the coming into force of the Fundamental law, when we observe the radical instrumentalisation of parliamentary law-making with sharp consequences for the whole political system. This trend has been facilitated by the high party discipline of Fidesz MPs, the party which has permanently held a majority since 2010 of two-thirds of the Hungarian Chamber. Additionally, the different composition of the Assembly, which was reduced from 364 to 200 parliamentarians in 2014, has enabled a more rapid approval of government bills.

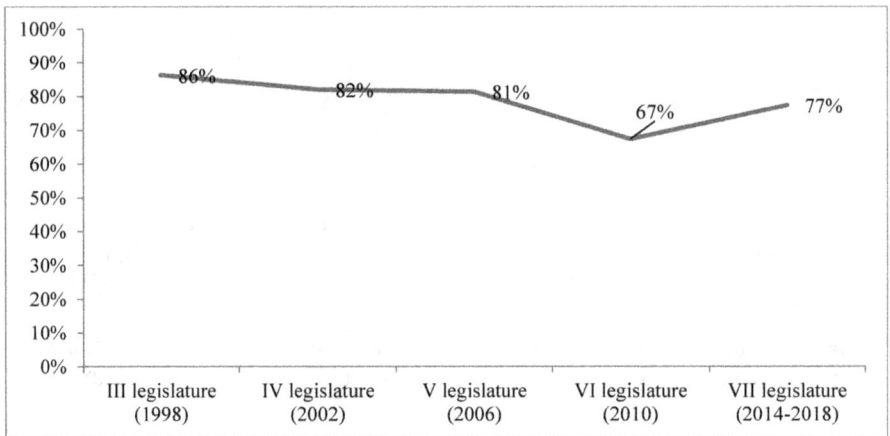

Figure 5: Evolution over time of government legislative initiatives (%) in Hungary. *Source:* own elaboration on data from CAP (Centre for social sciences), https://cap.tk.hu/en

Preferential procedures were also introduced in order to speed up parliamentary procedures[80]. In this respect, empirical evidence has highlighted that between 2010 and 2014 a law proposed by Fidesz reached its final vote in just 34 days (Boda and Sebok 2019), thus raising the suspicion that the new parliament served 'no other purpose than to rubberstamp and entrench the cabinet's political wishes' (Kazai 2019, 7).

---

[80] The new procedures favoured the volume of government sponsored bills. Indeed, while during the first Orbán government 397 bills were enacted, the total amount increased to 565 during his third government.

Nevertheless, the main change introduced by the 2010 constitutional reform refers to the deconstruction of the parliamentary opposition (Várnagy and Ilonszki, 2018), that now has very little chance to see its proposals approved. The percentage of bills coming from the parliamentary opposition decreased significantly from 11.3% during the socialist governments (2006–2010) to 8.7% in the period 2010–2014. During the third Orbán government, a further reduction can be registered, reaching a value of 6.7% (2014–2018). In addition, the ruling party and the executive have systematically used amendments to make the scrutiny of legislative proposals extremely difficult, with the result of marginalising the role of opposition parties. In such a scenario, the absence of meaningful discussion in parliament, along with the absence of consultation and opposition, has sustained the autocratic turn in Hungary.

Similarly, the experience of Italy confirms the trend of a more powerful presence of the executive in legislative activities. As the Italian Constitution (articles 71 and 87) includes the executive among actors which may propose a law, from the XIII legislature until today the majority of the legislative bills have come from the governmental branch (Figure 6). Indeed, over the last six legislatures, the executive initiatives have reached the significant figure of 75% per year. This trend has been even more marked under the Berlusconi III (2001–2006) – the longest Italian government – and the Prodi II governments (2006–2008), when the governmental legislative initiatives reached the highest percentage in the recent history of Italian politics (88.3%). Moreover, in the aftermath of the 2008 financial crisis, data show that the executive took even stronger control over the agenda of the parliament.

This is particularly true under the technocratic government led by Mario Monti, who succeeded Silvio Berlusconi as the head of the Italian executive in 2011, when 'the executive has not confined itself to the presentation of emergency decrees but has very often had recourse to votes of confidence and has done so in a strategic way, in order to give ironclad protection to a specific 'package' of important measures' (Marangoni 2012, 147). Finally, similar patterns can be observed during the XVII legislature when, along with an increase in the number of government proposals, the government increasingly resorted to a series of constitutional weapons (i.e. the vote of confidence had been 67 during the Renzi government and 64 during the Gentiloni's one) showing the desire to quicken the legislative process or preclude legislative interference by parliament. An exception to this trend since 1996 is represented by the last legislature, when the success rate for governmental proposals was below 60%. Here, the heterogenous majority led by Giuseppe Conte seemed to affect the quantity of government

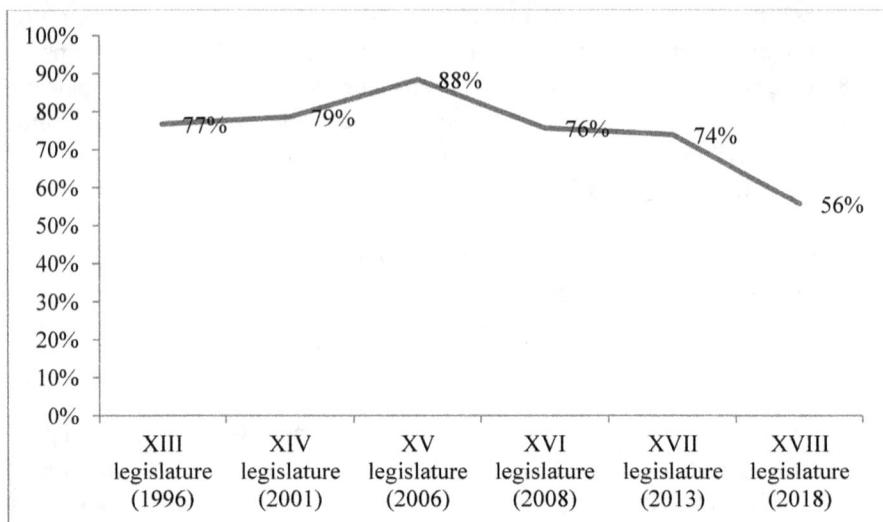

Figure 6: Evolution over time of government legislative initiatives (%) in Italy. *Source:* own elaboration on data from Italian Chamber of Deputies and Senate.

sponsored bills, especially during its second term (2019 – 2020) when only 44 proposals have been approved out of the total amount of 127[81] (34.5%).

Moreover, it is very significant that in recent times there has been an increasing involvement of the chief executives in the draft of legislation (Saiegh 2009). In Italy, the *Presidente del Consiglio* seems to affect patterns of policymaking in a very significant way. As data in Figure 7 shows, the Prime Ministers' legislative success rates, namely the percentage of bills presented as *'primo firmatario'*[82] (first signatory) that have been published in the Official Gazette from 1992 to 2019, has clearly increased.

Over the last thirty years, for the most part, the Prime Ministers' proposals had become, law thus confirming the highly personalised nature of the Italian executive. The rate of success rapidly increased at the beginning of the 2000s and reached its peak during the Berlusconi IV (2008 – 2011) government and Renzi's (2014 – 2016) government when the rate of success was over 80% of the proposed laws. Most parts of these legislative proposals concerned emergency de-

---

81 See the official statistics on Italian national legislation provided by the Senate, http://www. senato.it/leg/18/BGT/Schede/Statistiche/Governi/77/DDLGovernoPerNatura.html
82 The transparency of the actor who initiates a parliamentary initiative represents a mechanism that favours the accountability of political processes and the understanding of the actors involved in the legislative production.

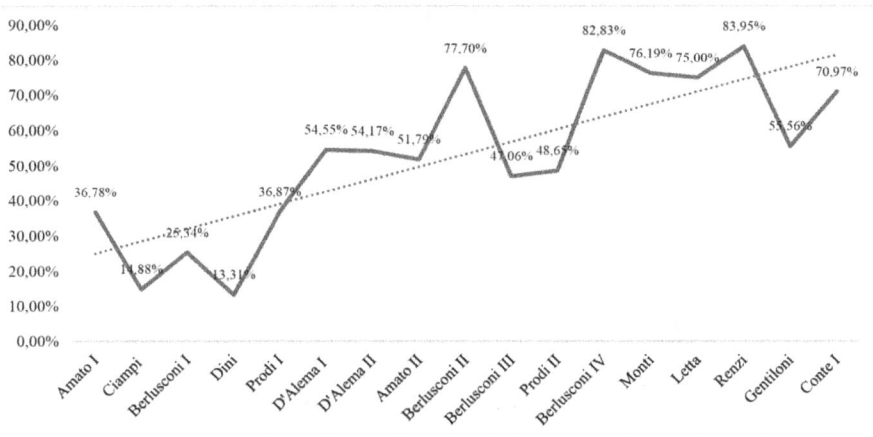

Figure 7: Chief Executives' Legislative Proposals. Success Rates in Italy (1992 – 2019). *Source:* own elaboration on data from Italian Chamber of Deputies and Senate.

crees to be converted into ordinary law, suggesting the activism of the prime minister in 'getting things done', and the need to act efficiently and rapidly.

Finally, the crucial role of government in law-making does not come as a surprise in Westminster democracies, which have, in their long history, demonstrated the 'efficient secrecy' of governmentality: the superiority of the English Constitution was identified by Walter Bagehot (1867) in a 'nearly complete fusion of executive and legislative powers'. Focussing on more recent times, in the United Kingdom, where bills can be presented by the government, individual MPs or lords and private individuals or organisations, our data show the rise of the executive as the main law-making actor.

As observed by Dorey (quoted in Kerrouche 2006, 362) 'whilst the Westminster Model continues to provide a normative framework concerning the role which many believe Parliament ought to play, the empirical reality discerned by most political commentators during the last one hundred years suggests something rather different. Indeed, the control over the activity of deputies reflects the fact that the effective initiation of laws is dominated by the executive'. As Figure 8 shows, more than 80% of the laws have come from government initiatives.

The trend in the executive–legislative relationship remained relatively stable until 2019, when the increased number of government bills reached the total amount of bills approved. Therefore, while the presence of coalition governments from 2010 (under David Cameron and Theresa May) seemed to slightly affect the percentage of government bills, from 2019 – 2020 the pattern of UK law-making

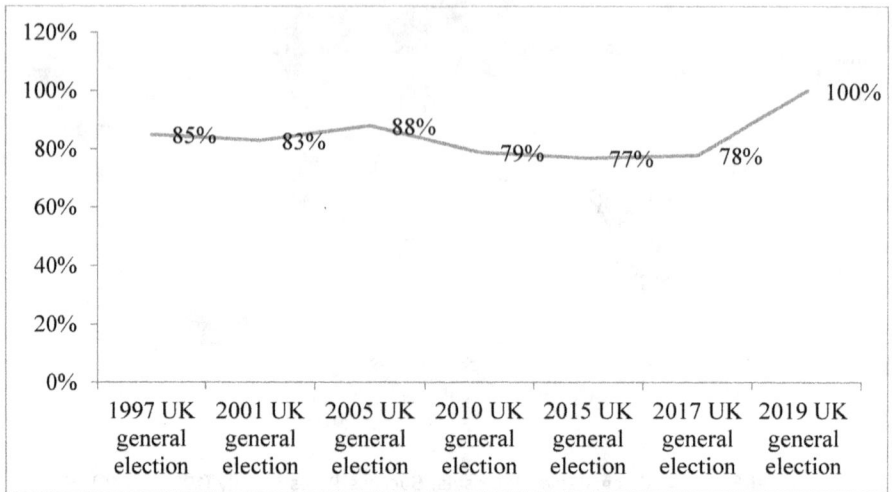

Figure 8: Evolution over time of government legislative initiatives (%) in the United Kingdom. *Source:* Loft and Apostolova (2019) and own elaboration from legislation.gov.uk

has unquestionably shown executive domination, a phenomenon that 'is closely related to the Government's greater control of the Parliamentary timetable, greater support given to ministers in the drafting of legislation, and the expectation of majority support for Government bills in the House of Commons' (Loft and Apostolova 2019, 7).

Shifting our attention to the Spanish case, as the Spanish Constitution (articles 87–88) also provides for government legislative initiatives, the most significant trend concerns the growing number of laws enacted from the early 2000s to 2010. As Figure 9 shows, government bills reached a success rate of above 85% between the VI and X legislatures. The lowest success rate was in the VI legislature (76%). Later, up until 2010, governments enjoyed a progressive concentration of executive power (Field 2009). The pattern of Spanish law-making shows a peak during the X legislature, thus confirming how 'national politics is driven by a strong concentration of power around the executive, and particularly the prime minister (*Presidente del Gobierno*) vis à vis the cabinet and the parliament' (Rodríguez-Teruel et al. 2018, 248; Rodríguez-Teruel 2020). In addition, the low rate of government legislative success falls in the short-term XI and XIII legislatures. These results are mainly linked to the high instability caused by the former lasting only 111 days from January to summer 2016, and the latter only lasting 126 days. During these periods, the government has had evident difficulties in overcoming (in a small amount of time) the resistance (if not the interlocking vetoes) of a heterogeneous parliamentary majority. Besides, the government bills success returned to higher levels during the last legislature (73%).

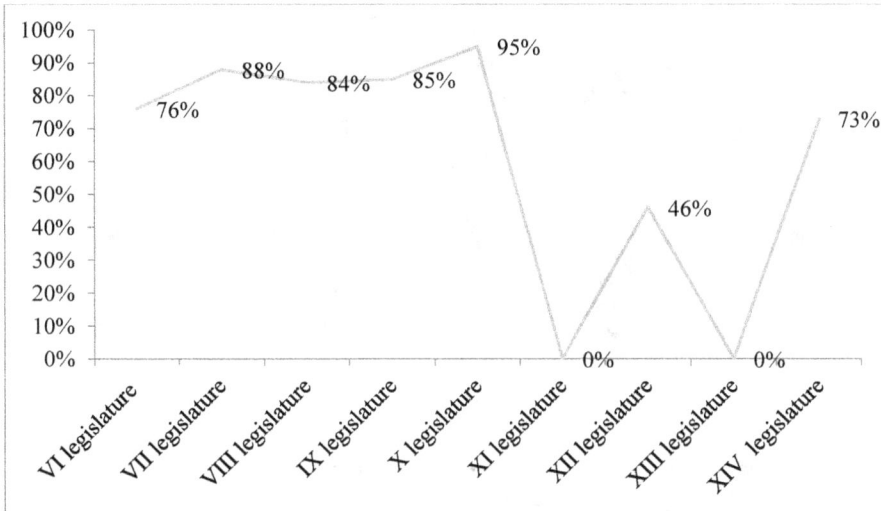

Figure 9: Evolution over time of government legislative initiatives (%) in Spain (2000–2020). *Source:* own elaboration on data from Boletín Oficial del Estado (BOE), https://www.boe.es/

The comparative analysis of the role of governments in legislative processes clarifies the strong role they have played throughout the last twenty years, with an average of 74% of laws originating in the executive in our set of democracies (Figure 10). Particularly, this trend is even more evident in the UK, which displays the highest percentages of legislative initiatives from the government (85%). This confirms the idea of a 'marginalization of parliament', that is so relevant that it has led scholars to talk about 'deparliamentarisation' to indicate the deprivation of parliaments of many of their long-entrenched powers (Baldwin 2004; Elgie and Stapleton 2006; Musella 2019).

In a nutshell, the government has become the main actor presenting legislative proposals and getting them approved, as well as demonstrating the extent to which the executive proposals have become an integral part of the legislative procedures. As Figure 11 shows, the expansion of the executive at the expense of other branches of government can be transversally noted in Europe. The trend over time confirms the government's prominence in all our selected countries thus suggesting how the marginalisation of parliaments in legislative processes represents a peculiar feature of contemporary monocratic governments.

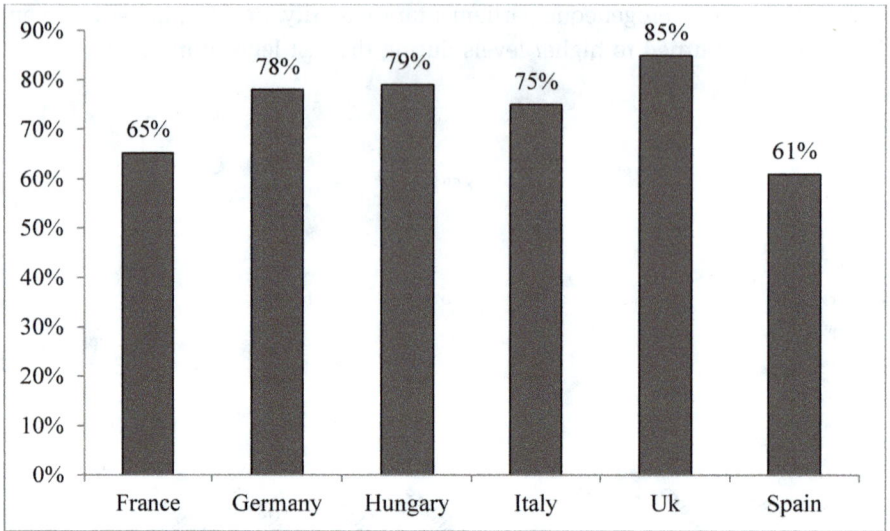

Figure 10: Legislative initiatives of the executive in all countries on average (2000 – 2020). *Source:* own elaboration, see Appendix B.

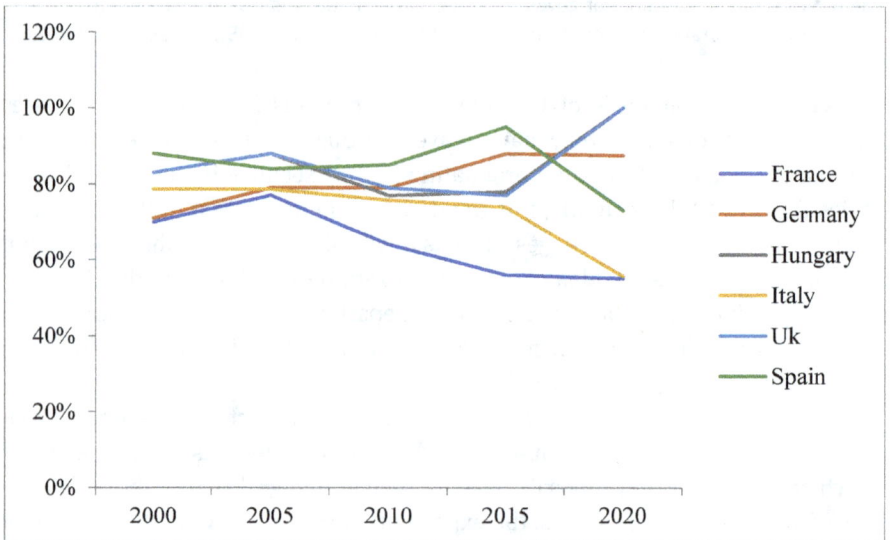

Figure 11: Legislative initiatives of the executive in all countries (2000 – 2020). *Source:* own elaboration, see Appendix B.

4.5 Three arenas of executive expansion

In this chapter, three different fields of legislative activities have shown the strengthening of the executive as it has developed over time. First, we have concentrated attention on how presidents and prime ministers have been endowed with unilateral legislative powers, so that they have used decrees and executive orders as the main instruments to realise their political programme. For instance, the increasing number of executive orders approved by American presidents is concurrent with the growing relevance of issues they deal with: with a stroke of a pen, the chief executives have made 'policy on their own without interference from either Congress or the courts', and can 'reorganize the executive branch agencies, alter administrative and regulatory processes, affect how legislation is interpreted and implemented, and take whatever action is permitted within the boundaries of their constitutional or statutory authority' (Mayer 1999, 445, 2001). In the same way, the Italian *decreto legge* or Spanish *decreto-ley* were introduced by the constitutions of the two European countries to provide a way for the executive to cope with sudden emergencies that does not allow for ordinary parliamentary deliberation. Yet although the formal dispositions suggested a restricted use of these tools, they became a frequent channel for substantive legislation, and as a way to overcome parliamentary gridlocks or slowdowns: legislating without parliaments has become an ordinary and diffuse mechanism of contemporary democracies.

In addition to this, delegation of legislative prerogatives from the parliamentary assemblies to the government represents a common trend in both parliamentary and presidential regimes, where legislative assemblies tend to delegate powers towards the executive more and more frequently. Indeed, although the systems of strong separation of powers would prevent any forms of passage from parliament to the executive, the constitutional jurisprudence in several democratic states has been progressively more indulgent in allowing for delegated legislation. The path of the US Supreme Court is particularly significant: although it had defined the legislative competencies of the Congress as 'strictly and exclusive legislative' at the beginning of the nineteenth century[83], during the Wilson presidency some of its determinations started to concede that the presidential powers were 'given in general terms'[84]. This has been the constitutional foundation of a presidency that was not only devoted to the executive

---

[83] See the sentence Wayman vs Southard (23 US 1, 1825).
[84] Myers vs United States 272 US 52, 1926.

will of the Congress (Corwin 1927). And this path was followed, with differences related to institutional designs, by other Western countries.

Finally, we may observe how the executive intervenes directly in parliamentary activities. An increasing part of the overall legislation comes from executive initiatives, especially in Westminster democracies where constitutional bodies realise a close collaboration in the law-making process. In other countries, the government may choose to avoid whatever form of parliamentary intervention by seeking approval of a bill through a vote of confidence, the shortest way to 'overcome dissension inside the majority as well as the opposition's obstructionism' (Onida 2004; Lupo 2006), thus forcing the parliament to pass a totally pre-defined document. Instead, in the presidential system, the elected head of state may refuse to approve a legislative bill that has been passed by the legislature and thus prevent its enactment into law is through veto powers. Thus, political leaders have gained a very significant power to enact and block legislation even when compared to the recent past. As it has been noted with reference to US institutions, the Framers tried to establish a government of limited powers as 'they feared a tyrannical national legislature' (Spitzer 1988, 303). Conversely, today the greatest concern is about the *sceptre* – and the *spectre*[85] – of an unbound president in direct communication with their supporters.

---

[85] The expression comes from the introductory chapter by D. Albertazzi and D. McDonnell to their edited volume *Twenty-First Century Populism. The Spectre of Western European Democracy*, Basingstoke, Palgrave, 2008.

5 Digital presidents: political engagement and decision

5.1 Introduction

Personalisation is one of the most widespread phenomenon in contemporary politics. As a very rich strand of literature has been documenting different dimensions and aspects of the concentration of power in the hands of monocratic figures in several countries (Karvonen 2010; Costa Lobo and Curtice 2014; Rahat and Kenig 2018), a key element in such a process is the development of a direct relationship with citizens that is not mediated by political parties and that is often emotional. Indeed, there is strong empirical evidence that leaders have been acting as a political representative 'above the party' in both democratic and autocratic countries thanks to the intensive use of mediatic instruments (Calise 2011; Musella and Webb 2015), thus progressively becoming the focus of popular attention – and expectations (Lowi 1985).

Digital media has added an extra and more relevant chapter to this story, with 'a manifestation of a more systemic return of strong leadership in contemporary society, after a time at which prevalent processes of leadership took a technocratic and anti-charismatic form' (Gerbaudo 2019a, 145). Initially digital technologies have revolutionised political campaigning[86], with very high potential for leaders to 'develop an immediate relationship – in the dual sense of instantaneous and free of mediation – with millions of citizens acting as individual, but interconnected in the digital environment' (Calise and Musella 2019, 80; Parmelee and Bichard 2011; Enli and Skogerbø 2013). A turning point for the

---

86 Most of the contributions in this field concentrate attention on the role of new technologies in presidential campaigns, see J. Stromer-Galley, *Presidential campaigning in the Internet age*, Oxford, Oxford University Press, 2019; D. Lilleker, K. Koc-Michalska, R. Negrine, R. Gibson, T. Vedel, and S. Strudel (eds.), *Social Media Campaigning in Europe*, London, Routledge, 2019; R.K. Gibson, *When the Nerds Go Marching in: How Digital Technology Moved from the Margins to the Mainstream of Political Campaigns*, Oxford, Oxford University Press, 2020; also with reference to specific case studies, J. Katz, M. Barris and A. Jain, *The social media president: Barack Obama and the politics of digital engagement*, New York, Springer, 2013. Nevertheless, more attention would be devoted to the use of digital instrumentation during governmental activities, see D. Taras and D. Richard (eds.), *Power Shift? Political Leadership and Social Media: Case Studies*, in *Political Communication*, London, Routledge, 2019.

https://doi.org/10.1515/9783110721720-005

rise of neo-leadership[87] has been the intensive use of digital data analytics and profiling techniques ending in effective political propaganda[88], along with tools used to gain and maintain the attention of users on the web. Moreover, what is appearing as increasingly clear over time is that political leaders have been using social media to both inform and make an impact on the public during governmental activities as well, as has been also registered by an emerging field of research[89] (Davis and Taras 2020; Bracciale, Andretta and Martella 2021; Boin et al. 2021). Thus, while social media has helped new political formations to emerge, bringing their leaders into the limelight, digital instruments are becoming part of the strategies of presidents and prime ministers, too (Groll 2015; Barberá and Zeitzoff 2018).

This leads to the use of social media in the decisional arena. Once at the top, political leaders have been elaborating a new way to decide through social posts, which seeming to be overcoming procedures – and the rituals – of traditional decision-making. As very often 'heads of state and heads of government are more popular on social media than the institutions they represent' (Mickoleit 2014, 2)[90], they also use social media to preview their decisions to their millions of followers, with immediate effects on other actors' behaviour at the national and international levels. In a context of high fragmentation of the web's publics, where each citizen elaborates his convictions in the self-referential autonomy of the social networks, new technologies open the field for innovation in the way political leaders communicate and decide. This chapter will focus on some of the more active current chief executives to investigate the perils and opportunities of the new political phase.

---

87 A new paradigm of leadership is emerging in the new digital environment according to the recent book by A. Kasińska-Metryka and T. Gajewski, (eds.), *The Future of Political Leadership in the Digital Age: Neo-Leadership, Image and Influence*, Arbingdon, Routledge, 2020.
88 It is no coincidence that the term 'propaganda' is being used again in the democratic context, see S.C. Woolley and P.N. Howard, (eds.), *Computational propaganda: political parties, politicians, and political manipulation on social media*, Oxford, Oxford University Press, 2018; D. Kreiss, *Prototype politics: Technology-intensive campaigning and the data of democracy*, Oxford, Oxford University Press, 2016; L. Morlino and M. Sorice (eds.), *L'illusione della scelta. Come si manipola l'opinione pubblica in Italia*, Roma, Luiss University Press, 2021.
89 More recently, studies on the pandemic crisis have confirmed how political leaders have been using digital channels to 'make meaning' during the year that will be remembered in the collective memory as the 'annus horribilis' (Haman 2020; Lilleker et al. 2021; Rullo 2021).
90 The impact of social media on leader popularity as well as on the process of rebuilding confidence between government and citizens has been examined in the OECD report: Arthur Mickoleit, *Social media use by governments: a policy primer to discuss trends, identify policy opportunities and guide decision makers*, OECD Working Papers on Public Governance No. 26, 2014.

5.2 Direct communication

The development of a new technology brings about relevant changes in governor–citizens relationships. The entry of the radio into the American political system enabled Franklin D. Roosevelt to start a direct dialogue with electors, for the first time not mediated by the parties. While before the introduction of the 'new medium' the president channelled his messages through party-controlled newspapers on a local basis, through the radio he became able to deliver his speeches in direct connection with several millions of Americans. The FDR fireside chats remained a clear example of how familiar and intimate presidential communication could be, in what was later described as a 'revolutionary experiment with a nascent media platform'[91]. As a mass ritual, the chat was fundamental in helping the president to mobilise and organise a mass public behind his New Deal policies, so paving the way for 'a new form of mass politics that featured a more politically and rhetorically assertive presidency' (Ryfe 1999, 81; Tulis 1987; Milkis 1993). At the same time, Roosevelt may also be remembered as the first president who revealed their intimate private lives, thus anticipating a tendency that would become typical of political communication in most contemporary – and media-saturated – democracies (Van Aelst et al. 2011; Stanyer 2013). Thus, radio broadcasting had a radical impact on the presidency and its functioning.

Political leaders take great advantage of a personal, and even emotional, relationship with citizens, with ample opportunities to monitor – and often manipulate – users' perceptions and opinions. In the following decades, the advent of television created new opportunities for direct communication between political leaders and people. Indeed, the role played by television has been clearly acknowledged as a vehicle of political personalisation, especially with reference to voting behaviour (Mughan 2000; Barisione 2015). Research on political leadership has underlined the television effect in reinforcing the leader's image and message, while removing the dividing line between the public and the private spheres[92]. As the major source of political information for a vast majority of vot-

---

91 The way Roosevelt used the radio to unify the nation appears in high contrast with the recent Trump communications to citizens, which very often assumes an extremely divisive style, see A. LaFrance, *Donald Trump is Testing Twitter's Harassment Policy*, in *The Atlantic*. Archived from the original on January 26, 2021. Retrieved July 3, 2017.

92 As it has been noted 'Television has in effect transformed political communication: the audience of news bulletins, the debates between political leaders or the interviews with journalists imply the existence of a strong personalisation of the leader', see J. Blondel and J.L. Thiébault (eds.), *Political leadership, parties and citizens: the personalisation of leadership*, London, Routledge, 2009, pp. 32–33.

ers, television has been also an opportunity for leaders to create their own 'public' by stimulating political identification (Di Gregorio 2010; Garzia 2013). With the spread of political spectatorship, the emphasis has been placed on how citizens see and feel the leader's image. Moreover, as 'democracy hitherto has been conceived as an empowerment of the People's voice' (Green 2010, 3), an important element in the construction of presidential consensus was 'polling', which became a more a more institutionalised practice as a means to measure and influence public opinion (Eisinger 2000). It is no surprise that in 1940 the Office of Public Opinion was founded at the White House to provide the president with in-depth analysis on the trends of citizens' orientations on the main social and political issues[93]. Besides offering a tool for dialogue and the engagement with public opinion, polling facilitated direct contact between the president and the people, and contributed to the formation of an autonomous consensus circuit for the government leader. Since Roosevelt, the American Presidents showed an increasing propensity to take 'the pulse of the people'[94].

After the digital revolution, political leaders move in a very different landscape from the past, which confirmed – and radicalised – the direct contact between governors and citizen-users. The first change concerns the massive character of the public the leader may appeal to. It is worth noting some data on the impressive development of the Internet: in the last four years, the global connected inhabitants – the Internet users – have gone from 2.2 billion to over 4.5 billion, with the majority of them also engaged in social networks (4.2 billion active users)[95]. These quantities appear to be growing fast, if we consider that during the pandemic there was a jump of 7.3% in the number of global users,

---

93 On the evolution of the American presidency to cope with the necessity of studying and orienting public opinion see: R.M. Eisinger and J. Brown, *Polling as a means toward presidential autonomy: Emil Hurja, Hadley Cantril and the Roosevelt administration*, in *International Journal of Public Opinion Research*, 10, 3, 1998, pp. 237–256; R.M. Eisinger, *The Evolution of Presidential Polling*, Cambridge, Cambridge University Press, 2003; V. Reda, *I sondaggi dei presidenti. Governi e umori dell'opinione pubblica*, Milano, Bocconi, 2011.

94 Roosevelt devoted great attention to postal correspondence, which amounted to about five to eight thousand letters a day, also as a result of the president's invitations to citizens to write to him directly. This correspondence was the object of precise quantitative analysis, so that the letters of each day were classified by topic. Roosevelt himself also read some of them according to a scientific sampling procedure, see R.W. Steel, *The pulse of the people. Franklin D. Roosevelt and the measurement of American public opinion*, in M. Vaudagna, *Il New Deal*, Bologna, Il Mulino, pp. 237–247, p. 237.

95 See the annual report published by *We Are Social and Hootsuite*, Digital Report 2021, https://datareportal.com/reports/digital-2021-global-overview-report

each with an average use of digital technologies that reaches the astonishing level of seven hours a day. At this level information technologies are able to affect citizen's behaviour, while shaping – to use a far-sighted formula – their 'brainframes'[96].

Parallel to these incredible developments of the Internet, we can notice a significant increase of leaders' online activism, which leads to a very high number of posts and interaction with users: Donald Trump reached the number of twenty-five million followers on Facebook in 2019, by posting an average of nine posts a day. Moreover, Trump's pages registered an increase of about ten million users during the pandemic year (Figure 1). European leaders, from Giuseppe Conte to Boris Johnson, dedicate three posts a day to target of a millions of followers, which have registered, however, a significant increase during recent months: the expansion of Conte's followers is very significant, having grown from one million to more than three million (Figure 2).

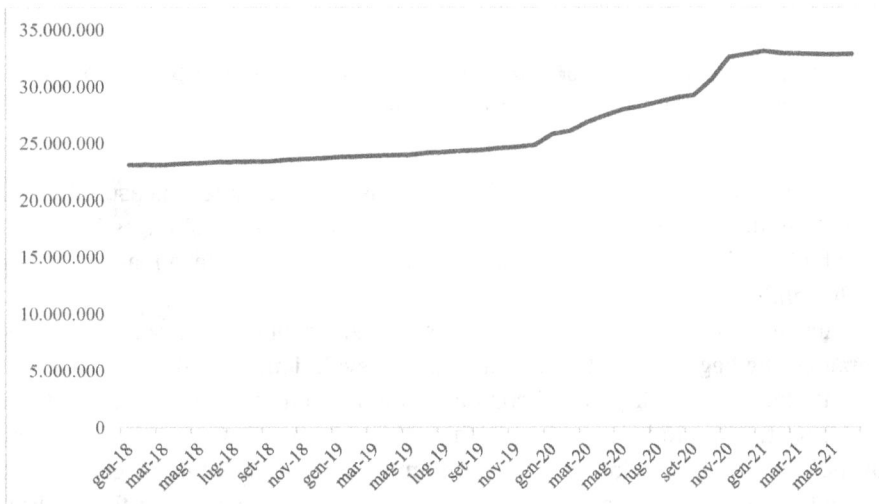

Figure 1: Number of fans on Donald Trump's Facebook account (January 2018–May 2021). *Source:* own elaboration on data from FanPage Karma.

In the following figure, the waves of political engagement with the European political leaders' webpages are represented; this is the number of reactions by citi-

---

96 See D. De Kerckhove on how information and knowledge processing technologies end up forging the cognitive and sensorial perception structures of reality (*Brainframes: Technology, Mind and business*, Utrecht, Bosch & Keuning, 1991).

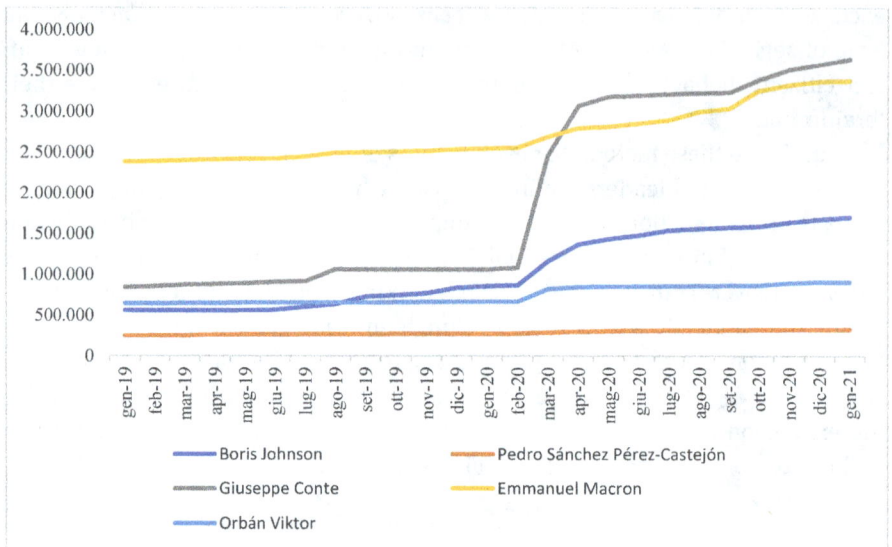

Figure 2: Number of fans of European leaders on Facebook (January 2019–January 2021). *Source:* own elaboration on data from FanPage Karma.

zens to the leaders' posts, such as likes, comments, and shares, measured daily. Especially during the coronavirus crisis, the vitality of leaders' pages has been very high so that some of them, such as Conte and Orbán, have reached about twelve million reactions per day.

According to these very rapid changes, the advent of digital technologies has heralded the beginnings of a communication revolution, strongly dominated by digital platforms. Yet if political communication becomes even more direct than in the past, it would be a mistake to think that it is even less mediated. Indeed, in the new society 'social, economic, interpersonal traffic is largely channelled by an (overwhelmingly corporate) global online platform ecosystem that is driven by algorithms and fueled by data' (Van Dijck et al. 2018, 4). The distance from the past is marked by the passage from 'connectedness' to 'connectivity' based on algorithms and other technical features of a platform (Van Dijck et al. 2018). The new epoch has been produced by the shift 'from connectedness, the result of the relationships that each of us weaves of his own free will, to connectivity, the cybernetic relationships that machines sew on us. From the actor who makes the network, to the networks that make the actors' (Calise and Musella 2019, viii). Consequently, the reputation of individuals and products is linked to the quantitative measures of their circulation on the Internet, in an en-

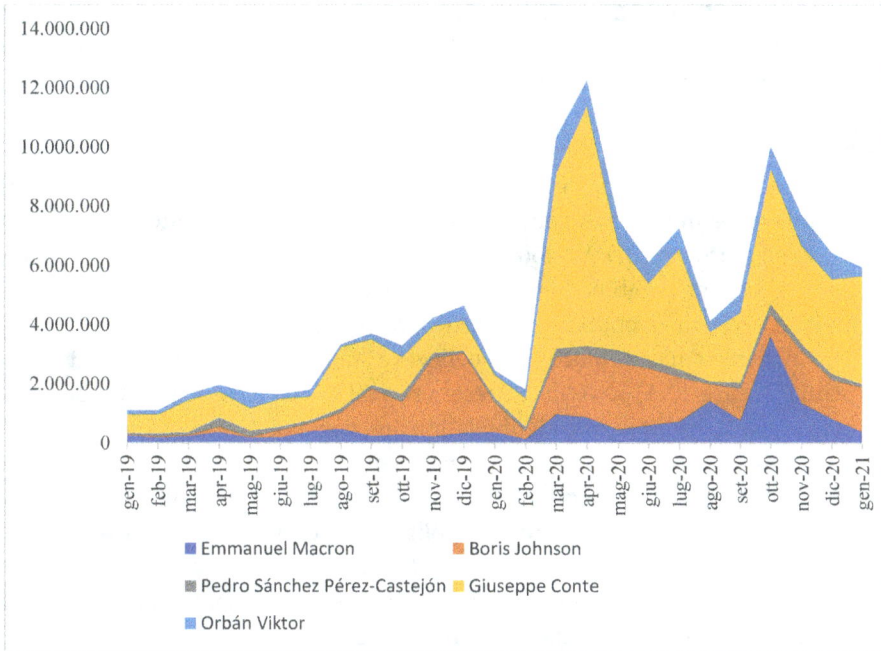

Figure 3: Engagement. European leaders on Facebook (January 2019–January 2021). *Source: own elaboration on data from FanPage Karma.*

vironment that was expected to be free, but which is instead managed and regulated by the big corporations of the web.

The combination of the global diffusion of social networks and the rise of digital platforms' oligopolies allows political presidents to have a one-to-one relationship with citizens. On the one hand, such individualisation of public opinion provides political leaders with new instruments to build consensus, so as to be able to communicate with billions of users in an autonomous way. On the other hand, it renders them more and more dependent on the new digital intermediaries, so that the disintermediation that started with American presidents has resulted in a new digital remediation. This was a lesson that Donald Trump has been recently taught when, after the Capitol riot in January 2021, Facebook and Twitter banned Donald J. Trump from their platforms so depriving him of direct access to his most powerful megaphones[97].

---

97 D. Alba, E. Koeze and J. Silver, *What Happened When Trump Was Banned on Social Media*, in *The New York Times*, June 7, 2021.

5.3 Algorithmic leadership

The digital leadership needs two ingredients. The first is very ancient, and it does not change a lot in the new world. According to Max Weber, the leader's extraordinary personal qualities are a necessary condition to create a group of followers, and to acquire consensus among them especially in pre-modern political settings: this takes the form of compliance based on inspiration induced by single individuals (Turner 2001). Yet looking at contemporary politics, the role of leaders has been often combined with the collegial working typical of large modern organisations such as political parties, where 'a combination of charismatic and patrimonial resources replaces the collective and legal-rational original party structure' (Calise 2015, 304). In the recent revival of charismatic power, the leader becomes a focus for public identification and comes at the top of mass parties. More recently, in the relationship between political leaders and electors, charisma still plays a significant role in the digital environment as well. The spread of social networks reinforces the role of political leader vis à vis political parties, thanks to the leader's increasing capacity to direct and have continuous contact with citizens. Indeed, looking at the Italian Five Star Movement as an example of a political party fostering digital innovation, it is difficult to imagine its rise without Beppe Grillo, and the party 'has shared, in fact, the main features of the personal party model' (Gerbaudo 2019b; Diamanti 2014).

The second – and more disruptive – element of digital leadership is the use of algorithmic mechanisms applied to political communication (Nunziata 2021). Political leaders can take the pulse of electors and continuously react to their expectations and demands. Political leaders take great advantage of a personal, and even emotional, relationship with citizens, with ample opportunities for them to monitor – and often manipulate – users' perceptions and opinions. Micro-targeting – based on the use of computational statistics to collect immediate information on the public by observing the digital behaviour of web users – has become the new magic word in the field of consensus building. The United States has provided the first examples of online political micro-targeting used in presidential and parliamentarian elections to influence the electorate's political views[98] (Kenski, Hardy and Jamieson 2010). The clearest case

---

98 On the evolution of micro-targeting see R. Blaemire, *The Evolution of Microtargeting*, in *Campaigns and Elections American Style*, New York, Routledge, 2018, pp. 217–236; O. Papakyriakopoulos, S. Hegelich, M. Shahrezaye and J.C.M. Serrano, *Social media and microtargeting: Political data processing and the consequences for Germany*, in *Big Data & Society*, 5, 2, 2018; M. Lavigne, *Strengthening ties: The influence of microtargeting on partisan attitudes and the vote*, in *Party Politics*, 2020.

has been provided by Donald Trump, whose hybrid media (Chadwick 2017) campaigns represented a breaking point in political communication – in addition to raising doubts on the controversial use of data from millions of citizens. More recently, one may think of the pervasive digital machinery and the algorithm set up by Matteo Salvini and his staff, significantly named 'the Beast', that allows the League leader to know what people want in real-time – through sophisticated computational statistics concerning social media pages – and to dominate the public agenda. While mobilising an anti-elite protest, Salvini has tried to represent the real interest of the people as they immediately emerge from the Internet: he 'uses social media to not only speak to the electorate directly, but also uses data collection to create specific targets and adapt its message to them'[99], in a 'complex digital media infrastructure through which to distribute his messages'. There is a general tendency towards an increasing use of digital platforms – even in an unconventional way – to galvanise grassroots support for political leaders.[100] This is an important aspect of the process of individualisation of the leader/users relationship which the spread of the digital ecosystem largely contributes to the development of, and which is the process of the 'personalisation of masses' (Calise and Musella 2019).

Algorithmic leadership relies on a high – and unexpected – level of professionalisation. Digital disruption has significantly improved the degree of professionalisation of electoral campaigns (Negrine and Lilleker 2002). Political leaders rely on new digital machines composed by personal staffers and structures tasked with the leader's personal consensus-building and which are independent from the party organisation[101]. They hire more talent from outside the political field, especially from the tech industry. Some scholars have seen this tendency as a countertrend in political communication and pointed towards

---

99 I. Maly, *Algorithmic populism*, in *Diggit Magazine*, 26 November 2019.

100 The best known (and studied in literature) platforms are LiquidFeedback (Pirate Parties), participa.podemos (Podemos, We Can), Rousseau (Movimento Cinque Stelle). See: M. Deseriis, *Digital movement parties: a comparative analysis of the technopolitical cultures and the participation platforms of the Movimento 5 Stelle and the Piratenpartei*, in *Information, Communication & Society*, 23, 12, 2020, pp 1770–1786; P. Gerbaudo, *Are digital parties more democratic than traditional parties? Evaluating Podemos and Movimento 5 Stelle's online decision-making platforms*, in *Party Politics*, 27, 4, 2021, pp. 730–742.

101 The category of 'platform politics' has been introduced by Federica Nunziata to analyse how the emergence of digital leaders have been based on a new organisational structure independent from – if not antagonistic to – traditional party organisation. From Trump to Jair Bolsonaro and Narendra Modi, social networks have represented the most important arena to monitor and maintain popular consensus, see F. Nunziata, *Il platform leader*, in *Rivista di Digital Politics*, 1, 2021.

an amateurish style of election campaigns (Enli 2017). However, studies of the professionalisation of leaders' campaigning has shown an increased specialisation of technology and data analytics services in political campaigns (Kreiss and Jasinski 2016), suggesting a trend towards hyper-professionalisation. For instance, Donald Trump was also seen as an outsider in terms of the individuals and organisations that he hired for his campaign (Karpf 2017), and his strategy was described as amateurism (Enli 2017). By contrast, Trump's digital campaign was far more professionalised than the one run by the Democratic party. He hired external firms and digital specialists to handle key activities of the campaign strategy, and channelled substantial economic resources to technologies previously unseen in an electoral contest. Likewise, Matteo Salvini's digital factory enlisted staffers with low – or even non-existent – political experience but who were well qualified in the digital area. The so-called 'Beast' was actually founded in collaboration with digital specialists. These hyper-professionalised organisations, in terms of digital skills and tools, provided both Trump and Salvini a great technological advantage in electoral campaigning.

5.4 Digital decisions

While the diffusion of new technologies represents a crucial element of the personalisation of politics in contemporary democracies, by stimulating an ongoing and direct relationship between top political figures and citizens, it plays an important – and often undervalued – role in the decisional arena as well. Indeed, political leaders have shown an increasing capacity to channel autonomous legislation, so that the gross of legislative production has been transferred from the parliamentary body to the executive, and the decrees have been used as an ordinary instrument of government, from the historical trend towards the increase of the executive order in the United States to the recent use of decrees of the Italian *Presidente del Consiglio*[102]. New technologies have ended up relaunching this trend, by allowing the rapid communication, or rather the anticipation, of decisions taken by political leaders. At the same time the immediacy of social interaction leads chief executives to speed up the formal protocols of official procedures, so that 'after the emergency decree – which had marked the rise of the prime-ministerial executive – we have the immediate decree by tweet, the supreme stage of presidential government' (Calise and Musella 2019, 106). This is

---

[102] A comparative analysis is provided in F. Musella (ed.), *L'emergenza democratica. Presidenti, decreti, crisi pandemica*, Napoli, Editoriale Scientifica, 2020.

the reason why digital innovation may be assumed to be the last and definitive component of the primacy of heads of government.

Once again, the United States has shown the world its destiny. Throughout his presidency, Trump frequently appeared to issue orders through his tweets. This helped him to get the attention and votes necessary to win a presidential race even though tweets were not official directives. American courts are still debating whether a presidential tweet may be considered an official statement, and whether it falls within the 'outer perimeter' of his official duties (McKechnie 2017). However, what is clear is that a presidential declaration through social media produces political effects immediately, and it may lead other actors to take the decision into account and behave accordingly.

An important area in terms of presidential social media declarations concern foreign relationships. As has been noticed, Twitter has become an integral part of contemporary international relations, so that the term "Twiplomacy" has been coined to refer to the increasing tendency by which 'social media platforms allow government officials to broadcast their views on pertinent issues and developments in the public domain without the need for formal diplomatic channels or jargon' (Chhabra 2020, 3). Indeed, when a leader expresses their view through a social channel, a political figure in another country may react, so that the posts could be the premise to reach an agreement on a particular policy issue or the opening to a conflictual phase. Sometimes tweets have aggravated conflictual escalation such as in the conflict between North Korea and the United States in 2017, with social posts used as ammunition: thus, 'instead of mending relationships, bridging gaps and building trust between counterparts, irresponsible Twitter exchanges result in misunderstandings and increase distrust, leading to an unnecessary escalation in conflict' (Chhabra 2020, 8).

Also, European prime ministers have been noticing a significant quantity of posts aimed at transmitting 'a frame of authority without contention from opposing parties or media', by taking advantage of a 'a more "individuated" politics in which people experience politics as an expression of individual autonomy, direct interaction with leaders, and choice among sources of information and support' (Ie 2020, 164, 159). Very often, before taking a decision, a chief executive invokes the support of public opinion to force other decisional bodies, such as the Parliament, to follow the leader's line.

The leaders' activism on social media has been very evident during the coronavirus emergency with political leaders communicating their decisions in day-by-day press conferences held on social media pages, like Twitter or Instagram, as a major means of communication. First studies in this field show that social media has been used extensively by world leaders 'as [a] powerful tool to rapidly communicate with citizens during public health crises: to inform, to boost morale and even to politicize', resulting in extensively viral effects on the diffusion of their message (Rufai and Bunce 2020). An example of change in modes of communication produced by the pandemic was provided by the Italian Prime Minister Conte who announced several decrees through his personal Facebook page before they were published in the Official Gazette. On the 8th of March 2020, Conte proclaimed a nationwide lockdown, under which people would only be allowed to leave their homes for work or health reasons, before this decision was announced by an official decree. Such a declaration caused an immediate reaction on the part of Italian citizens, as 'video footage on social media showed people rushing to get on the last train out and escape a virtual lockdown that will see people housebound'[103], in a last attempt to move from the northern top to the southern regions of Italy.

As Conte centralised policy-making though an innovative use of prime-ministerial decrees (DPCM) resulting in a rapid and effective response to the spread of the virus across the country (Criscitiello 2020), by ending the marginalisation – by necessity as well as political choice – other constitutional bodies (Musella 2020c), the *Presidente del Consiglio* also changed remarkably the way in which he communicated to citizens during the pandemic. Indeed, 'digital platforms were at the basis of a metamorphosis of Conte's political leadership. Facebook became the main channel of Prime Ministerial communication to promote governmental activities, broadening public knowledge, and communicate official decisions and forthcoming decrees' (Rullo and Nunziata 2021; Ceccobelli and Vaccari 2021).

5.5 Forms and borders of government

A rich strand of literature shows the increasing use of media technologies that allow political leaders to construct and maintain personal consensus. In line with the logic of the permanent campaign, leaders adapt their behaviour and communication to meet electors' preferences in real time through an intensive use of digital technologies. Yet little attention has been devoted to how such radical processes have impacted systems of government, starting with changes regarding how presidents reinforce their position in relation to parliaments and political parties. The direct relation of the chief executive gives them a surplus

---

103 *Italy's Conte puts 16 million around Milan under lockdown to combat virus*, 8 March 2020, https://www.japantimes.co.jp/news/2020/03/08/world/science-health-world/italy-milan-lockdown-coronavirus/.

of legitimation in both presidential and parliamentary regimes, so that this may suggest the transcending of the governmental setting as fixed in the Constitution (Carnevale 2019, 277). At the same time, the potential of the web to shift decisional power toward a monocratic figure can be emphasised, as leaders can anticipate relevant measures before their discussion and deliberation by competent organs. Thus, although the constitutional doctrine tends to consider forms of government in their static nature, the spread of new technologies stimulates a more accurate understanding of the dynamics related to political institutions, putting emphasis on the necessity of evaluating and measuring increasing presidential powers in contemporary democracies as they evolve over time (Matcalf 2000; Palanza 2018; Doyle 2020).

At the same time, the relationship between political leaders and digital networks appears as highly controversial. The leader takes great advantage of them, especially in electoral processes, as a mean for financing campaigns though micro-donations, as shown by the Move-On movement, as well as using them as an intensive instrument of online persuasion with negative effects demonstrated by the Cambridge Analytica scandal. Moreover, social networks help leaders to make a continuous and emotive linkage with electors, so gaining a prominent position over their political parties. Nevertheless, digital presence tends to be very expensive for political leaders in terms of political autonomy. First, while adapting messages to algorithmic analysis, they lose their capacity to define the political agenda. This is the problem already evidenced for catch-all parties, and now readapted to digital catch-all political leaders: while they continuously follow electors' preferences, their identity and political positions remain fluid and highly influenceable. Moreover, digital corporations may ban those political figures of whom they do not approve.

To make a recent and crucial example, digital media has offered instruments to sway voters and can amplify the messages of populists such as Donald Trump. Digital corporations have not been able to combat the battle against bots and fake accounts, which were the basis of Russian foreign interference in the American elections. Following this controversial behaviour, however, they have acted to defend democracies under the attack manifested by the Capitol Hill invasion. In particular, Twitter's decision to ban Donald Trump has made it appear to be a defender of democratic values by simply toning down the megaphone of 'the most powerful and platformed man in the world'[104] The unprecedented Twitter

---

104 A. Haroun, *Trump still has the biggest voice on the planet as president. As he becomes increasingly isolated in his final days in office, his suspension from Twitter could help stave off potential disaster*, in *Insider*, 9 January 2021.

decision to sanction Trump after the Capitol insurrection seemed justified, and so was accepted in Western countries, 'due to the risk of further incitement of violence'. Yet this poses the problem, or at least is a manifestation of it, of a private actor having the last voice in the most delicate circumstances of democratic countries. Twitter's move shows the digital companies' potential to silence strong political leaders when they found their strategies on the Internet. One may remember the famous Carl Schmitt position according to which the sovereign is he who decides on the state of exception, that is the imposition of a rule in an unregulated territory such as current cyberspace. For his part, Donald Trump announced the launch of his own digital platform that would gather millions of supporters, so initiating a new trend in contemporary leadership: the almost desperate attempt of leaders who have gained success thanks to a social media platform, to reach autonomy by controlling digital architectures.

6 Heads of government from primacy to emergency

6.1 Introduction

While the statement that we are living in a democratic emergency is becoming progressively more frequent, this should not be interpreted as alluding to the moribund condition of contemporary democracies. Instead, emergency has become a permanent state of democracies, by paving the way to the expansion of the role of the government over the last decades[105]. More recently, it relates to how democracies have been facing the most severe crisis since the Second World War, with the COVID-19 pandemic confirming the primacy of heads of government in contemporary real-world politics.

On American soil, the shift in power away from legislatures to personalised executives, and the further break with the traditional liberal model, has been anticipated since the 1960s (Lowi 1979), when scholars reflected on a new constitutional order which started with the New Deal[106]. Since then, presidential decree authority has extended its scope and improved its effectiveness in line with an institutional framework that has ensured presidents both an increasingly cen-

---

[105] In this chapter we will try to combine the two meanings given by Norberto Bobbio to the concepts of normality and exception, by bearing in mind his definition: 'the term "norm" originally denotes a measuring instrument, such as the cord or the square that is used by architects. The "norm" is divided in both "normality" and "normativity". These two are very similar. So what are the differences between them? Following Hume and Kant, normality is conceived as a plethora of descriptive rules, and normativity as a complex of prescriptive rules. The descriptive rules lead to questions of fact, whereas the prescripted ones lead to questions of law. Human behavior is subject to two dimensions: normality and normativity', see N. Bobbio, *Contributi ad un dizionario giuridico*, Torino, Giappichelli, 1994. Indeed, by starting from the constitutional prescription of a state of emergency, it aims at understanding similar trends followed by compared democracies.

[106] As President Roosevelt rewrote the American constitutional system when he stated that 'first, the Executive Office was no longer confined to its duty to merely "take care that the laws be faithfully executed" and second, the federal government as a whole was no longer confined to the powers provided to it by a strict interpretation of the Constitution with regard to federalism concerns and civil liberties'. From that time on, an implicit 'doctrine of emergency powers' found a welcome in the US constitutional framework, see Roger I. Roots, *Government by Permanent Emergency: The Forgotten History of the New Deal Constitution*, in *Suffolk University Law Review*, 33, 2, 2000, p. 259–292, p. 269. On the 'implicit' amendments to the American constitution see B. Ackerman, *We the People, Volume 2: Transformations*, Cambridge, Harvard University Press, 2000.

https://doi.org/10.1515/9783110721720-006

tralised control in policymaking and new modes of political communication. Presidential decree authority has exerted an increasing control over nearly every arena of policy, often granting effective responses to deal with a dangerous situation, from an economic crisis to terrorism, from war to domestic risks[107]. In the end, the extensive use of emergency powers has ushered in a 'new normality' in American politics to the point that some authors have emphasised that 'practically during all of the twenty-first century to date, the United States has been under a presidentially declared state of emergency' (Gross 2015, 785; Scheppele 2005).

European parliamentary systems have followed the same path (Andeweg et al. 2020)[108]. The use of executive emergency decrees has extended its scope and relevance over the last few decades. This trend has led prime ministers to become 'the main governmental driving force and the point of concentration of mass expectations' (Musella 2018, 97). Most recently, these challenges in executive power dynamics seem to be exalted and further accelerated during the unprecedented COVID-19 pandemic crisis. As observed by Ginsburg (2020, 1–2), the sanitary emergency 'has posed a grave challenge to governance systems everywhere. Indeed, it is hard to imagine that there has ever been a shock that affected all governments in the world in such a short period of time'. Indeed, while younger liberal democracies have been facing a concrete risk of 'autocratic involution', a vertiginous institutional rise of executive power has taken place in consolidated democratic countries as well. Hence, 'the participation of parliaments in decision-making has been confined in scope [...], since their legislative prerogatives were reduced to little more than ratifying executive proposals' (Griglio 2020, 50).

This chapter focusses on our set of Western countries (Usa, Italy, Germany, Spain, Hungary, UK, France) and it is structured into three sections. First, it discusses how these countries constitutionalised the state of emergency. Second, it shows how – well before the current pandemic – the use of emergency bills al-

---

107 An ample list of contributions focusses on the specific escalation of emergency powers. See M. Neocleous, *The problem with normality: Taking exception to 'permanent emergency'*, in *Alternatives*, 31, 2, 2006, pp. 191–213; J.C. Paye, *From the state of emergency to the permanent state of exception*, in *Telos*, 136, 2006, pp. 154–166; F. Schurmann, *Emergency Powers. The New Paradigm in Democratic America*, in *New California Media*, December 23, 2002.

108 The political reinforcement of the executive branch of government is also evidenced by the wide diffusion of studies dedicated to this topic on the international scenario. See R.B. Andeweg, R. Elgie, L. Helms, J. Kaarbo, and F. Müller-Rommel, *The Political Executive Returns: Re-empowerment and Rediscovery*, in R.B. Andeweg, R. Elgie, L. Helms, J. Kaarbo, and F. Müller-Rommel (eds.), *The Oxford Handbook of Political Executives*, Oxford, Oxford University Press 2020, pp. 1–24.

ready represented an 'ordinary' instrument of government, thus realising a 'stabilized emergency'. Third, it observes the key role played by presidents and prime ministers in handling the COVID-19 pandemic crisis, and how it has further developed the concentration of strategic decision-making powers in their hands.

6.2 Constitutionalising emergencies

Emergency phases typically work to strengthen monocratic figures (Rossiter 1948). This phenomenon meets the need to ensure rapid reactions during unforeseeable and dangerous situations, which cannot accommodate the involvement of collegial bodies and traditional deliberative procedures. A clear-cut example can be found in ancient Rome where the dictator – whose magistrature was instituted *de iure,* and was very far from contemporary authoritarian leadership – was appointed to restore order for a fixed period of no more than six months during an emergency (Sartori 1972; Stoppino 2004). Even modern democracies allow for the temporary suspension of general rules (Mortati 1973; Agamben 2003) to deal with the sudden and unexpected appearance of danger[109]. These special legal regimes are designed to overcome extraordinary circumstances, such as war, internal upheavals, and natural disasters, and have the potential to entail restrictions on citizens' constitutional freedoms and to give chief executives extraordinary powers.

Most national constitutions adopt a dualistic perspective that contrasts the state of normality to the state of exception, with 90 % of them containing explicit provisions for regulating emergencies (Bjørnskov and Voigt 2018). The underlying idea shared by most liberal democracies consists of the possibility of providing temporary and complementary measures to address the state of emergency with a 'conservative' aim, as emergency powers cannot make permanent changes to the system[110] (Ferejhon and Pasquino 2004). Therefore, the choice of constitu-

---

109 Although the reference to the classical theory of the state of exception by C. Schmitt, (*Die Diktatur. Von den Anfängen des modernen Souveränitätsgedankens bis zum proletarischen Klassenkampf*, Berlin, Duncker & Humblot, 1921; translated in *Dictatorship*, New York, John Wiley & Sons, 2014) allows us to state that the 'Sovereign is he who decides on the exception', the aim of democratic architectures stays in regulating periods of radical crisis through concrete constitutional provisions.
110 As Ferejhon and Pasquino notice (2004, 211) 'this conservative purpose is reflected in the fact that the executive is not permitted to use emergency powers to make any permanent changes in the legal/constitutional system'.

tionalising the emergency seems to exalt one of the main vocations of modern constitutions, which were born as instruments to 'limit power' (Böckenförde 2017), and to confine exceptional powers to exceptional situations (Lazar 2009).

Moreover, looking in more detail, two prevailing orientations emerge: 'an integral coverage that governs any power that can be activated in a crisis, or a minimal provision that proceeds in broad lines, describing types and classes of powers' (Di Minico 2018, 8; Vedaschi 2020). The common belief shared by both approaches is that governmental action should be carried out in the fastest and most productive way during periods of crisis when it is framed, and be limited, by specific rules, that are the 'normative architecture of the emergency' (Bjørnskov and Voigt 2017).

The pivotal role played by parliaments underlies the regulation of the state of emergency. It is worth recalling that 73% of the democratic constitutions in force reserve to the parliament the capacity to declare a state of emergency or delegate authority to the government, while others – such as in Spain and France – prevent the parliament from being dissolved during an emergency phase (Ginsburg and Versteeg 2020b; Khakee 2009). Yet the variability of emergency management opens up to different cases, either because of different constitutional provisions or the frequent circumstance of 'when countries "legalize" states of emergency by embedding them in domestic constitutions, such provisions are almost never used in a formal way' (Scheppele 2008, 174).

In Table 1, a frame is provided for emergency regulation for each country and the way it has been used in the past. The French legal system provides three rules that allow exceptions to the constitution in case of crisis and/or emergency: art. 16 Cost. attributes exceptional powers to the President of the Republic; article 36 Cost. provides for a state of siege, which is triggered by 'an imminent danger resulting from a foreign war or an armed insurrection'; and Law No. 55–385 of 3 April 1955, explicitly regulates the state of emergency. By contrast, in Germany, post-war politicians were very hesitant to provide any constitutional basis for a state of emergency. Nevertheless, while the 1949 constitution did not refer to emergencies, this provision has been added through the 1968 Amendment to the Basic Law. The 1968 reform – which took place after ten years of discussions – introduced one of the most detailed examples in the European scenario (Jakab 2006) and distinguished between an internal State of Emergency (or State of Tension/Spannungsfall) and an external State of Emergency (State of Defence/Verteidigungsfall). The former ends whenever the Bundestag so decides, the latter is terminated whenever the Bundestag, with the approval of the Bundesrat, so decides. These constitutional provisions have never been activated to deal with any emergency until now. In Hungary, the 2012 Fundamental Law provided for special legislation to cope with crisis and introduced a series of extraordinary measures (artt. 48–54) to the point that some authors have spoken of an 'emergency Constitution'. Indeed, the Fundamental Law introduced in 2012 displays a well-defined, constitutionally based structure for dealing with emergencies. It is worth noting that in 2016 'terrorism' was explicitly included among the contingencies justifying the call for an emergency. There are five cases which allow for exceptional measures: a state of national crisis, a state of emergency, a state of preventive defence, unexpected attack, and a state of danger.

Table 1: Normative basis to face the COVID-19 pandemic in six European countries and USA.

	Measures adopted at national level	Temporality	Parliamentary oversight	Used before
Italy	Decree Law (art. 77 Cost.), DPCM, Law 833/1978, Code of Civil Protection (art. 24)	Yes	Yes	Yes
Germany	Infektionsschutzgesetz, paragraph 5	Yes	Yes	No
Spain	State of alarm (art. 16 Cost. and art. 4–12 Organic law 4/1981), decree law (art. 86 Cost.)	Yes	Yes	Yes
Hungary	Cardinal Law XII/2020, Decree 40/2020 (11 March)	No	Yes	Yes
France	Code of Public Health, Act of Parliament of 23 March 2020	Yes	Yes	No
UK	Public Health (control of disease) Act 1984, Health Protection Regulation 2020, Coronavirus bill 2019–2021	Yes	Yes	Yes
USA	National Emergencies Act, Stafford Act	Yes	Yes	Yes

Source: own elaboration, see Appendix B.

Nevertheless, at the onset of the COVID-19 pandemic crisis, with the exception of Spain that declared the 'state of alarm'[111], European democracies such as Germany and France have governed without the state of emergency constitutional framework. For instance, in France, the emergency has been managed under the 'State of sanitary emergency' declared for the first time through an Act of Parliament on 23 March 2020. According to this Act, the prime minister can dispose of a range of exceptional powers to tackle the pandemic, and the government has been allowed to legislate by decree on a significant number of issues (Haguenau-Moizard 2021). Indeed, as Table 1 shows, of the US and European democ-

---

111 The state of alarm (*estado de alarma*) is one of the several constitutional provisions provided for exceptional regimes enshrined in the Spanish Constitution (artt. 55 and 116 of the Spanish Constitution and Organic Law 4/1981).

racies included in our cluster for analysis, the US have used 'original' tools not explicitly determined by the national emergency provisions, with no reference to specific constitutional provisions for the state of emergency[112].

The 1948 Italian Constitution does not contain any emergency section, unlike other European democracies such as Spain, France, Germany, and Hungary (Rolla 2015; Baldini 2020a; 2020b). Nevertheless, other strategies allow the government to cope with an emergency. First, article 77 of the Constitution provides that in cases of extraordinary necessity and urgency the government may adopt decree laws, which are subject to ordinary legislative procedure. Decree laws require parliamentary approval within 60 days for them to be converted into law, but they remain in force during this span of time. Second, article 78 of the Constitution regulates the State of War by assigning specific powers to both parliament and government in case of national conflict. However, this article 'gives no room – either in broad interpretation or misinterpretation – to the particular exercise of governmental power' beyond a war event' (Bertolini 2018, 513). Additionally, article 120 of the Constitution, amended with Constitutional Law 3/2001, provides that the government can subsume the authority of a region, metropolitan city, province, or municipality in case it fails to comply with international rules and treaties or EU legislation, or in case of grave danger to public safety and security. Nevertheless, among the kaleidoscope of measures adopted at both national and subnational levels, the decrees of the President of the Council of Ministers (DPCM) represent the main executive instrument to face the current COVID-19 pandemic crisis. This phenomenon highlights how crisis management may give power and autonomy to the executive in contemporary Italian politics.

The US Constitution seems to remain relatively silent when it comes to emergency provisions to the point that the US Supreme Court once stated that 'the Constitution of the United States is a law for rulers and people, equally in war and in peace, and covers with the shield of its protection all classes of men, at all times, and under all circumstances' (quoted in Fisch 1990, 393). The Constitution, indeed, provides that emergency powers are granted to the Congress in case of war, invasion, or rebellion, along with the suspension of the writ of habeas corpus in particular delineated circumstances[113]. Nevertheless, despite this general statement, political processes follow different paths. While the US Constitution formally allocates the responsibility of coping with emergencies to the

---

112 See the special issue edited by T. Ginsburg on *Legislatures in the Time of COVID-19*, in *The Theory and Practice of Legislation*, 8, 1–2, 2020.
113 The suspension of the writ of habeas corpus has occurred only twice in American history: during the Civil War and after the 9/11 terrorist attack. See B. Ackerman, *The emergency constitution*, in *Yale International Journal*, 113, 5, 2003, pp. 1029–1091.

Congress, American political reality has taught us that 'the emergency is the hour of the executive' (Scheuerman 2012, 745; Gerstle and Isaac 2020).

Presidents represent the most powerful political actor in times of emergencies. Indeed, the president has been delegated powers that the Constitution expressly reserves for the Congress during difficult times. The prominence of presidents – also justified by the vague wording of the Vesting clause (Art. II) – was expanded after the Roosevelt and Nixon presidencies, when the Congress passed the 1976 National Emergencies Act[114], giving the president the ability to activate provisions of law via an emergency declaration, through the compromise for which 'the president alone may declare an emergency and Congress may terminate it. Which is the same as saying that presidential declarations remain in force so long as Congress does not volunteer to end them' (Klieman 1979, 62).

Along with the further strengthening of the American presidency in the last decades, its prerogative to produce emergency decrees has grown. In particular, the Bush presidency intensified the expansion of emergency powers to the point that some scholars warned that under the Bush presidency 'Madison's nightmare' had become a reality, namely the collapse of the liberal division of power (Shane 2009). This trend was prolonged during the term of President Obama who signed the *National Defense Order Preparedness* (Executive order 16303) in 2012[115] which acted as a new source for the expansion of the role of president during an emergency. More recently under Donald Trump's presidency, some policies such as immigration were approached as a national emergency[116].

---

114 Other fundamental examples include the Public Health Service Act and the Stafford Act. For a detailed account on the vast number of laws that greatly enhanced presidential powers during emergencies see *A Guide to Emergency Powers and Their Use*, Brennan Center for Justice (2018), available at: https://www.brennancenter.org/sites/default/files/2019-10/AGuideToEmergencyPowersAndTheirUse_2.13.19.pdf.
115 The executive order clarifies its general aims as follows : to 'a) identify requirements for the full spectrum of emergencies, including essential military and civilian demand; (b) assess on an ongoing basis the capability of the domestic industrial and technological base to satisfy requirements in peacetime and times of national emergency, specifically evaluating the availability of the most critical resource and production sources, including subcontractors and suppliers, materials, skilled labor, and professional and technical personnel; (c) be prepared, in the event of a potential threat to the security of the United States, to take actions necessary to ensure the availability of adequate resources and production capability, including services and critical technology, for national defense requirements (...)', see Administration of Barack Obama, 2012, Executive Order 13603—National Defense Resources Preparedness.
116 The risks that the use and abuse of executive power may have on contemporary American and international politics have been clear under the Trump presidency and its attempt to reduce the flow of immigrants. We may think, for instance, of the executive order that put in place the highly controversial 'Muslim ban' restricting travel and immigration to a large list of countries in

Yet it was the pandemic crisis that has shown how the president is the only actor in charge when the nation faces threats to its security, leading Trump to claim 'total authority' in imposing or leaving restrictions over citizens[117].

6.3 The stabilisation of emergency

In the practice of consolidated democracies, the oxymorons 'permanent state of emergency' (Greene 2018; Alford 2017) and 'permanent emergency' (Neocleous 2006) signal the 'breaks' with the conceptual coupling of the normality–exceptionality of politics.

Indeed, from the United States to Europe, 'emergency powers have found a home within the processes of normal governance' (Scheppele 2005, 862). The main characteristics related to this 'new normality' share two fundamental elements: the stabilisation of the emergency and the expansion of executive decree authority to cope with it. Notably, the use – and/or abuse – of emergency bills to face different types of emergencies – terrorist attacks, wars, health, environmental and humanitarian crises – is the result of long-term structural changes and the clearest indicator of the shift in decision-making power resources away from parliaments to governments.

It is easy to understand the difference from the past. The expression 'rule by decree' has often been used to refer to situations of martial law (Carey and Shugart 1992). At the same time, government by decree has for a long time been a peculiar trait of some geographical areas. For instance, 'bypassing the parliament is endemic, and often epidemic, in much of Latin America' (Sartori 1994, 178). However, although from a theoretical point of view we need to talk about emergency acts at the onset of specific contingencies, the expansion of governmental decree/emergency bills emphasises that their use is no longer exceptional but essential in the practice of today's politics. Indeed, political executives have increasingly resorted to emergency legislation as part of their autonomous action, along with the tendency to gain control of the legislative agenda (Musella 2018). Mainly due to the high fragmentation of the party system and difficult law-

---

order to protect national security, or the declaration of national emergency concerning the southern border of the United States (Proclamation 9844).

117 These were the words of the presidents: "'When somebody's president of the United States, the authority is total", Trump said at a press briefing Monday when asked about the governors' plans. "And that's the way it's got to to be. It's total. It's total. And the governors know that'", in Jeremy B. White, *Trump claims 'total authority' over state decisions*, in *Politico.com*, April 13th, 2020.

making in contentious and divided assemblies, the 'stabilisation of the emergency' has become a new source of political stability in most established democracies. Additionally, the most recent process of the personalisation of politics has transformed emergency bills into the most effective tools to ensure heads of government both effective decision-making and strong media impact.

As has been often shown in this volume, the US has anticipated such phenomena resulting from the expansion of executive powers and the rising predominance of presidents in an increasingly vast array of policy arenas. During the twentieth century, presidents have been able to exploit a new centrality in the political system and have emerged as the dominant political and administrative force at the federal level (Gitterman 2017). Largely due to increased polarisation, Congress' capability and productivity has gradually reduced and has ended up favouring the sustenance and expansion of executive power (infra. Chapter 5). Additionally, claiming existing or 'potential' emergencies has represented a new source for the expansion of presidential power. The strengthening of the executive has been particularly evident in the law-making arena, where the expansion of presidential decree authority at the expense of the Congress has been reached through a growing series of instruments of direct presidential governance and executive orders[118].

In this scenario Italy represents one of the clearest cases regarding the use (or abuse) of emergency decrees. Indeed, the copious, and extremely versatile, production of decree-laws and extra-ordinem orders has led some authors to speak about a country in 'perennial emergency' (Biondi Dal Monte 2011), 'infinite emergency' (Simoncini 2006), 'stabilized emergency' (Staiano 2006) or 'normalization of emergency' (Cardone 2011). The Italian case highlights a growing inclination to frame different situations under the emergency label. Very significantly, the decree has become an alternative instrument to present legislative proposals, as well as an integral part of the legislative process in Italian politics (Frosini 2019). Over the first fifty years of the Italian Republic, during the so-called integral parliamentarism, executive emergency decrees increased because of the common practice of 'reiterating' them after their limited period of validity[119].

---

118 In this respect, the Roosevelt administration revolutionised the presidential law-making prerogatives. Indeed, with 3,522 executive orders issued and 4,422 days in office he almost issued one order per day.

119 Whenever the decrees were not converted into laws within the terms provided by the Constitution (within 60 days), they were issued again and therefore gained an additional 60 days of validity consequently overloading parliamentary activities through a continuous 'mechanism of decay-reiteration'. The Constitutional Court stopped this praxis through judgement 360/1996. Indeed, the Court argued that 'the constitutional requirements of extraordinary urgency are lost

While this praxis highlighted a particular form of collaboration between government and Parliament, the executive became the main driver – and beneficiary – of the use of government decrees in recent times (Musella 2012b). Indeed, the executive has extended its competences permanently out of necessity and urgency. This phenomenon 'seems to respond less and less to an irresistible and exceptional contingency, and more to a diffuse "technique" that subverts the standards laid down in laws or [the] Constitution' (Agosta 2011, 373).

The expansion of the role of the executive has led to an 'infinite emergency' because the emergency bill could not be used 'to produce certain types of measures, certain types of legislation, it was not, in other words, the specialized instrument to cope with particular types of (emergency) interventions. Indeed, due to the parliamentary decisional paralysis [...], art. 77 Cost. represented the compulsory avenue for legislation tout court; the urgent decree coincided and overlapped with the whole spectrum of primary regulatory production' (Simoncini 2006, 34). Despite the role of the Constitutional Court, which has restricted the expansion of government legislative power over the last two decades, a watershed in the use of decrees cannot be traced. On the one hand, some aspects have been corrected, and certain limits have been put in place. On the other hand, this has not led to a drastic reduction in the use of decree laws, that still represent a fundamental part of the legislative process in Italian politics.

As shown in Chapter 5, Italy is not an isolated case. In many European democracies, the expansion of executive authority has been achieved through the increased use of emergency bills or other forms of autonomous legislation on the part of the government. In Spain, the erosion of the law-making powers of parliament for the benefit of national executives led the *decreto-ley* to become so diffuse as to suggest the eloquent formula '*gobernar por decreto*'[120] (Iglesia-Chamarro 1997; Pomed Sanchez 2020). Executive decrees have also grown in quantity

---

when a measure is reiterated [...] and legal certainty is jeopardized when, as a consequence of repeated reissuance it becomes impossible to predict how long the decree law will be in effect [because] there is no fixed end point of conversion' (M. Volcansek, *Constitutional politics in Italy*, London, Palgrave, 1999, p. 46). Other landmark decisions on decree laws are rulings 171/2007, 22/2012 and 32/2014. See also: M. Troisi, *Il governo nelle decisioni della Corte costituzionale*, in F. Musella (ed.), *Il governo in Italia. Profili costituzionali e dinamiche politiche*, Bologna, Il Mulino, 2019, pp. 95–122.

120 This trend has been widespread in territorial autonomies as well, introducing the possibility of resorting to this legislative act in their statutes (F.J. Rodríguez Gutiérrez, *El Decreto-Ley como instrumento ordinario de gobierno en Andalucía*, in *Revista general de derecho constitucional*, 11, 2011, pp. 8–38; R. Fittipaldi, *The Rise of Presidents in Coronavirus Emergency: national and sub-national evidence in Italy and Spain*, in *Partecipazione e Conflitto*, 14, 1, 2021, pp. 132–151).

and relevance in other European democracies. In France, the expansion of the role of the executive resulted in an established phenomenon, which has become particularly evident in recent years because of the terrorist attacks that threatened the country. Indeed, government rulemaking has progressively extended its scope, through both primary and secondary sources.

The United Kingdom became detached from the 'glossy' image that its institutional model offered to the world. The Westminster myth was one of the most admired models on the international scenario, with its 'efficient secrecy' (Bagehot 1868) achieved through the nearly complete fusion of the executive and legislative powers through the majority party. In accordance with this ideal type, the British government finds in Parliament an easy channel of legislation. Nevertheless, parliamentary majority, in line with the transformations of most contemporary democracies, have been crumbling in recent decades. Since the late 1980s, the number of parliamentary defeats suffered by the government has increased, especially in the House of Lords. Moreover, the acts of delegated legislation (the statutory instruments) enacted by the government exceeded the number of ordinary laws, and since then these two types of legislation have become progressively different. Over the last 40 years, the expansion of regulatory powers enjoyed by the British cabinet has combined with the definition of government tools that can guarantee quick reactions in times of insecurity as in the case of the 2008 financial crisis. As Valbruzzi (2020) observed, English history can be read as 'permanent crisis and permanent emergency'.

In Germany, the massive shift of law-making authority to the executive from the legislative branch has led some authors to talk about 'chancellor's democracy' since the early 1990s. Indeed, despite the complex institutional balancing system – both horizontal and vertical – which characterises the German political system, this process seemed to enhance the development of the era of personal politics. Recently, chief executives have been able to exploit the levers of power. Thus, they become among the most authoritative European prime ministers in coordinating the government team and issuing priorities on the agenda. Although this does not translate into the definition of autonomous governmental powers, prime ministers manage to play 'the lion's share in quantitative terms both concerning the bills and even more about their actual approval' (Vercesi 2020). This trend has accelerated during the current health emergency. Angela Merkel turned out to be a point of reference in emergency management, by holding a strident position within the intricate power scheme of co-responsibility between the central government and regional executives. Very significantly, as already observed during Merkel's past terms, the Chancellor faced serious crises, such as the Fukushima nuclear disaster (2011), the eurozone crisis (around 2009 – 2015), and the peak of migratory flows of Syrian refugees to Europe

(2015). Therefore, the COVID-19 pandemic emergency may be listed as the most recent experience of crisis management that explicitly underlines the key role played by the chancellor in German politics. This process has become evident even in a German institutional context that has always been hostile to the rise of 'heroic leadership' (Padgett 1994), and that tends to strongly oppose the overwhelming power of a monocratic figure.

The Hungarian case follows a radical path. Here, the idea of a state of exception has represented a *fil rouge* between the significant 2012 constitutional reform and the process of centralisation of power (Sadecki 2014; Szente et al. 2015). While during the 1990s the augmented number of executive staff was a sign of the prime minister strengthening, and the 2010s marked the ascent of Viktor Orbán's personal power. Under his leadership, a combination of executive dominance and a weak form of separation of powers took place. Therefore, 'constitution-making did not become an exceptional, dedicated moment, separated from the normal political process, but it has become a permanent feature' (Körösényi et al. 2020, 139 – 140). Looking at policymaking, one of the most evident trends concerns the exponential increase of governmental decrees to accomplish its policy goals (see Figure 1).

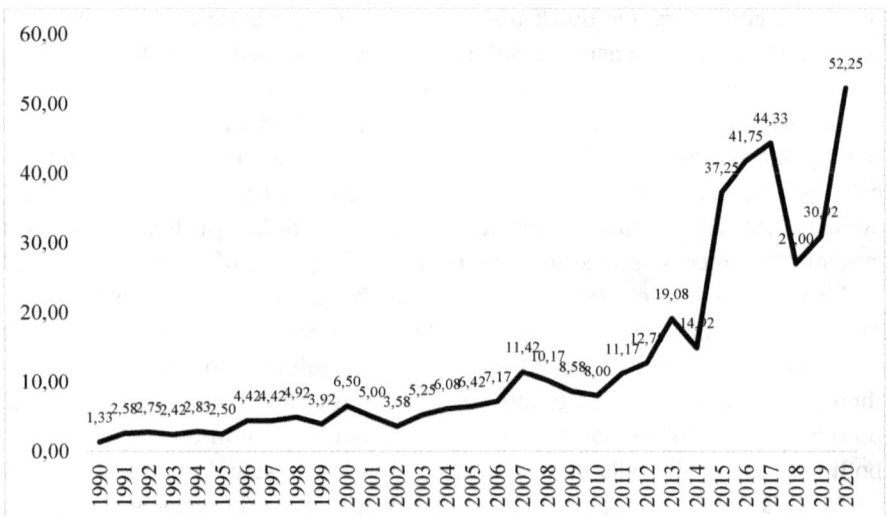

Figure 1: Governmental decrees on a monthly basis in Hungary (1990 – 2020). *Source:* own elaboration from Hungarian government official data. (*) 2020 until 31st August.

Hence, a breaking point can be observed with the phase of democratic transition, when the scarce use of decrees was found to be 'a counterreaction to the communist period during which governance was almost exclusively by decree' (Körösényi 2001, 212). This trend became particularly evident during the 2014 migration crisis, when the Hungarian government expanded the use of decrees to outline a wide range of policy areas, often showing detrimental attention to the protection of fundamental rights. Therefore, over the last two decades, governmental decrees steadily increased from an average of 63 decrees per year between 1990 and 2010 to 318 during the most recent period. Very significantly, despite the resolution of the immigration issue, the state of crisis has been renewed eight times. The last renewal – on 5 March 2020 – highlighted the instrumental character that the state of emergency could assume. This confirmed that very often 'what counts as an emergency is largely in the eye of the beholder' (Gross and Aolain 2006, 5).

6.4 The COVID-19 outbreak

The role of presidents and prime ministers becomes steadily more relevant in the wake of COVID-19 outbreak. The current pandemic crisis represents an unprecedented challenge to health, freedom, and democracy across the globe. It has posed several challenges to governments worldwide by requiring extraordinary measures to limit the spread of infection in order to save lives. The measures adopted have often imposed severe restrictions on individual rights. Massive resources have been mobilised to purchase medical supplies and to introduce extraordinary welfare policies to help workers, family, and companies by instituting wage guarantee funds and parental leave. While governmental responses followed different trajectories and dynamics regarding both timing and strategies adopted, the current pandemic crisis has accelerated and deepened established political process in contemporary democracies. Thus, during the emergency executive leaders have dominated national decision-making, with the shift of a large part of law-making away from assemblies to executives and the use of the governmental decree as an 'ordinary' instrument of government.

The key role played by political leaders in coping with the emergency has led to the most advanced stage of presidential politics in contemporary regimes. The need to generate quick reactions with measures that directly affect democratic fundamental rights and liberties has called for centralised decisions, thus leading to a new centrality of monocratic bodies. Therefore, the COVID-19 outbreak may be considered as the last step of the dynamics of the presidentialisation of politics and, for many countries, a point of no return concerning the evolution of their political regime. In some cases, these dynamics have led to the definition and stabilisation of policy structures that have favoured presidential autonomy.

By contrast, in others, they revealed even more clearly the authoritarian spectrum: the concentration of powers in a single person.

6.4.1 Italy

Italy represents an ideal type of presidentialisation of the political system in the international scenario (Calise 2005, 88, 2016). The management of the COVID-19 pandemic has accelerated the rise of presidential rulemaking that represents one of the most remarkable novelties forced by the COVID-19 outbreak. Although the Italian Constitution identifies decree-law as the main instrument provided by the Constitutional Charter to face emergencies (Art. 77), the current COVID-19 pandemic crisis has revealed a centralised control of executive decisions by the prime minister. Indeed, after the enactment of decree law 6/2020, the prime minister Giuseppe Conte has increasingly resorted to autonomous normative power through Decrees of the President of the Council of Ministers (DPCM) (Musella 2020a; 2020b). DPCMs are secondary normative sources that represent the most used instruments to provide political directions to citizens. The use of DPCMs had already increased during the 2008 economic crisis leading to the strengthening of the role of both the minister of finance and the prime minister, particularly in respect of the curbing of public expenditure. Although they are not constitutionally delineated, DPCMs differ from the decree law that the Constitutional Charter provides in order to deal with situations of necessity and urgency (Art. 77). Indeed, they do not involve the Council of Ministers along with the intervention of Chambers in the process of converting decree. Besides, DPCMs are not subject, like decree-laws, to the control of the president of the Republic in the enactment of governmental acts that have the force of law. Therefore, while DPCMs have gained increasing political significance, there is still a lack of proper publicity tools (Piccione 2017), thus realising 'a disqualification of the sources of laws and regulations that become even more disturbing because they are not subject – in general – to the control of the Council of State' (Di Porto 2016, 13).

In such a scenario, during the pandemic phase, the *Presidente del Consiglio* adopted immediate measures that escaped the control of constitutional actors, ensuring a substantial monopoly for the government.

Figure 2 shows the widespread use of government decrees and the increase in presidential decrees over the last two decades, thus confirming that '"governing by decree" and "governing by Dpcm" are certainly not new but have become the guiding thread of the executive led by Giuseppe Conte during the COVID-19 outbreak' (Criscitiello 2020). Indeed, during the COVID-19 era, DPCMs and decree

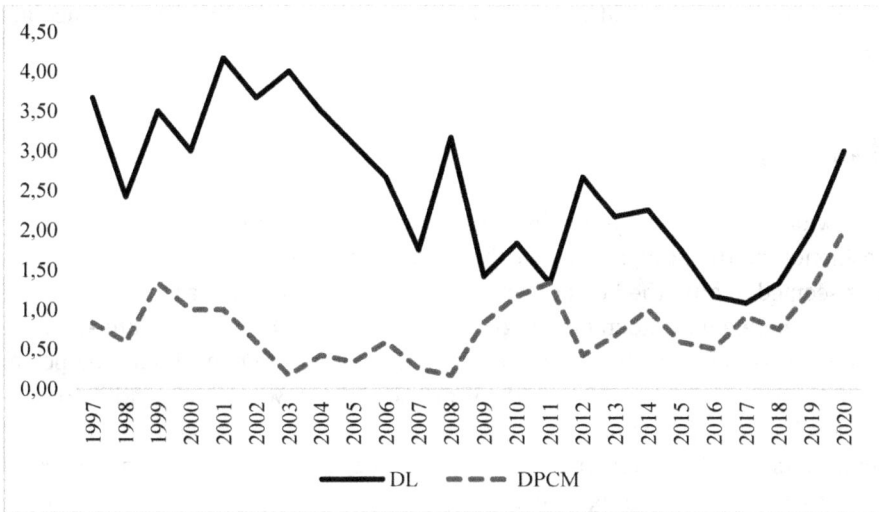

Figure 2: Decree law and Decree of the President of the Council of Ministers on a monthly basis (1997–2020). *Source:* own elaboration from Normattiva.it (*) 2020= until 28 October 2020.

laws have sharply increased, ultimately becoming the main instrument of emergency intervention. The institutional centralisation of Giuseppe Conte has easily translated into mediatic presence, which has increased his popularity[121]. The decrees have been presented through empathetic press conferences and speeches to the nation in which the prime minister speaks personally. Moreover, they have been broadcast through national television channels as well, and what counts as an emergency is largely in the eye of the beholder according to the prime minister's personal Facebook account and social messaging. Indeed, the communication crisis management relates not only to the presentation of the activities of the government, but also to the announcement of acts, and of the anticipation of decrees whose content is rumoured or circulated, and which will acquire official status only in the following hours (or days). The only political actors who could undermine the prime minister's prominence during the emergency phase, in both decision-making and mediatic arenas, have been the demo-elected Italian regional presidents. They were the only figures who have contest-

---

121 Giuseppe Conte is at the top of the leaders' confidence ranking, reaching a consensus rate of 64% at the end of phase 1 of the emergency period, compared to a lower value of 19 percentage points in February, see *Da Salvini a Speranza, come cambia la popolarità dei leader*, in *La Repubblica*, May 2nd, 2020.

ed an area that is crucial for the chief executive: that of direct and immediate relationship with citizens (Musella 2020a).

6.4.2 Hungary

The widespread use of prime ministerial rulemaking raises concerns about the resilience of the Hungarian constitutional system where the pandemic crisis has seemed to offer the head of government Viktor Orbán the last piece he needed to complete his autocratic design. Indeed, the law 'On the containment of the Coronavirus' has become an extraordinary instrument to consolidate the power of the prime minister and his party. It provides the power to suspend by decree the application of specific laws and derogate from legal provisions, and instead empowers the chief executive to adopt extraordinary measures. In a context of the progressive weakening of the checks and balances mechanism, the protection of individual rights, and the 'capture' of the economic and media circuits of the country, the pandemic has accelerated a process of autocratic involution that many authors had already been signalling for some years (Agh 2016; Bankuti et al. 2012; Körösényi et al. 2020). The absence of time limits related to its exercise makes the law on the containment of coronavirus a unicum, from a comparative point of view. It opens the way to govern by decree without the approval of Parliament. In addition, several highly restrictive laws on freedom of expression have been particularly controversial. In this respect, there has also been the introduction of one to five-year prison sentences for anyone 'who, during the period of special legal order and in front of a large audience, states or disseminates any untrue fact or any misrepresented true fact that is capable of hindering or preventing the efficiency of protection [and] is [therefore] guilty of a felony and shall be punished by imprisonment for one to five years' (art. 337 of the Penal Code, c.2). The Hungarian case shows how the personalisation of politics can lead to radical transformation of the form of the state and to the establishment of autocracy in the heart of Europe.

6.4.3 France and UK

The centralisation of power in the hands of the head of government has been remarkable in the French case. President Macron appeared to assume the role of 'commander in chief' of the nation, with the prime minister relegated to a mere executive function of presidential decisions. After the first month of emergency and confinement, Macron appeared as the leader of the emergency. As observed by Hassentaufel (2020, 174) 'the main decisions have been taken by the 'Defence Council,' convened and chaired by the French president and composed of the prime minister and the ministers discretionarily selected by the President'. The management of the pandemic seems to confirm the inclination of the Macron Presidency to centralise and, above all, personalise the action of government, which is also forcefully pushing the leverage of the executive decree powers. In the meantime, the push towards presidential power finds its containment and rebalancing in the institutional logic of the semi-presidential system (Vittoria 2020). Given this scenario, the COVID-19 outbreak reiterates a particular trait of French politics: the 'national tradition of state monocracy' (Hayward 2013, 44), or rather the persistence of a structurally monocratic dimension in the system of government.

In the United Kingdom, the measures adopted by Boris Johnson fits into the framework of the extension of the regulatory activities of the government. Indeed, starting from the 1980s, the growth of delegated legislation represented a rupture of the classic English model, suggesting the progressive establishment of an autonomous regulatory area of the executive. The exceptional nature of the pandemic phase, however, brought further developments, along with the shift in Prime Minister Boris Johnson's lack of activity to contain the coronavirus with the implementation of a large body of restrictive measures. Indeed, while the Public Health (Control of diseases) Act already allowed for restrictions of movement, the pandemic has come under the Coronavirus Act 2020, which has largely affected fundamental individual freedoms by giving extensive powers to the police (Ewing 2020). These are the reasons why the adoption of the Coronavirus Act 2020 led some authors to underline how the Parliament 'surrender[ed] control to the Government at a crucial time' (Hale 2020, 4), or to interpreting the Act as 'an example of an authoritarian seizure of power' by the Johnson government (Kirton-Darling et al. 2020, 307).

6.4.4 Spain and Germany

Moving elsewhere in Europe, the Spanish and German cases have displayed common contours in the crisis management of COVID-19. In these countries, the executive has immediately centralised the decision-making process and policy interventions, by acting as the focal point in the institutional structure of the government. It is worth noting that during the first months of the pandemic

(March–May 2020), the Spanish decision-making process was so executive-centred that 13 Presidential decrees[122] and 15 decree-laws[123] were produced.

Nevertheless, the powers of chief executives have been counterbalanced by other forces. First, both Spain and Germany have a form of government (respectively regional/autonomous and federal) which usually leaves ample room for manoeuvre at the sub-state levels. Consequently, during the current pandemic, the centralisation of powers has led to an overlap – not always harmonious – between the two levels of government. As far as the German case is concerned, it has indeed been observed, that 'the COVID-19 pandemic has served as a stress test for the German federal system. Many issues that needed to be regulated in the wake of the crisis fall under the jurisdictions of the Länder including, for instance, policies related to schools, kindergartens and universities, as well as those related to businesses'[124]. Thus, it has been calculated that the German federal government only produced 23 policy decisions to deal with the COVID emergency by June 2020, while in the same period the *Länder* legislated 335 times in 13 policy sectors[125].

Second, in both cases a shared management of the emergency occurred because of the peculiar role played by political parties compared to other European countries: the counterweight to the leadership of the presidents comes essentially from the party system that produces coalition governments. In Germany, despite the general climate of cooperation among the coalition partners, there has been 'an increasingly vociferous debate about how fast and how far restrictions should be lifted'[126]. In order to deal with such difficulties, Angela Merkel has led an inner cabinet (a Corona-Kabinett) made up of health, finance, interior, foreign, and defence ministers which meets on a weekly basis (on Mondays).

---

122 Decrees approved by the government presidency and the Ministry of the Presidency (*Presidencia de Gobierno*). Source: Boletín Oficial del Estado (BOE), https://www.boe.es/.
123 This is the number of approved decree-laws. Source: http://www.congreso.es/portal/page/portal/Congreso/Congreso/Iniciativas/LeyesAprob?_piref73_1335447_73_1335446_1335446.next_page=/wc/busquedasLeyesAprobadas&anoLey=2020&selectLey=tituloListadoRealesDecretos
124 See M.B. Siewert, S.Wurster, L. Messerschmidt, C. Cheng, and T. Büthe, *A German Miracle? Crisis Management During The COVID-19 Pandemic In A Multi-Level System, in Executives, presidents and cabinet politics (PEX)*, https://pex-network.com/, 25 June 2020.
125 See M.B. Siewert, S. Wurster, L. Messerschmidt, C. Cheng, and T. Büthe, *A German Miracle? Crisis Management During the COVID-19 Pandemic In A Multi-Level System*, cit., p. 5.
126 P. Bochum, *Germany's coalition government under COVID-19*, in *Policy Network*, 29 April 2020.

Moreover, this 'cabinet' was extended from time to time to the ministers whose sector was at the centre of the discussion[127].

Furthermore, the monocratisation of governments has been strongly evident in the high degree of personalisation of institutional communication. Indeed, the president of the Spanish government and the German chancellor have strongly personalised their relationship with citizens through frequent and punctual press conferences held to update the public on the trends of the pandemic. Some scholars have noticed that Angela Merkel has seemed to be a 'caring mother attempting to explain the complexity and dilemmas of the crisis step by step' (Wodak 2020, 12). Also, the leader has remained confirmed as the focal point in a grand coalition, at least in the eyes of citizens.

6.4.5 United States

Moving to the other side of the Atlantic, Donald Trump's handling of the pandemic played a pivotal role in his defeat in the 2020 US election. Similarly, for Bolsonaro in Brazil and Johnson in the UK, the COVID-19 outbreak has revealed all of the fragilities of right-wing populist leaders. Donald Trump contended over 27 times that the 'China flu' would 'simply go away'[128], promoted the malaria drug hydroxychloroquine as a cure for COVID-19, and raised international concerns by cutting funds to the WTO. During the pandemic, Trump strongly criticised the role of scientific committees and experts to the point that the immunologist Dr. Fauci – appointed as part of the White House coronavirus task force and head of the National Institute of Allergy and Infectious Diseases since 1984 – became the symbol of Trump's 'war on expertise' (Rutledge 2020). The president's scepticisms seamlessly turned into deficiencies of adequately implementing measures to beat the virus. Indeed, 'his administration declared a public health emergency in late January, but it was slow to exercise the powers this declaration could have unlocked [...]. The president downplayed the crisis and delayed declaring a national emergency or a Stafford Act emergency for several weeks' (Goitein 2020, 28). Very significantly, this came as a surprise when considering that –

---

127 On the internal mechanisms of the German executive, with particular reference to the COVID emergency, see M. Vercesi, *L'autonomia decisionale del cancelliere tedesco tra resistenza istituzionale e gestione della crisi*, in F. Musella, *L'emergenza democratica. Presidenti, decreti, crisi pandemica*, Napoli, Editoriale Scientifica, 2020, pp. 89 – 132.

128 See P. Bump, *Yet again, Trump pledges that the coronavirus will simply go away*, in The Washington Post, 28 April 2020, available at: https://www.washingtonpost.com/politics/2020/04/28/yet-again-trump-pledges-that-coronavirus-will-simply-go-away/ (accessed 3 March 2021).

well before the current pandemic – President Trump had already declared a national emergency seven times, and in so doing had surpassed his predecessors (see Figure 3).

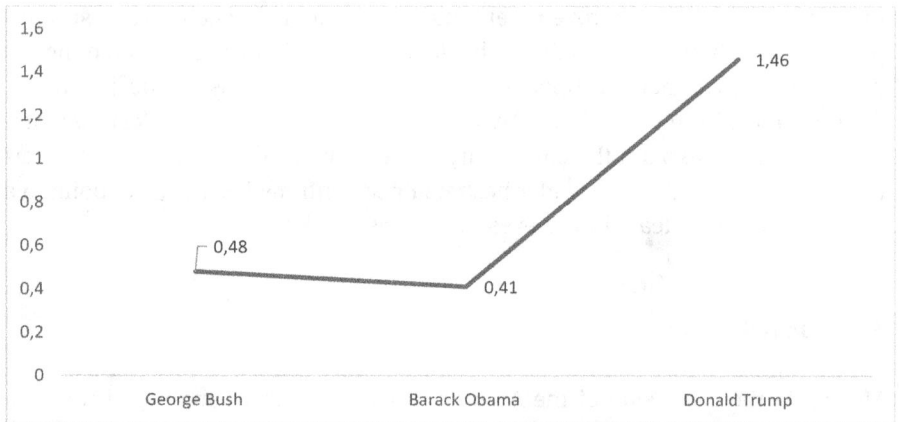

Figure 3: Presidential emergency declarations under the National Emergencies Act of 1976 by days in office (2001–2020). *Source:* own elaboration on the Brennan Center Justice data (https://perma.cc/G4V7-PVSH).

The Trump administration's delays drew strong criticisms from Democratic governors, ending in a constitutional showdown between US states and the federal government. Indeed, the president's struggle with governors over social distancing measures and the introduction of lockdown augmented disinformation campaigning and anti-lockdown protests. Notably, in mid-April, when the US had already had 42,500 deaths, Trump falsely claimed that as president, he had 'total' authority to lift restrictions governors had imposed to fight the coronavirus pandemic[129]. Therefore, the pandemic became a new source to accomplish policy goals such as the reduction of immigration flows, in an incessant attempt to shift attention to issues that would give him victory in his presidential run against Joe Biden.

---

129 The president claimed that 'when somebody's the president of the United States, the authority is total, and that's the way it's got to be'. See K. Liptak and J. Hoffmann (2020), *Trump lashes out in grievance-filled briefing claiming 'total' authority as president*, CNN, 14th April.

6.5 The democratic emergency

The COVID-19 emergency represents a test bench for contemporary democracy. It has facilitated a movement towards the monocratisation of power in the world's advanced industrial democracies, and highlighted the increasing expansion and autonomy of presidents and prime ministers in contemporary politics. Simultaneously, once these extraordinary contingencies turn into a stabilised emergency, the potential for a strong executive to continue to accumulate power represents a peril to the health of contemporary democracies. For these reasons, we need to reflect on the risks of this new era because 'a state of emergency does not only provide leaders with the opportunity to use additional powers. It also offers a good argument for why they need more power [...]. Thus, states of emergencies can help to dismantle democracy and subvert resistance to its demise' (Lührmann and Rooney 2020, 10).

Empirical evidence suggests a growing reduction of political liberties on the international stage. Freedom House noted a worsening of human rights and democratic conditions in 80 of 192 countries (41.7%), thus highlighting the increased abuse of power by the government, the increased use of violence, and extensive restrictions on the freedom of expression of the media at the global level[130]. The V-Dem Institute, through the pandemic democratic violations index, has highlighted a deterioration of democratic standards by analysing governments' responses to the pandemic[131]. This trend has been particularly evident in the US and in Hungary, where Trump and Orbán's autocratic tendencies have been more marked (see Figure 4).

The resilience of European democracies has been under stress during the pandemic crisis, thus confirming repeatedly acknowledged difficulties of democratic systems when facing radical crises. In several national contexts, we observed how executive power largely increases at the expense of a diminished legislature and marginalises the role of intermediate bodies. On the one hand, this trend has been necessary because of the urgent need to minimise procedural and regulatory obstacles to the action of monocratic leaders. On the other hand, it has made clear the shift of important decisions from the representative circuits

---

130 The report is available here: https://freedomhouse.org/report/special-report/2020/democracy-under-lockdown.
131 The V-Dem Liberal Democracy Index scores the strength of democratic institutions from weak to strong (0 – 1). The index aggregates variables across several dimensions, including suffrage rights, clean elections, equality before the law, constraints on the executive, and freedom of association and expression.

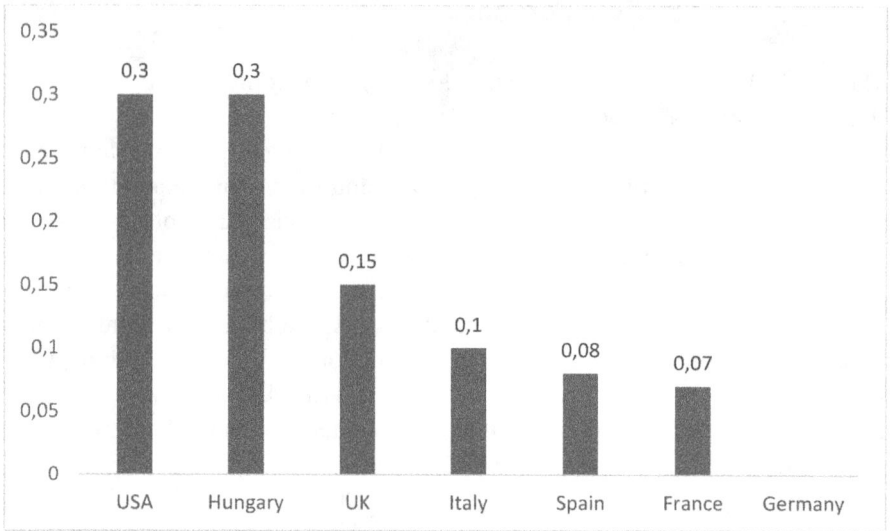

Figure 4: Pandemic Violations of Democratic Standards Index (March–December 2020) in selected countries. *Source:* own elaboration from V-Dem Institute (https://www.v-dem.net/en/analysis/PanDem/).

often in favour of technocratic solutions (Flinders 2020)[132]. Notably, the current COVID-19 pandemic has accelerated another 'great transformation of government: the return of a technical power far from the circuit of democratic legitimacy' (Calise 2019, 321). The need for specific knowledge has been a response to the twofold need to legitimise restrictive policies while offering quick responses to deal with the emergency. Therefore, the role of technocrats and experts has supported some of the key functions of political leaders during a crisis such as sense-making and decision-making (Boin et al. 2012). In Italy, in addition to the support of the ministerial offices, Prime Minister Conte has employed the Civil Protection Operational Committee and a series of task forces set up for emergency management. Very significantly, during the first phase of the pandemic crisis, Giuseppe Conte seemed to favour the technical-scientific advice of the task forces, often bringing their indications into the DPCMs and decree-laws. Also, in France the government 'has created new expert advisory bodies, instead of relying on existing agencies, including the High Council for Public Health,

---

132 The role of experts is supported by public opinion as shown by the Edelman Eurobarometer on a sample of 10,000 individuals. The report is available here https://www.edelman.com/research/trust-2020-spring-update.

Public Health France, and the High Authority for Health' (Hassentaufel 2020, 174). This strategy has been common in many Western democracies, and it has not been free of tensions in some cases. Nevertheless, we can also think of the conflictual relationship between the Brazilian President Jair Bolsonaro and his scientific committee or that of the immunologist Dr Anthony Fauci and President Donald Trump in the United States.

Additionally, in Europe, the COVID-19 pandemic crisis has highlighted some countertendencies compared to the recent past, especially with regard to public trust in institutions. According to a recent Eurobarometer survey, support for the measures adopted by the national government has exceeded 54% in European Union countries. Furthermore, 56% of respondents were totally or very satisfied with the measures adopted. These attitudes have been more evident in those countries where leaders have better recognised the large-scale threat of the virus, communicated well with citizens, and carried out rapid measures to limit the spread of the virus. On the one hand, European democracies demonstrated their strengths even in an emergency by introducing robust plans to support national economies at the European level. On the other hand, public trust of a particular form of democratic leader has gained momentum. For instance, according to a research study on Italian public opinion, three months after the COVID-19 outbreak, four out of ten respondents accepted the suspension of certain rules of democracy in the emergency phase, and there were similar results with regard to the matter of 'strong leaders'[133]. In contrast, the election of Joe Biden offered a ray of hope to the increasingly polarised American democratic regime which – as the assault on Capitol Hill underlined – seemed to be seriously threatened. The COVID-19 pandemic has brought a high rate of unpredictability and uncertainty to democratic systems, and this will characterise the coming months. Restoring confidence in competence and expertise could help to channel the efforts to overcome the challenges that the current crisis has provoked. The future of democratic politics still requires strong and active commitment on the part of citizens.

---

[133] Demos&P research published by Ilvo Diamanti, *L'emergenza giustifica uno stop alla democrazia per 4 italiani su 10*, in *La Repubblica*, 31 May 2020.

7 Combining *demos* and *kratos:* a mission impossible for the future of democracy?

Personalisation at a turning point

Impersonal rule was considered the destiny of the Western world. In the Weberian tripartite classification of legitimate power, Max Weber pointed to the rise of bureaucratic authority as the winning alternative to two classical traditional and charismatic forms of power, both united by the centrality of political figures. Bureaucracy, conceived in a coherent set of rules and obligations set forth by a legislative body, paved the path to modernity. However, the application of the Weberian ideal type of bureaucracy remained quite 'limited' (Boudon and Borricaud 1989; Calise and Lowi 2010), with different experiences leading to greater or lesser fulfilment on a national basis, and very often to resistance and a significant return to the past in even more industrialised societies (Roth 1990). Nevertheless, the rule of law, and its ability to constrain politics in a virtuous process of the defence of citizen's rights, was at the basis of the development of democratic regimes: 'whether the bureaucrats are fanatical ascetics or, more likely, eager claimants of privilege, their ideology systematically evades the question of who rules with bland assurances of impersonality and unbelievable assertions of universality' (Mansfield 1989, 282). Instead, when power was not strongly embedded in abstract rules, this brought the spectre of autocracy to the surface.

This is the reason why democratic leadership has always been seen with circumspection. We can even argue that the expression which puts together leadership and democracy has taken on the traits of an oxymoron. Three decades on from Giovanni Sartori's statement, his judgment is still valid: 'the vital role of leadership is frequently acknowledged; nonetheless it obtains only a negligible status within the theory of democracy' (Sartori 1987, 171; Körösényi 2005). On the one hand, the concept of leadership risks being considered a pre-democratic one, as the main paradigm of modernity was founded on the prevailing of impersonal power (Musella 2018). On the other hand, leadership may appear as an anti-democratic concept: scholars have noticed that the basic mission of democratic theory is how to limit the power of single actors, avoiding an excessive concentration of power (Costa Lobo and Curtice 2014), so that the 'fear of leadership is the basic justification of democracy' (Ruscio 2004, ix; Kane and Patapan 2012). This resulted in the fallacious idea that personal power would be ousted by modernity, but it has become evident – and progressively so – that this concept has been contradicted during recent years. Yet when the idea of leadership occupies a larger space in the practice of democracy, it may occur only through

https://doi.org/10.1515/9783110721720-007

the definition of an affective institutional architecture that ensures the division of power.

The marriage of leadership and democracy has been tried in the American context where, starting from the nineteenth century, a new idea of the presidential mandate was elaborated. This was a quite unnatural marriage, which, for some enthusiastic authors, gave way to a superior form of plebiscitary democracy. In the democratic laboratory of the US, for the first time it appears clear that strong political leadership is compatible with the ideals and boundaries of liberal regimes. In the words of President Wilson, a crucial political figure at the turn of two centuries, his mandate was superior to the Congressmen's one:

> 'Members of the House and Senate are representatives of localities, are voted for only by sections of voters, or by local bodies of electors like the members of the state legislatures. There is no national party choice except that of President. No one else represents the people as a whole, exercising a national choice.... The nation as a whole has chosen him, and is conscious that it has no other political spokesman. His is the only national voice in affairs.... He is the representative of no constituency, but of the whole people. When he speaks in his true character, he speaks for no special interest.... (T)here is but one national voice in the country, and that is the voice of the President' (Wilson 1908, cited in Dahl 1990, 360)

Yet, even in the case of presidential regimes, the probability of a democratic outcome depends on the capacity of constitutional bodies, such as parliaments, to balance presidential power – that is to realise a new division of powers. Although several variables lead to the recognition of how the American polity is different from that of other industrialised countries, especially because of its radical group activism (Kingdon 1999), a basic principle of democratic life may be enlarged to the whole democratic world: as politics becomes more personal in so large a number of national cases, the power exercised by chief executive officers has to be tamed in a check and balances structure (Vile 1967; Mansfield 1989; Fabbrini 2011). The 'division of powers' has been largely conceived as the primary means to prevent the rise of an arbitrary or repressive regime, with different schools of thought concentrating at one point on the horizontal distribution of government in a structure of government, and for another on the vertical distinction among layers of government[134] (Vanoni and Baraggia 2017).

---

134 More generally speaking, this leads us to consider the principle of the 'division of power' as a relationship between state and society. 'Since the principle role of the state is, inside the state, to protect 'separated' civil society, it must adopt a governance structure fit for this purpose', see G. Bognetti, *Per il bicentenario del federalista*, in *Giurisprudenza costituzionale*, 12, 1986, now republished in M. Iacometti, *Scritti scelti di Giovanni Bognetti*, Giuffrè, Milan, 2015, p. 160.

In recent times, with the expansion of political leaders' roles along with the process of fragmentation regarding the democratic electorates, this objective is more and more difficult to arrest, in America as well as on other continents.

Political science literature has documented a progressive shift of power from parliament to government in the last two decades. Empirical analyses have become more and more precise in recognising such a phenomenon with all its variants and ramifications. While underlining one of the most relevant trends in contemporary democracy, which cuts across both presidential and parliamentary regimes, studies remained quite cautious in considering the consequence of these institutional transformations on the future of democracy: once changed, forms of government still seemed to express an efficient system of division of power in most of the contributions which analysed them. It was when the increasing personalisation of leadership was combined with a widespread personalisation of the masses that the democratic regimes started to shake, and that political science started to change its hitherto optimistic view on the triumphal progression of democracy. Along with the growth in the number of explicit dictatorships[135], this is due to what is happening in more consolidated democracies with their undisputed revival of personal power, in a trend shared – at a different level and speed – by presidential and parliamentary systems.

A particular conception of the form of governments has been presented in this volume. On the one hand each form of government has to be considered from a dynamic perspective: although classical constitutional classifications tend to refer to a few ideal types to deal with very rich political experiences, our definition of government aims to understand processes of change beyond traditional regime types. On the other hand, it tries to overcome a restricted conception of forms of government, that is frequently based on few formal elements (such as modality of presidential election and duration of the government), by considering other political and constitutional elements strongly affecting the principle of division of power, such as the role of political parties, the character-

---

135 Carothers (2002) ties the break of the 'transition paradigm', which supposed the general affirmation of the liberal order, to the following trends which 'converged to change the political landscape of the world: 1) the fall of right-wing authoritarian regimes in Southern Europe in the mid-1970s; 2) the replacement of military dictatorships by elected civilian governments across Latin America from the late 1970s through the late 1980s; 3) the decline of authoritarian rule in parts of East and South Asia starting in the mid-1980s; 4) the collapse of communist regimes in Eastern Europe at the end of the 1980s; 5) the breakup of the Soviet Union and the establishment of 15 post-Soviet republics in 1991; 6) the decline of one-party regimes in many parts of sub-Saharan Africa in the first half of the 1990s; and 7) a weak but recognizable liberalizing trend in some Middle Eastern countries in the 1990s'.

istics of civil society, and the level of autonomy. Indeed, the ascendency of strong leaders has been facilitated by the two actors that had limited their expansion during the past.

First, the way in which political parties are formed and structured influences the form of government, as it defines the form and limits of democratic leadership. Moreover, it is worth noting that 'the party actors exert a direct influence on the system when they interpret constitutional rules and integrate them by establishing constitutional conventions' (Ferraiuolo and Praino 162; Elia 2006, 2601; Staiano 2019). With the spread of personal parties, the concentration of power in a single political figure may be too hastily accused of modifying, or even violating, the basic principle of democracy. Indeed, the leader may even be relevant in providing a new version of democracy, with their strength relying on restoring 'the relationship between leaders and people that the old parties had worn out', and acting as an alternative 'while state institutions appear increasingly incapable of fulfilling their historical role of container and reference for the associated life' (Calise 2016, 39). Nevertheless, as the personalisation of politics has progressed, one may ask to what extent monocracy can be controlled and limited according to the rules of the democratic game.

Political parties have acted as both the main political support for the leader's political action and the organisation that is able to determine their rise and fall. Yet today political parties have become the machinery for personal support. As the Berlusconi model of personal party has clearly expressed (Calise 2010), and after two decades of the transnational diffusion of that archetype, political leaders have largely increased their party organisation and decision-making. Conversely political parties are not capable of dismissing the political leaders who had often founded and created them, because they depend on the financial and/or mediatic resources of the party leaders – in several aspects it appears neo-patrimonial in its form (Kefford and McDonnell 2018). Thus, we expect that a personal party has a lifespan strongly correlated to the political – and/or biological – life of its founder/leader; there is no alternative leadership inside the party and, even following heavy electoral defeats, no internal debate can be launched in order to evaluate mistakes and the possibility of renewal (Bosco and Morlino 2007). Yet, if the leader is the absolute dominus of its creature, whose rationale is the political advancement of its head, and how can we expect political parties to represent the ultimate bulwark of democracy?

The second element regards the ghost – or holy spirit – of democracy. Studies on how democracy emerged in the Western world consider the formation of public opinion to be its most indispensable ingredient. Indeed, an alternative definition of 'division of powers' lies in the statement by which 'democracy is government by consent' (Dicey 1914), as it 'postulates a public opinion which establishes a permitted government, that is, governments that are conditioned by the consensus of that opinion' (Sartori 1979). The functioning of democratic institutions requires an active and critical citizenship, starting from its basic procedures such as elections. In a period when democracy has been assailed by internal and external attacks, public opinion is in charge to put it back on the right path. Yet, in the last two decades, the process of individualisation of public opinion, also prompted by the spread of new technologies, makes this role more uncertain. While political leaders take great advantage of a personal, and even emotional, relationship with citizens, with ample opportunities for them to monitor – and often manipulate – users' perceptions and opinions, public opinion shows high vulnerability with the spread of pervasive instruments of digital communication, and computational statistics to collect immediate information on massive numbers of the public and observe the digital behaviour of web users. Despite the promising advent of the Internet, these technological innovations do not allow a free and independent public opinion, by exploiting the enormous cognitive potential of the networks (Calise and Musella 2019, XIII). As has become evident during the pandemic crisis, when our democracy becomes more fragile and our freedoms are limited, an increasing pressure has been put on media freedoms and the space for civil society across many contemporary regimes[136].

It is too early to state if monocratic governments are turning into autocratic ones. This volume aims to show that the personalisation of politics is an established fact. Yet it is also an evolutionary process that is progressing at both leadership and mass levels. And at every hairpin bend it becomes increasingly difficult to conform to the original democratic asset as it was posited in the past.

---

[136] See the report by the Civil Liberties Union for Europe, 2020: Demanding on Democracy. Country & Trend Reports on Democratic Records by Civil Liberties Organisations Across the European Union, March 2021, EU.

Appendix
Monocratic Government Dataset: Personalisation of Leaders and Masses in Democracy

Appendix A: Variables and dataset structure

The book investigates on the dataset "Monocratic Government Dataset" created by Fortunato Musella, Raffaella Fittipaldi and Luigi Rullo, as part of a Relevant Research Project of National Interest (PRIN) 2020 – 2023 "Monocratic Government. The Impact of Personalisation on Contemporary Political Regimes" (Principal Investigator: Fortunato Musella).

The dataset is freely available at the De Gruyter website.

The analysis of monocratic government increases our knowledge about the nature and challenges of the impact of personalisation on contemporary political regimes. To this end, the first step in the creation of the dataset has been deciding on the list of countries to include in the study. The countries selected had to provide an opportunity for cross-country comparison and all countries had to be members of the democratic genus. In particular, we focused on countries belonging to either the category 'full democracies' or 'flawed democracies' in line with the *EIU 2020 Democracy Index* ('Democracy Index 2020 In sickness and in health?' available at: https://www.eiu.com/n/campaigns/democracy-index-2020/). Our groups of countries were made up of seven: France, Germany, the United Kingdom, Italy, Spain, Hungary, and the US. The second step was related to gathering information about each government in office between 2000 and 2020.

The dataset contains a list of 56 governments and a total of 34 individuals who served as presidents in semi-presidential or presidential regimes and as prime ministers in parliamentary regimes. This list included the names of each president and prime Minister, their gender, the number of years in office, the number of term/legislatures, and their party affiliation. Then, we collated information related to each government by examining the executive decree authority, the main characteristics of the party systems, and the elections thus collecting a total of 17 variables which are outlined in detail below.

Then, we structured our dataset into three main blocks: government, party, and election.

https://doi.org/10.1515/9783110721720-008

Monocratic Government

Government

Constitutional reforms
Decrees
Veto powers
Governmental legislative initiatives

Party

Effective number of parties (parliament)
Party membership
Total party membership as percentage of electorate
Party switching
Average age of parties (since having at least one parliamentary seat)
Average age of parties (since parties obtained at least 3% of votes)
Number of new parties
Number of groups in parliament (lower chamber)
Number of groups in parliament (upper chamber)

Election

Effective number of parties (election)
Electoral volatility
Electoral volatility (Total)
Polarisation

Executive decree authority: this variable observes the patterns of executive law-making in the form of primary and secondary legislation. We gathered information related to decree laws and legislative delegated authority. In France we examined the *'ordonnance'*, in Spain the *'decreto ley'*, in Italy the *'decreto-legge'* and *'decreto legislativo'*, in Hungary the government decree (primary or based on powers delegated to it by Acts), in the US we took into consideration the 'executive orders', and in the UK the statutory instruments.

Governmental legislative initiatives: this variable documents the role of government in parliament by looking at its impact on the policy-making process. We collected information related to each government in office then calculating the rate of success of government sponsored bills.

Constitutional reforms: this variable sheds light on constitutional reforms, namely the number of amendments to the national constitution. This information relates to each amendment which took place at the time when a specific government was in office, and it is useful to understand the dimension of constitutional law-making.

Veto powers: this variable refers to the powers of presidential veto on legislation passed by the Congress in the USA (Article I, section 7 of the American Constitution), which grants the president the authority to veto legislation passed by Congress. This power is useful especially when the majority in Congress belongs to a party other than that of the president (i.e. in the case of divided government). Thus, using the veto or the threat of a veto, the president can enable legislation or negotiate with their counterpart.

Effective number of parties (in parliament and in an election): the variable measures the number of parties present in a party system (i.e. how many political parties are in the parliament of such a country) adjusted according to the weight of each party. The effective number of parliamentary parties is calculated with the following formulae: $ENPP=1/\Sigma si^2$ where si is the proportion of seats of the ith party and $ENEP=1/\Sigma vi^2$ where vi is the proportion of votes of the ith party. Defining the 'real' format or the size of a party system, the effective number of parties coincides with the number of parties only when all existing parties have equal strength or weight. As a rule, the effective number of parties is lower than the actual number of parties. Fragmentation is generally measured with the ENPP or ENEP indices, which are particularly useful for cross-country comparisons.

Total party membership and total party membership as percentage of electorate: these figures show the total number of individual party members. The sum of party membership is relative to the single legislature of each country, and it takes into consideration the membership of the parties in each national election. This variable registers the general declining trend not in relation to the electorate, as well as in relation to the absolute numbers of party members.

The party switching variable represents the interparty movement that is any change in party affiliation, based on parliamentary archives. We have included all switchers in certain legislatures, counting the switching once only. Therefore, deputies who have changed parties more than once in the same legislature have not been recounted.

Average age of parties (with at least one parliamentary seat) and average age of parties (since the parties obtained at least 3% of votes): this refers to party system institutionalisation.

The number of new parties: this variable is constructed based on Sikk's consideration on this argument. According to him, new parties are those that are 'not successors to any previous parties, have a novel name and structure', and are not mergers (or electoral coalitions) of pre-existing political parties. For more details on the emergence and success of new political parties see: P. Lucardie, *Prophets, Purifiers and Prolocutors: Towards a Theory on the Emergence of New Parties*, in *Party Politics*, 6, 2, 2000, pp. 175–185. For the dispute on the new parties' emergence see: A. Sikk, *Newness as a winning formula for new political parties*, in *Party Politics*, 18, 4, 2005, pp. 465–486. Other useful research articles are: S. Bartolini and P. Mair, *Policy competition, spatial distance and electoral instability*, in *West European Politics*, 13, 4, pp. 1–16; N. Bolleyer and E. Bytzek, *Origins of party formation and new party success in advanced democracies*, in *European Journal of Political Research*, 52, 6, pp. 773–796.

The variables of the **number of groups in parliament (Lower Chamber) and the number of groups in parliament (Upper Chamber)** make it possible to count the bodies that collect political requests and representations within a parliament. For a deep understanding of parliamentary party groups as central actors in most European democracies, see: K. Heidar and R. Koole (eds.), *Parliamentary Party Groups in European Democracies. Political Parties Behind Closed Doors*, Routledge, London, 2000.

Electoral volatility refers to the degree of change in voting behaviour between elections. This variable stresses the electors switching between parties following the dealignment thesis. **Net volatility** is measured by the Pedersen index using the following formula: $TEV = \Sigma |Vi,t\text{-}1\text{-}Vi,t|/2$, in which Vi,t is the vote share for a party *ith* at a given election (t) and Vi,t-1 is the vote share of the same party *ith* at the previous elections (t-1). It concerns the vote shares for each party. **Total volatility** is instead the total proportion which changed between the two elections. This can be measured with respect to those who voted at both elections, those who were eligible at both elections, or those who were eligible at either election.

Polarisation relates to ideological distance between the parties or the voters along a relevant political issue. Giovanni Sartori (*Parties and Party Systems: A Framework. Giovanni Sartori,* New York, Cambridge University Press, 1976, pp. 131–145) argues that the centrifugal competition will produce a pattern of polarised pluralism that is likely to occur in party systems characterised by fairly large numbers of relevant parties and by high levels of ideological polarisation, and these characteristics, in turn, are believed to reflect the number and depth of the political cleavages. According to the Dalton Index, the formula to calculate the polarisation is: $PI = SQRT\{\sum(\text{party vote share } i)*([\text{party L/R score }^i - \text{party system average L/R score}]/5)^2\}$ (i represents individual parties). Party vote share is calculated as a percentage for parties. Party system average L-R score is weighted by size of each party – namely $\sum[(\text{party vote share}i*\text{party L-R score}i)/\sum(\text{party vote share}i)]$, where the sum of party vote share falls short of 100 per cent in some elections. The division by 5 is an arbitrary adjustment to centre the index on the 0–10 scale. The resulting index has a range from 0 when all parties are located at the same position on the Left–Right scale to 10 when all parties are located at extreme positions on the Left–Right scale.

Appendix B: Notes on sources

We extracted and developed digital and published data available from official and online sources. In more detail:

Both data about the **Executive Decree Authority** and data about **Governmental Legislative Initiatives** stemmed from official sources. In France we collected and elaborated data from Legifrance.fr, which is the official website of the French government for the publication of legislation, regulations, and legal information; in Italy we consulted the official websites of the Chamber of Deputies (Camera.it) and Senate (Senato.it), and from official compendia published annually by the Research Centre of the Italian Parliament, and the official laws dataset Normattiva.it; for Germany data came from the official statistics published on the Bunderstat website (https://www.bundesrat.de/DE/dokumente/statistik/sta tistik-node.html) and the federal report on enacted legislation (Statistik der Gesetzgebung); as far as Hungary is concerned, data was from the CAP (Centre for Social Sciences) dataset (https://cap.tk.hu/en/datasets-and-codebooks-national-assembly) and the National Legislation Dataset (https://njt.hu); in the UK we extracted and developed our data from the National Archives on enacted legislation (https://www.legislation.gov.uk) and from P. Loft and V. Apostolova (2017), *Acts and Statutory Instruments: the volume of UK legislation 1950 to 2016*, https://commonslibrary.parliament.uk/research-briefings/cbp-7438/; in Spain data came from the official government website Boel.es; finally we gained our data for the case of the USA from the National Archives Federal Register (https://www.fed eralregister.gov/presidential-documents/executive-orders) and from T.J. Lowi, B. Ginsberg, K.A. Shepsle and S. Ansolabehere, *American government: Power and purpose*, New York, Norton, 2017.

Our data on **constitutional reforms,** came from Z. Elkins and T. Ginsburg, *Characteristics of National Constitutions, Version 3.0,* in *Comparative Constitutions*

Project, 2021. Other useful sources are: Hein's Online World Constitutions illustrated and Z. Elkins, T. Ginsburg and J. Melton, *The endurance of national constitutions*, Cambridge, Cambridge University Press, 2009.

Veto Powers data came from the official website of the Senate of the USA (https://www.senate.gov/legislative/vetoes/vetoCounts.htm)

Data about the **Effective number of parties (ENPP and ENEP)** are available at whogoverns.eu. (F. Casal Bértoa, *A database on WHO GOVERNS in Europe and beyond*, PSGo, 2021). For more details on the Effective number of parties in parliament and its measurement see: M. Laakso, R. Taagepera, *Effective' Number of Parties: A Measure with Application to West Europe*, in *Comparative Political Studies*, 12, 1, 1979, pp. 3–27 and P. Dunleavy and F. Boucek, *Constructing the Number of Parties*, in *Party Politics*, 9, 3, 2003, pp. 291–315. Additionally, see M. Gallagher and P. Mitchell (eds.), *The Politics of Electoral Systems paperback edition*, Oxford and New York, Oxford University Press, 2008, and the useful and updated 2019 online appendix(https://www.tcd.ie/Political_Science/people/michael_gallagher/ElSystems/Docts/ElectionIndices.pdf)

Data about **total party membership** are basically collected from direct party sources and E. van Haute, and E. Paulis (2016), *MAPP Dataset*, Zenodo. When the data was not available, other useful digital and published sources have been used from official and online sources. To calculate the **total party membership as a percentage of electorate**, the electoral turnout was taken from the institutional archives of the general legislative election of each country.

On party membership trends see: R. Katz and P. Mair (eds.), *Party Organisations: A Data Handbook*, London, Sage, 1992; P. Mair and I. van Biezen, *Party Membership in Twenty European Democracies, 1980–2000*, in *Party Politics*, 7, 1, 2001, pp. 5–21.

Party switching data are the result of our own elaborations from a wide range published data available in parliamentary archives of each country and on digital websites such as Wikipedia, as in the case of United Kingdom (https://en.wikipedia.org/wiki/List_of_elected_British_politicians_who_have_changed_party_affiliation). See also the appendix provided by E. Klein, *The personal vote and legislative party switching*, in *Party Politics*, 24, 5, 2018, pp. 501–510.

Data on the **average age of parties (since parties obtained at least 3% of votes)** are available at: F. Casal Bértoa, *Database on WHO GOVERNS in Europe and beyond*, PSGo, 2021. Available at: whogoverns.eu; while data on the **average age of parties (with at least one parliamentary seat)** are the result of our own elaboration based on Parlgov dataset: http://www.parlgov.org/explore/.

Our own elaboration of the **number of new parties** data stemmed from: F. Casal Bértoa, *Database on WHO GOVERNS in Europe and beyond*, PSGo,

2021. Available at: whogoverns.eu. We have only included new parties with more than 0.5% of the vote, while independents are excluded.

Number of groups in parliament (Lower Chamber) and number of groups in parliament (Upper Chamber) the sources of data are the countries institutional archive of the lower and upper chambers.

With reference to the **volatility** our data on **electoral volatility** are from https://whogoverns.eu/party-systems/electoral-volatility/. It refers to the conceptualisation offered by M.N. Pedersen, *The dynamics of European party systems: changing patterns of electoral volatility*, in *European Journal of Political Research*, 7, 1, 1979, pp. 1–26. See also R. Dassonneville, *Net Volatility in Western Europe: 1950–2014 Dataset*, Leuven, Centre for Citizenship and Democracy, 2015. Data related to the **total volatility** came from V. Emanuele, *Dataset of Electoral Volatility and its internal components in Western Europe (1945–2015)*, Rome, Italian Centre for Electoral Studies, 2015. The dataset is available here: http://cise.luiss.it/cise/dataset-of-electoral-volatility-and-its-internal-components-in-western-europe-1945-2015/.

Polarisation data stemmed from the comparative study of electoral systems dataset (https://cses.org/). Useful sources are: R.J. Dalton, *The Quantity and the Quality of Party Systems: Party System Polarisation, Its Measurement, and Its Consequences*, in *Comparative Political Studies*, 41, 7, 2008, pp. 899–920 and R.J. Dalton, and C.J. Anderson (eds.), *Citizens, context, and choice: how context shapes citizens' electoral choices*, Oxford, Oxford University Press, 2011. For more details on the crucial American case see: A.I. Abramowitz, and K.L. Saunders, *Is polarisation a myth?*, in *The Journal of Politics*, 70, 2, 2008, pp. 542–555; M.P. Fiorina, S.A. Abrams and J.C. Pope, *Polarisation in the American Public: Misconceptions and Misreadings*, in *The Journal of Politics*, 70, 2, 2008, pp. 556–560. See also: A.S. Gerber and E. Schickler (eds.), *Governing in a polarized age: Elections, parties, and political representation in America*, Cambridge, Cambridge University Press, pp. 223–242.

In the end, other general useful sources have been encyclopaedic texts such as the Encyclopaedia Britannica, Oxford University Press's Dictionary of Political Biography, Wikipedia, V-Dem (https://www.v-dem.net/en/analysis/PanDem/), and R. East and J. Thomas, *Profiles of people in power: the world's government leaders*, Routledge, London, 2014.

Bibliography

Aarts, K., Blais, A., Schmitt, H. (eds.), (2011), *Political Leaders and Democratic Elections*, Oxford, Oxford University Press.

Abamowitz, A., Saunders, K.L. (2008), *Is Polarization a Myth*, in *The Journal of Politics*, 70, 2, pp. 542–555.

Abramowitz, A., McCoy, J. (2019), *United States: Racial Resentment, Negative Partisanship, and Polarization in Trump's America*, in *The Annals of the American Academy of Political and Social Science*, 681, 1, pp. 137–156.

Abramowitz, A.I. (2018), *The great alignment: Race, party transformation, and the rise of Donald Trump*, New Haven, Yale University Press.

Acemoglu, D., Robinson, J.A. (2012), *Why Nations Fail: The Origins of Power, Prosperity and Poverty*, London, Profile Books.

Ackerman, B. (2000a), *New Separation of Powers*, in *Harvard Law Review*, 113, 633–725.

Ackerman, B. (2000b), *We the People*, Volume 2: Transformations, Cambridge, Harvard University Press.

Ackerman, B. (2003), *The emergency constitution, in Yale International Journal*, 113, 5, 2003, pp. 1029–1091.

Ackerman, B. (2010), *The decline and fall of the American republic*, Cambridge, Harvard University Press.

Ackerman, B. (2017), *The Failure of the Founding Fathers. Jeffeson, Marshall, And The Rise of Presidential Democracy*, Cambridge, Cambridge University Press.

Agamben, G. (2003), *Lo Stato di eccezione*, Torino, Bollati Boringhieri.

Ágh, A. (2016), *The Decline of Democracy in East-Central Europe. Hungary as the Worst-Case Scenario*, in *Problems of Post-Communism*, 63, 5–6, pp. 277–287.

Agosta, S. (2011), *Ruolo del Presidente della Repubblica e ordinanze contingibili e urgenti del governo*, in A. Ruggeri (ed.), *Evoluzione del sistema politico-istituzionale e ruolo del Presidente della Repubblica*, Atti di un incontro di studio, (Messina-Siracusa, 19–20 novembre 2010), Torino, Giappichelli, pp. 373–387.

Albert, R. (2009), *The fusion of presidentialism and parliamentarism*, in *The American Journal of Comparative Law*, 57, 3, pp. 531–578.

Albertazzi, D., McDonnell, D. (eds.), (2008), *Twenty-First Century Populism. The Spectre of Western European Democracy*, Basingstoke, Palgrave.

Alford, R. (2017), *Permanent state of emergency: unchecked executive power and the demise of the rule of law*, Montreal, McGill-Queen's Press-MQUP.

Andersen, J.G. (2006), *Political power and democracy in Denmark: decline of democracy or change in democracy?*, in *Journal of European Public Policy*, 13, 4, pp. 569–586.

Anderson, L.E. (2006), *The Authoritarian Executive? Horizontal and Vertical Accountability in Nicaragua*, in *Latin American Politics and Society*, 48, 2, 2006, pp. 141–169.

Andeweg, R., Elgie, R., Helms, L., Kaarbo, J., Müller-Rommel, F. (2020), *The Political Executive Returns: Re-empowerment and Rediscovery*, in R. Andeweg, R. Elgie, L. Helms, J. Kaarbo, F. Müller-Rommel (eds.), *The Oxford Handbook of Political Executives*, Oxford, Oxford University Press, pp. 359–381.

André, A., Depauw, S., Beyens, S. (2015), *Party loyalty and electoral dealignment*, in *Party Politics*, 21, 6, pp. 970–981.

Bagehot, W. (1867), *The English Constitution*, Oxford, Oxford University Press.

https://doi.org/10.1515/9783110721720-009

Baines, D., Brewer, S., Kay, A. (2020), *Political, process and programme failures in the Brexit fiasco: exploring the role of policy deception*, in *Journal of European Public Policy*, 27, 5, pp. 742–760.

Baldini, V. (2020a), *Emergenza costituzionale e Costituzione dell'emergenza. Brevi riflessioni (e parziali) di teoria del diritto*, in *Dirittifondamentali.it*, 1, pp. 893–905.

Baldini, V. (2020b), *Emergenza sanitaria e Stato di prevenzione*, in *Dirittifondamentali. it*, 1, 27 febbraio 2020.

Baldwin, N.D.J. (2004), *Concluding Observations: Legislative Weakness, Scrutinising Strength?*, in *Journal of Legislative Studies*, 10, 2–3, pp. 295–302.

Balkin, J.M. (2017), *Constitutional Crisis and Constitutional Rot*, in *Maryland Law Review*, 77, 1, pp. 147–160.

Bánkuti, M., Halmai, G., Scheppele, K.L. (2012), *Hungary's illiberal turn: disabling the constitution*, in *Journal of Democracy*, 23, 3, pp. 138–146.

Barber, M., McCarty, N. (2015), *Causes and consequences of polarization*, in J. Mansbridge, C.J. Martin (eds.), *Political negotiation: A Handbook*, New York, Brookings, pp. 39–43.

Barberá, P., Zeitzoff, T. (2018), *The new public address system: why do world leaders adopt social media?*, in *International Studies Quarterly*, 62, 1, pp. 121–130.

Bardi, L. (1996), *Anti-Party Sentiment and Party System Change in Italy*, in *European Journal for Political Research*, 29, 3, pp. 345–363.

Barisione, M. (2015), *Leadership, political*, in G. Mazzoleni, K.G. Barnhurst, K.I. Ikeda, R.C. Maia, H. Wessler (eds.), *The International Encyclopedia of Political Communication*, New York, Wiley.

Bartolini, S., Mair, P. (1990), *Policy competition, spatial distance and electoral instability*, in *West European Politics*, 13, 4, pp. 1–16.

Bauman, Z. (2013), *Liquid modernity*, New York, John Wiley & Sons.

Beck, U. (1992), *Risk Society: Towards a New Modernity*, London, Sage Publications.

Bertolini, E. (2018), *Democracy and the State of Exception. The Italian experience*, in *Zeitschrift für Politikwissenschaften*, 28, 4, pp. 507–520.

Best, J. (1987), *Legislative tyranny and the liberation of the executive: A view from the Founding*, in *Presidential Studies Quarterly*, 17, 1, pp. 697–709.

Bimes, T., Skowronek, S. (1996), *Woodrow Wilson's Critique of Popular Leadership: Reassessing the Modern-Traditional Divide in Presidential History*, in *Polity*, 29, 1, pp. 27–63.

Biondi Dal Monte, F. (2011), *La politica della perenne emergenza e i poteri extra ordinem del Governo*, Relazione all'incontro del Gruppo di Pisa, Milano.

Bjørnskov, C., Voigt, S. (2018), *The architecture of emergency constitutions*, in *International Journal of Constitutional Law*, 16, 1, pp. 101–127.

Blaemire, R. (2018), *The Evolution of Microtargeting*, in C.J. Nelson, J.A. Thurber (eds.), *Campaigns and Elections American Style: The Changing Landscape of Political Campaigns*, New York, Routledge, pp. 217–236.

Blanco Valdés, R. (2013), *España: división de poderes y calidad democrática*, in F.L. Agulló Leal, *Cátedra "Jorge Juan"*, ciclo de conferencias: curso 2011–2012. Servizo de Publicacións, Universidade da Coruña, pp. 117–136.

Blondel, J. (2001), *Government*, in N.J. Smelser, P.B. Baltes (eds.), *International Encyclopedia of the Social & Behavioral Sciences*, London, Elsevier, pp. 6321–6323.

Blondel, J. (2015), *The presidential republic*, London, Palgrave.

Blondel, J., Thiébault, J.L. (eds.), (2009), *Political leadership, parties and citizens: the personalisation of leadership*, London, Routledge.

Bobbio, N. (1994), *Contributi ad un dizionario giuridico*, Torino, Giappichelli.

Böckenförde, E.W. (2017 [1978]), *The Repressed State of Emergency: The Exercise of State Authority in Extraordinary Circumstances* [1978], in M. Künkler, T. Stein (eds.), *Constitutional and political theory. Selected writings*, Oxford, Oxford University Press, pp. 108–132.

Boda, Z., Sebők, M. (2019), *The Hungarian Agendas Project*, in F.R. Baumgartner, C. Breunig, E. Grossmann (eds.), *Comparative policy agendas: Theory, tools, data*, Oxford, Oxford University Press, pp. 105–113.

Bogaards, M. (2018), *De-democratization in Hungary: diffusely defective democracy*, in *Democratization*, 25, 8, pp. 1481–1499.

Bognetti, G. (2001), *La divisione dei poteri. Saggio di diritto comparato*, Torino, Giuffrè.

Bognetti, G. (2015 [1986]), *Per il bicentenario del federalista. Giur. Cost*, in M. Iacometti (ed.), Scritti *scelti di Giovanni Bognetti*, Milano, Giuffrè.

Boin, A., Hart, P.T., van Esch, F. (2012), *Political leadership in times of crisis: comparing leader responses to financial turbulence*, in L. Helms (ed.), *Comparative Political Leadership*, PalgraveMacmillan, London, pp. 119–141.

Boin, A., McConnell, A., 't Hart, P. (2021), *Governing the Pandemic: The Politics of Navigating a Mega-Crisis*, Cham, Palgrave.

Bolleyer, N. (2013), *New parties in old party systems: persistence and decline in seventeen democracies*, Oxford, Oxford University Press.

Bolsover, G., Howard, P. (2017), *Computational Propaganda and Political Big Data: Moving Toward a More Critical Research Agenda*, in *Big Data*, 5, 4, pp. 273–276.

Bolton, A., Thrower, S. (2016), *Legislative Capacity and Executive Unilateralism*, in *American Journal of Political Science*, 60, 3, pp. 649–663.

Bosco, A., Morlino, L. (eds.), (2007), *Party Change in Southern Europe*, London, Routledge.

Boudon, R., Bourricaud, F. (1989), *A Critical Dictionary of Sociology*, Chicago, University of Chicago Press.

Bowler, S. (2000), *Parties in legislature: Two competing explanations*, in R.J. Dalton, M.P. Wattenberg (eds.), *Parties Without Partisans: Political Change in Advanced Industrial Democracies*, Oxford, Oxford University Press, pp. 157–179.

Bracciale, R., Andretta, M., Martella, A. (2021), *Does populism go viral? How Italian leaders engage citizens through social media*, in *Information, Communication & Society*, pp. 1–18, doi: 10.1080/1369118X.2021.1874472.

Branum, T.L. (2002), *President or King. The Use and Abuse of Executive Orders in Modern-Day America*, in *Journal of Legislation*, 28, pp. 1–86.

Bréchon, P. (2010), *Francia: Un monarca repubblicano*, in G. Passarelli (ed.), *Presidenti della Repubblica. Forme di governo a confronto*, Torino, Giappichelli, pp. 97–117.

Broder, D.S. (1972), *The Party's Over. The Failure of Politics in America*, New York, Harper & Row.

Bryce, J. (1921), *Modern Democracies*, New York, Macmillan.

Bump, P. (2020), *Yet again, Trump pledges that the coronavirus will simply go away*, in *The Washington Post*, 28 April, available at: https://www.washingtonpost.com/politics/2020/04/ 28/yet-again-trump-pledges-that-coronavirus-will-simply-go-away/ (accessed 3 March 2021).

Buzogány, A. (2017), *Illiberal democracy in Hungary: authoritarian diffusion or domestic causation?*, in *Democratization*, 24, 7, pp. 1307–1325.

Byung-Chul, H. (2017), *In the swarm: digital prospects*, Cambridge, Mit Press.

Calandra, P. (1986), *Il governo della Repubblica*, Bologna, Il Mulino.

Calise, M. (1997), *Il governo*, in F. Barbagallo (ed.), *Storia dell'Italia repubblicana*, vol. III, Torino, Einaudi, pp. 347–397.

Calise, M. (2005), *Presidentialization, Italian style*, in T. Poguntke, P. Webb, (eds.), *The Presidentialization of Politics. A Comparative Study of Modern Democracies*, Oxford, Oxford University Press, pp. 88–106.

Calise, M. (2006), *La Terza Repubblica: Partiti contro Presidenti*, Roma-Bari, Laterza.

Calise, M. (2010 [2000]), *Il partito personale: I due corpi del leader*, Roma-Bari, Laterza.

Calise, M. (2011), *Personalisation of Power*, in B. Badie, D. Berg-Schlosser, L. Morlino (eds.), *International Encyclopedia of Political Science*, Los Angeles, Sage, pp. 1857–1860.

Calise, M. (2015), *The personal party: an analytical framework*, in *Rivista Italiana di Scienza Politica / Italian Political Science Review*, 45, 3, pp. 301–315.

Calise, M. (2016), *La democrazia del leader*, Roma-Bari, Laterza.

Calise, M. (2019), *Conclusioni. Il governo al tempo del potere personale*, in F. Musella, *Il governo in Italia. Profili costituzionali e dinamiche politiche*, Bologna, Il Mulino, pp. 319–322.

Calise, M. (2010 [2000]), *Il partito personale: I due corpi del leader*, Roma-Bari, Laterza.

Calise, M., Lowi, T.J. (2010), *Hyperpolitics: an interactive dictionary of political science concepts*, Chicago, University of Chicago Press.

Calise, M., Musella, F, (2019), *Il principe digitale*, Roma-Bari, Laterza.

Cameron, C.M. (2002), *Studying the Polarized Presidency*, in *Presidential Studies Quarterly*, 32, 4, pp. 647–663.

Cameron, C.M. (2009), *The presidential veto*, in G.C. Edwards III, W.G. Howell (eds.), *The Oxford Handbook of the American presidency*, Oxford, Oxford University Press, pp. 362–382.

Campbell, A., Converse, P., Miller, W., Stokes D. (1960), *The American voter,* New York, Wiley.

Canel, M.J., Sanders, K.B. (2012), *Government communication: An emerging field in political communication research*, in H.A. Semetko, M. Scammell (eds.), *The Sage Handbook Political Communication*, London, Sage, pp. 85–96.

Canel, M.J., Sanders, K.B. (2015), *Government communication*, in G. Mazzoleni, K.G. Barnhurst, K.I. Ikeda, R.C. Maia and H. Wessler (eds.), *The International Encyclopedia of Political Communication*, New York, John Wiley & Sons, pp. 1–8.

Capano, G. (2020), *Policy design and state capacity in the COVID-19 emergency in Italy: if you are not prepared for the (un) expected, you can be only what you already are*, in *Policy and Society*, 39, 3, pp. 326–344.

Cardone, A. (2011), *La "normalizzazione" dell'emergenza: contributo allo studio del potere extra ordinem del governo*, Torino, Giappichelli.

Caretti, P. (2001), *I gruppi parlamentari nella XIII legislatura*, in L. Carlassare (ed.), *Democrazia, rappresentanza e responsabilità*, Padova, Cedam.

Carey J.M., Shugart, M.S. (1995), *Incentives to Cultivate a Personal Vote: A Rank Ordering of Electoral Formulas*, in *Electoral Studies*, 14, 4, pp. 417–439.

Carey, J.M., Shugart, M.S. (1998), *Executive decree authority,* Cambridge, Cambridge University Press.

Carmines, E.G., Fowler, M. (2017), *The temptation of executive authority: How increased polarization and the decline in legislative capacity have contributed to the expansion of presidential power*, in *Indiana Journal of Global Legal Studies*, 24, 2, pp. 369–398.

Carnevale, P. (2019), *Conclusioni*, in D. Chinni (ed.), *Potere e opinione pubblica. Gli organi costituzionali dinanzi alle sfide del web*, Napoli, Editoriale Scientifica, pp. 211–228.

Carothers, T. (2002), *The End of the Transition Paradigm*, in *Journal of Democracy*, 13, 1, pp. 5–21.

Casal Bértoa, F. (2021), *Database on WHO GOVERNS in Europe and beyond*, PSGo. Available at: whogoverns.eu.

Casal Bértoa, F., Deegan-Krause, K., Haughton, T. (2017), *The volatility of volatility: Measuring change in party vote shares*, in *Electoral studies*, 50, 142–156.

Cassese, S. (2014), *Diritto amministrativo: una conversazione*, Bologna, Il Mulino.

Ceccanti, S., Vassallo, S. (2004), *Come chiudere la transizione*, Bologna, Il Mulino.

Ceccobelli, D., Vaccari, C. (2021), *Un virus nel sistema mediale ibrido: come il governo Conte ha comunicato la crisi Coronavirus*, in A. Giovannini and L. Mosca, *Politica in Italia. I fatti dell'anno e le interpretazioni, Edizione 2021*, Bologna, Il Mulino.

Ceron, A., Volpi, E. (2019), *Breakups hurt: Party switching and perceived proximity between politicians and their party*, in *Party Politics*, 27, 4, pp. 656–666.

Chadwick, A. (2017), *The Hybrid Media System: Politics and Power*, Oxford, Oxford University Press.

Cheibub, J., Elkins, Z., Ginsburg, T. (2014), *Beyond presidentialism and parliamentarism*, in *British Journal of Political Science*, 44, 3, pp. 515–544.

Cheibub, J.A. (2007), *Presidentialism, Parliamentarism, and Democracy*, New York, Cambridge University Press.

Cheibub, J.A., Przeworski, A., Saiegh, S.M. (2004), *Government Coalitions and Legislative Success under Presidentialism and Parliamentarism*, in *British Journal of Political Science*, 34, 4, pp. 565–587.

Cheibub, J.A., Rasch, B.E. (2021), *Constitutional parliamentarism in Europe, 1800–2019*, in *West European Politics*, pp. 1–32, Published online: 09 Feb 2021.

Chhabra, R. (2020), Twitter Diplomacy: A Brief Analysis, *Twitter Diplomacy: A Brief Analysis*, in *ORF Issue Brief*, Observer Research Foundation, 335, January.

Chiaramonte, A., Emanuele, V. (2017), *Party system volatility, regeneration and de-institutionalization in Western Europe (1945–2015)*, in *Party Politics*, 23, 4, pp. 376–388.

Clark, T.S. (2009), *Measuring Ideological Polarization on the United States Supreme Court*, in *Political Research Quarterly*, 62, 1, pp. 146–157.

Clarke, H., Stewart, M. (1998), *The decline of parties in the minds of citizens*, in *Annual Review of Political Science*, 1, 357–378.

Clift, B. (2008), *The Fifth Republic at Fifty: The Changing Face of French Politics and Political Economy*, in *Modern & Contemporary France*, 16, 4, pp. 383–398.

Cole, A. (2019), *Emmanuel Macron and the two years that changed France*, Manchester, Manchester University Press.

Collier, D., Levitsky, S. (1997), *Democracy with Adjectives: Conceptual Innovation in Comparative Research*, in *World Politics*, 49, 3, pp. 430–451.

Comba, M. (2007), *Il Presidente degli Stati Uniti d'America: la persistenza del modello roosveltiano*, in A. Di Giovine, A. Mastromarino (eds.), *La presidenzializzazione degli esecutivi nelle democrazie contemporanee*, Torino, Giappichelli.

Conley, R.S. (2002), *The Presidency, Congress, and Divided Government: A Postwar Assessment*, College Station, Texas A&M University Press.

Cooper, P.J. (1986), *By order of the president: Administration by executive order and proclamation*, in *Administration & Society*, 18, 2, pp. 233–262.

Corwin, E.S. (1927), *The President's Removal Power under the Constitution*, New York, National Municipal League.

Corwin, E.S. (1949), *The Presidency in Perspective*, in *The Journal of Politics*, 11, 1, pp. 7–13.

Costa Lobo, M. (2014), *Party dealignment and leader effects*, in M. Costa Lobo, J. Curtice (eds.), *Personality politics?: The role of leader evaluations in democratic elections*, Oxford, Oxford University Press, pp. 148–166.

Costa Lobo, M., Curtice, J. (eds.), (2014), *Personality Politics? The Role of Leader Evaluations in Democratic Elections*, Oxford, Oxford University Press.

Cox, G., Kernell, S. (2019), The politics of divided government, New York, Routledge.

Crewe, I., Denver, D.T. (eds.), (1985), *Electoral change in Western democracies: Patterns and sources of electoral volatility*, London, Croom Helm.

Criscitiello, A. (2004), *Il cuore dei governi. Le politiche di riforma degli esecutivi in prospettiva comparata*, Napoli, Edizioni Scientifiche, 2004.

Criscitiello, A. (2020), *Il potere normativo del Presidente del Consiglio in Italia*, in F. Musella (ed.), *L'emergenza democratica. Presidenti, decreti, crisi pandemica*, Napoli, Editoriale Scientifica, pp. 47–89.

Croissant, A. (2003), *Legislative Powers, Veto Players, and the Emergence of Delegative Democracy: A Comparison of Presidentialism in the Philippines and South Korea*, in *Democratization*, 10, 3, pp. 68–98.

Cross, W.P., Katz, R.S., Pruysers, S. (eds.), (2018), *The personalization of democratic politics and the challenge for political parties*, London and New York, Rowman & Littlefield International.

Crossman, R. (1963), *Introduction*, in W. Bagehot, *The English Constitution*, London, Fontana, pp. 1–57.

Currie, D.P. (2008), *Republication-Separation of Powers in the Federal Republic of Germany*, in *German Law Journal*, 9, 12, pp. 2113–2178.

Curry, J.M., Lee, F.E. (2020), *The Limits of Party: Congress and Lawmaking in a Polarized Era*, Chicago, University of Chicago Press.

D'Alimonte, R., Bartolini, S. (eds.), (2002), *Maggioritario finalmente? La transizione elettorale 1994–2001*, Bologna, Il Mulino.

Daalder, H. (1992), *A crisis of party?*, in *Scandinavian Political Studies*, 15, 4, pp. 269–288.

Dahl, R.A. (1990), *Myth of the presidential mandate*, in *Political Science Quarterly*, 105, 3, pp. 355–372.

Dahl, R.A., Tufte, E.R. (1973), *Size and democracy*, Stanford, Stanford University Press.

Dalton, R.J. (1996) *Comparative Politics: Micro-behavioral Perspectives*, in R. Goodin, H-D. Klingemann (eds.), *A New Handbook of Political Science*, Oxford, Oxford University Press.

Dalton, R.J. (2008), *The Policy Process*, in *Politics in Germany: The Online Edition*, Irvione University, avaialble at http://www.socsci.uci.edu/~rdalton/germany/ch9/chap9.htm.

Dalton, R.J. (2016), *Party identification and its implications*, in *Oxford research encyclopedia of politics*, Oxford. Published online: 09 May 2016.

Dalton, R.J., (2008), *The quantity and the quality of party systems: party system polarization, its measurement, and its consequences*, in *Comparative Political Studies*, 41, 7, pp. 899–920.

Dalton, R.J., Farrell, D.M., McAllister, I. (2011), *Political Parties and Democratic Linkage: How Parties Organize Democracy*, New York, Oxford University Press.

Dalton, R.J., Wattenberg M.P. (eds.), (2002), *Parties without partisans: Political change in advanced industrial democracies*, Oxford, Oxford University Press.

Dalton, R.J., Weldon, S.A. (2005), *Public images of political parties: A necessary evil?*, in *West European Politics*, 28, 5, pp. 931–951.

Dassonneville, R., Hooghe, M. (2011), *Mapping Electoral Volatility in Europe. An analysis of trends in electoral volatility in European democracies since 1945*, Paper presented at the *European Conference on Comparative Electoral Research*, 1–3 December, 2011, Sofia, Centre for Political Research.

Dassonneville, R., Hooghe, M. (2017), *Economic indicators and electoral volatility: economic effects on electoral volatility in Western Europe, 1950–2013*, in *Comparative European Politics*, 15, 6, pp. 919–943.

Davis, R., Taras, D. (eds.), (2020), *Power shift? Political leadership and social media*, London, Routledge.

De Gaulle, C. (1970), *27 juillet 1947, Rennes*, in C. de Gaulle (ed.), *Discours et Messages, 1946–1958*, vol. II, Paris, Plon.

de Kerckhove, D. (1991), *Brainframes: Technology, Mind and business*, Utrecht, Bosch & Keuning.

De la Torre, C., Peruzzotti, E. (2018), *Populism in Power: Between Inclusion and Autocracy*, in *Populism*, 1, 1, pp. 38–58, doi: https://doi.org/10.1163/25888072-01011002

De Luca, M. (2011), *Presidentialism*, in B. Badie, D. Berg-Schlosser, L. Morlino (eds.), in *International Encyclopedia of Political Science*, London, Sage, pp. 2124–2128.

De Micheli, C. (2020), *The Italian XVIII legislature: populism, law-making and procedures*, in *Italian Political Science*, 15, 2, pp. 191–208.

De Micheli, C., Verzichelli, L. (2004), *Il Parlamento*, Bologna, Il Mulino.

De Minico, G. (2018), *Costituzione ed emergenza*, in *Osservatorio sulle fonti*, 2, pp. 1–22.

De Siervo, U. (2006), *Introduzione*, in A. Simoncini (ed.), *L'emergenza infinita: la decretazione d'urgenza in Italia*, Macerata, EUM, pp. 9–18.

De Vergottini, G. (2004), *Guerra e costituzione: nuovi conflitti e sfide alla democrazia*, Bologna, Il Mulino.

Deering, C.J., Maltzman, F. (1999), *The politics of executive orders: Legislative constraints on presidential power*, in *Political Research Quarterly*, 52, 4, pp. 767–783.

Deseriis, M. (2020), *Digital movement parties: a comparative analysis of the technopolitical cultures and the participation platforms of the Movimento 5 Stelle and the Piratenpartei*, in *Information, Communication & Society*, 23, 12, pp 1770–1786.

Deseriis, M. (2020), *Two variants of the digital party: The Platform Party and The Networked Party*, in *Partecipazione e Conflitto*, 13, 1, pp. 896–917.

Di Gregorio, L. (2010), *Election*, in M. Calise, T.J. Lowi (eds.), *Hyperpolitics: An Interactive Dictionary of Political Science Concepts*, Chicago, Chicago University Press, pp. 100–101.

Di Porto V. (2016), *La carica dei DPCM*, in *Osservatorio sulle fonti*, 2, pp. 1–13.

Di Virgilio, A., Giannetti, D., Pinto, L. (2012), *Patterns of Party Switching in the Italian Chamber of Deputies 2008–2011*, in *Rivista Italiana di Scienza Politica*, 42, 1, pp. 29–58.

Diamanti, I. (2014), *The 5 Star Movement: A Political Laboratory*, in *Contemporary Italian Politics*, 6, 1, pp. 4–15.

Dicey, A.V. (1914), *Lectures on the relation between law and public opinion in England, during the nineteenth century*, London, Macmillan and Co.

Dickinson, M.J. (1999), *Bitter harvest: FDR, presidential power and the growth of the presidential branch*, Cambridge, Cambridge University Press.

Dickinson, M.J., Lebo, M.J. (2007), *Reexamining the Growth of the Institutional Presidency, 1940–2000*, in *Journal of Politics*, 69, 1, pp. 206–219.

Ditslear, C., Baum, L. (2001), *Selection of Law Clerks and Polarization in the U.S. Supreme Court*, in *The Journal of Politics*, 63, 3, pp. 869–885.

Douglass C.N., (1985), *The growth of government in the United States: an economic historian's perspective*, in *Journal of Public Economics*, 28, 3, pp. 383–399.

Dowding, K. (2013), *The prime ministerialisation of the British prime minister*, in *Parliamentary Affairs*, 66, 3, pp. 617–635.

Downs, A. (1957), *An Economic Theory of Democracy*, New York, Harper & Row.

Doyle, D. (2020), *Measuring Presidential and Prime Ministerial Power*, in R.B. Andeweg, R. Elgie, L. Helms, J. Kaarbo, F. Müller-Rommel, F. (eds.), *The Oxford Handbook of Political Executives*, Oxford, Oxford University Press, pp. 382–401.

Drummond, A.J. (2006), *Electoral Volatility and Party Decline in Western Democracies: 1970–1995*, in *Political Studies*, 54, pp. 628–647.

Duffy, B., Hewlett, K. A., McCrae, J., Hall, J. (2019), *Divided Britain? Polarisation and fragmentation trends in the UK*, London The Policy Institute at King's College, https://www.kcl.ac.uk/policy-institute/assets/divided-britain.pdf.

Duverger, M. (1963), *Political Parties: Their Organization and Activity in the Modern State*, New York, Wiley.

Duverger, M. (1974), *La monarchie républicaine ou comment les démocraties se donnent des rois*, Parigi, Robert Laffont.

Dyzenhaus, D. (2006), *The constitution of law: Legality in a time of emergency*, Cambridge, Cambridge University Press.

Easton, D. (1953), *The Political System. An Inquiry into the State of Political Science*, New York, Knopf.

Eaton, K. (2000), *Parliamentarism versus Presidentialism in the Policy Arena, Reviewed Work(s): Executive Decree Authority by John M. Carey, M.S. Shugart; Structure and Policy in Japan and the United States, by P.F. Cowhey, M.D. McCubbins (eds.), Do Institutions Matter? Government Capabilities in the United States and Abroad by B.A. Rockman, R.K. Weaver*, in *Comparative Politics*, 32, 3, 2000, pp. 355–376.

Edwards III, G.C., Barrett, A, Peake, J. (1997), *The legislative impact of divided government*, in *American journal of political science*, 41, 2, pp. 545–563.

Eisinger, R.M. (2000), *Gauging public opinion in the Hoover White House: Understanding the roots of presidential polling*, in *Presidential Studies Quarterly*, 30, 4, pp. 643–661.

Eisinger, R.M. (2003), *The evolution of presidential polling*, Cambridge, Cambridge University Press.

Eisinger, R.M., Brown, J. (1998), *Polling as a means toward presidential autonomy: Emil Hurja, Hadley Cantril and the Roosevelt administration*, in *International Journal of Public Opinion Research*, 10, 3, pp. 237–256.

Elgie R. (1999), *Semi-presidentialism in Europe*, Oxford, Oxford University Press.

Elgie, R. (2011), *Semi-presidentialism: Sub-types and democratic performance*, Oxford, Oxford University Press.

Elgie, R., Moestrup, S. (eds.), (2008), *Semi-presidentialism in Central and Eastern Europe*, Manchester, Manchester University Press.

Elgie, R., Passarelli, G. (2020), *The Presidentialization of Political Executives*, in R. Andeweg, R. Elgie, L. Helms, J. Kaarbo, F. Müller-Rommel (eds.), *The Oxford Handbook of Political Executives*, Oxford, Oxford University Press, pp. 359–381.

Elgie, R.M., Stapleton, J. (2006), *Testing the Decline of Parliament Thesis: Ireland 1923–2002*, in *Political Studies*, 54, 3, pp. 465–485.

Elia, L. (1970), *Governo (forme di)*, in *Enciclopedia del diritto*, vol. XIX, Milano, Giuffrè Editore, pp. 634–675.

Elia, L. (2006), *La presidenzializzazione della politica*, in *Teoria politica*, 1, pp. 5–11.

Emanuele, V., Chiaramonte, A., Soare, S. (2020), *Does the Iron Curtain Still Exist? The Convergence in Electoral Volatility between Eastern and Western Europe*, in *Government and Opposition*, 55, 2, pp. 308–326.

Enli, G. (2017), *Twitter as Arena for the Authentic Outsider: Exploring the Social Media Campaigns of Trump and Clinton in the 2016 US Presidential Election*, in *European Journal of Communication*, 32, 1, pp. 50–61.

Enli, G.S., Skogerbø, E. (2013), *Personalized campaigns in party-centred politics. Twitter and Facebook as arenas for political communication*, in *Information, Communication and Society*, 16, 5, pp. 757–774.

Enyedi, Z. (2014), *The Discreet Charm of Political Parties*, in *Party Politics*, 20, 2, pp. 194–204.

Epstein, L.D. (1967), *Political Parties in Western Democracies*, New York, Pall Mall.

Erdmann, G. (2011), *Decline of democracy: loss of quality, hybridisation and breakdown of democracy*, in *Zeitschrift für Vergleichende Politikwissenschaft/Comparative Governance and Politics*, 1, pp. 21–58.

Erdmann, G., Kneuer, M. (eds.), (2011), Introduction, in Special Issue: *Regression of Democracy?*, in *Zeitschrift für Vergleichende Politikwissenschaft/Comparative Governance and Politics*, 1, pp. 9–20.

Escobar-Lemmon, M.C., Taylor-Robinson, M. (2020), *Executive-Legislative Relations in Democratic Regimes: Managing the Legislative Process*, in R. Andeweg, R. Elgie, L. Helms, J. Kaarbo, F. Müller-Rommel (eds.), *The Oxford Handbook of Political Executives*, Oxford, Oxford University Press, pp. 547–565.

Ewing, K.D. (2020), *Covid-19: Government by Decree*, in *King's Law Journal*, 31, 1, pp. 1–24.

Fabbrini, S. (1993), *Il presidenzialismo americano. Governare gli Stati Uniti*, Roma-Bari, Laterza.

Fabbrini, S. (2011), *Addomesticare il Prìncipe*, Venezia, Marsilio.

Ferejohn, J., Pasquino, P. (2004), *The law of the exception: A typology of emergency powers*, in *International Journal of Constitutional Law*, 2, 2, pp. 210–239.

Ferraiuolo, G., Praino, D. (2018), *The role of political parties in the Italian electoral reforms*, in *Revista Catalana de Dret Públic*, 57, pp. 154–165.

Ferrajoli, C.F. (2018), *Rappresentanza politica e responsabilità. La crisi della forma di governo parlamentare in Italia*, Napoli, Editoriale Scientifica.

Ferreira Rubio, D., Goretti, M. (1998), *When the president governs alone: The decretazo in Argentina, 1989–93*, in J.M. Carey and M.S. Shugart (eds.), *Executive decree authority*, Cambridge, Cambridge University Press, 1998, pp. 33–61.

Field, B.N., (2009), *A Second Transition in Spain? Policy, Institutions and Interparty Politics under Zapatero (2004–8)*, in *South European Society and Politics*, 14, 4, pp. 379–397.

Fieldhouse, E., Green, J., Evans, G., Mellon, J., Prosser, C., Schmitt, H., van der Eijk, C. (2019), *Electoral shocks: the volatile voter in a turbulent world*, Oxford, Oxford University Press.

Fine, J.A., Warber, A.L. (2012), *Circumventing Adversity: Executive Orders and Divided Government*, in *Presidential Studies Quarterly*, 42, pp. 256–274.

Finer, S.E. (1997), *The History of Government from the Earliest Times: Ancient monarchies and empires*, Oxford, Oxford University Press.

Fiorina, M. (2002), *Parties and partisanship: A forty-year retrospective*, in *Political Behavior*, 24, 93–115.

Fiorina, M.P. (1992), *An era of divided government*, in *Political Science Quarterly*, 107, 3, pp. 387–410.

Fiorina, M.P., Abrams, S.J. (2008), *Political polarization in the American public*, in *Annual Review of Political Science*, 11, pp. 563–588.

Fioritto, A., (2008), *L'amministrazione dell'emergenza tra autorità e garanzie*, Bologna, Il Mulino.

Fisch, W.B. (1990), *Emergency in the constitutional law of the United States*, in *The American Journal of Comparative Law*, 38, pp. 389–420.

Fischer, M. (2014), *Coalition structures and policy change in a consensus democracy*, in *Policy Studies Journal*, 42, 3, pp. 344–366.

Fisher, L. (1971), *The efficiency side of separation of powers*, in *Journal of American Studies*, 5, 2, pp. 113–31.

Fisher, L. (2011), *Separation of powers*, in B. Badie, D.Berg-Schlosser, L Morlino (eds.), *International Encyclopedia of Political Science*, 1, London, Sage, pp. 2402–2407.

Fittipaldi, R. (2021), *The Rise of Presidents in Coronavirus Emergency: national and sub-national evidences in Italy and Spain*, in *Partecipazione e Conflitto*, 14, 1, pp. 132–151.

Fleischer, J., Parrado, S. (2010), *Power distribution in ambiguous times: The effects of the financial crisis on executive decision-making in Germany and Spain*, in *dms-der moderne staat-Zeitschrift für Public Policy, Recht und Management*, 3, 2, pp. 15–16.

Foa, R.S., Mounk, Y. (2016), *The democratic disconnect*, in *Journal of Democracy*, 27, 3, pp. 5–17.

Foley, M. (1993), *The rise of the British presidency*, Manchester, Manchester University Press.

Fortin-Rittberger, J. (2017), *Strong Presidents for Weak States. How Weak State Capacity Fosters Vertically Concentrated Executives*, in P. Harfst, I. Kubbe, and T. Poguntke (eds.), *Parties, Governments and Elites: The Comparative Study of Democracy*, Wiesbanden, Springer, pp. 205–226.

Frosini, T.E. (2019), *L'espansione dei poteri normativi dell'esecutivo*, in Musella, F. (ed.), (2019), *Il governo in Italia. Profili costituzionali e dinamiche politiche*, Bologna, Il Mulino, pp. 153–164.

Fry, G.K. (2019), *The Growth of Government, The Development of Ideas about the Role of the State and the Machinery and Functions of Government in Britain since 1780*, London, Routledge.

Fusaro, C. (2007), *La legge elettorale del 2005: profili ordinamentali e costituzionali*, in R. D'Alimonte, A. Chiaramonte (eds.), *Proporzionale ma non solo: le elezioni politiche del 2006*, Bologna, Il Mulino, pp. 89–119.

Gaffney, J. (2015), *France in the Hollande presidency: The unhappy republic*, Basingstoke, Palgrave.

Ganghof, S. (2021), *Beyond Presidentialism and Parliamentarism. Democratic Design and the Separation of Powers*, Oxford, Oxford University Press.

Garrett, T.A., Rhine, R.M. (2006), *On the size and growth of government*, in *Federal Reserve Bank of St. Louis Review*, 88, 1, pp. 13–30.

Garzia, D. (2013), *The rise of party/leader identification in Western Europe*, in *Political Research Quarterly*, 66, 3, pp. 533–544.

Garzia, D. (2019), *Personalization of politics and electoral change*, London, Palgrave Macmillan.

Geddes, B., Wright, J., Frantz, E. (2014), *Autocratic Breakdown and Regime Transitions: A New Data Set*, in *Perspectives on Politics* 12, 2, pp. 313–331.

Gerbaudo, P. (2019a), *The Digital Party. Political Organisation and Online Democracy*, London, Pluto Press.

Gerbaudo, P. (2019b), *The Age of the Hyperleader: When Political Leadership Meets Social Media Celebrity*, in *New Stateman*, 12 March.

Gerbaudo, P. (2021a), *Are digital parties more democratic than traditional parties? Evaluating Podemos and Movimento 5 Stelle's online decision-making platforms*, in *Party Politics*, 27, 4, pp. 730–742.

Gerbaudo, P. (2021b), *The Great Recoil: Politics After Populism and Pandemic*, London, Verso Books.

Gerstle, G., Isaac, J. (eds.), (2020), *States of Exception in American History*, Chicago, University of Chicago Press.

Gibson, R., Ward, S. (2009), *Parties in the Digital Age. A Review Article*, in *Representation*, 45, 1, pp. 87–100.

Gibson, R.K. (2020), *When the Nerds Go Marching in: How Digital Technology Moved from the Margins to the Mainstream of Political Campaigns*, Oxford, Oxford University Press.

Ginsberg, B. (2016), *Presidential Government*, New Haven, Yale University Press.

Ginsberg, B., Lowi, T.J., Tolbert, C.J., Weir, M. (2017), *We the people. An introduction to American Politics*, New York-London, W.W. Norton & Company.

Ginsburg, T. (2020), *Foreword for Special Issue on Legislatures in the Time of Covid-19*, in *The Theory and Practice of Legislation*, 8, pp. 1–2.

Ginsburg, T., Huq, A.Z. (2018), *How to save a constitutional democracy*, Chicago, University of Chicago Press.

Ginsburg, T., Versteeg, M. (2020a), *Binding the Unbound Executive: Checks and Balances in Times of Pandemic*, in *Virginia Public Law and Legal Theory Research Paper*, 52, University of Chicago Public Law, Working Paper 747.

Ginsburg, T., Versteeg, M. (2020b), *The bound executive: Emergency powers during the pandemic*, in *Virginia Public Law and Legal Theory Research Paper*, 52.

Gitterman, D.P. (2017), *Calling the shots: The President, executive orders, and public policy*, New York, Brookings Institution Press.

Goitein, E. (2020), *Emergency Powers, Real and Imagined: How President Trump Used and Failed to Use Presidential Authority in the COVID-19 Crisis*, in *Journal of National Security Law and Policy*, 11, pp. 27–60.

González, L. (2014), *Unpacking delegative democracy: digging into the empirical content of a rich theoretical concept*, in D. Brinks, M. Leiras, S. Mainwaring (eds.), *Reflections on Uneven Democracies: The Legacy of Guillermo O'Donnell*, Baltimore, Johns Hopkins University Press, pp. 240–268.

Graber, M.A., Levinson, S., Tushnet, M. (eds.), (2018), *Constitutional democracy in crisis?*, Oxford, Oxford University Press.

Graham, M., Svolik, M.W. (2020), *Democracy in America? Partisanship, Polarization, and the Robustness of Support for Democracy in the United States*, in *American Political Science Review*, 114, 2, pp. 392–409.

Green, J.C., Coffey, D.J. (2010), *The state of the parties: The changing role of contemporary American parties*, Lanham, Rowman & Littlefield Publishers.

Green, J., Prosser, C. (2016), *Party system fragmentation and single-party government: the British general election of 2015*, in *West European Politics*, 39, 6, pp. 1299–1310.

Green, J.E. (2010), *The eyes of the people: democracy in an age of spectatorship*, Oxford, Oxford University Press.

Greene, A. (2018), *Permanent states of emergency and the rule of law: constitutions in an age of crisis*, London, Bloomsbury Publishing.

Greene, A. (2020), *Emergency Powers in a Time of Pandemic*, Bristol, Policy Press.

Griglio, E. (2020), *Parliamentary oversight under the Covid-19 emergency: striving against executive dominance*, in *The Theory and Practice of Legislation*, 8, 1–2, pp. 49–70.

Groll, E. (2015), *These are the Most Influential World Leaders on Twitter and Why That Doesn't Matter*, in *Foreign Policy*, 28 April.

Gross, O. (2015), *Emergency Powers*, in M. Tushnet, M.A. Graber and S. Levinson, *The Oxford Handbook of the US Constitution*, Oxford, Oxford University Press.

Gross, O., Aoláin, F.N. (2006), *Law in times of crisis: emergency powers in theory and practice*, Cambridge, Cambridge University Press.

Gunther, R., Diamond, L. (2003), *Species of political parties: A new typology*, in *Party Politics*, 9, 2, pp. 167–199.

Haggard, S., Kaufman, R. (2021), *Backsliding: Democratic Regress in the Contemporary World*, Cambridge, Cambridge University Press.

Haguenau-Moizard, C. (2021), *The French Habeas Corpus and Covid-19: The decision of the Constitutional Council on pre-trial detention*, in *VerfBlog*, February 2, https://verfassungs blog.de/the-french-habeas-corpus-and-covid-19/.

Hajnal, Z., Lee, T. (2011), *Why Americans don't join the party: Race, immigration, and the failure of parties to engage the electorate*, Princeton, Princeton University Press.

Hale, B. (2020), *The Pandemic and the Constitution*, in J. Brennan, M. Groves, R. Friedman, S. James, S. Mullings (eds.), *Justice Matters: Essays from the Pandemic*, London, Legal Action Group.

Haman, M. (2020), *The use of Twitter by state leaders and its impact on the public during the COVID-19 pandemic*, in *Heliyon*, 6, 11, pp. 1–9.

Harmel, R., Robertson, J.D. (1985), *Formation and success of new parties: A cross-national analysis*, in *International political science review*, 6, 4, pp. 501–523.

Harms, P.D., Wood, D., Landay, K., Lester, P.B., Lester, G.V. (2018), *Autocratic leaders and authoritarian followers revisited: A review and agenda for the future*, in *The Leadership Quarterly*, 29, 1, pp. 105–122.

Hart, J. (1995), *The Presidential Branch. From Washington to Clinton*, New York, Chatham House.

Hassenteufel, P. (2020), *Handling the COVID-19 crisis in France: Paradoxes of a centralized state-led health system*, in *European Policy Analysis*, 6, 2, pp. 170–179.

Hayward, J. (2013), *Hyperpresidentialism and the Fifth Republic State Imperative*, in *The Presidents of the French Fifth Republic*, London, Palgrave Macmillan, pp. 44–57.

Hazan, R.Y. (2003), *Does Cohesion Equal Discipline. Towards a Conceptual Delineation*, in *Journal of Legislative Studies* (special issue on cohesion and discipline in legislatures), 9, 4, pp. 1–11.

Heffernan, R. (2005), *Exploring (and explaining) the British prime minister*, in *The British Journal of Politics and International Relations*, 7, 4, pp. 605–620.

Heffernan, R. (2013), *There's no need for the '-isation': the prime minister is merely prime ministerial*, in *Parliamentary Affairs*, 66, 3, pp. 636–645.

Heith, D.J. (2004), *Polling to govern: Public opinion and presidential leadership*, Stanford, Stanford University Press.

Heller, W., Mershon, C. (eds.), (2009), *Political parties and legislative party switching*, New York, Springer.

Helms, L. (2005), *The Presidentialisation of Political Leadership: British Notions and German Observations*, in *Political Quarterly*, 76, 3, pp. 430–438.

Helms, L. (2015), *Is there a presidentialization of US presidential leadership? A European perspective on Washington*, in *Acta Politica*, 50, 1, pp. 1–19.

Hennett V., Kirton-Darling E., Carr, H., Varnava, T. (2020), *Legislating for a pandemic: exposing the stateless State*, in *Journal of law and Society*, 47, pp. 302–320.

Hetherington, M. J. (2009), *Putting Polarization in Perspective*, in *British Journal of Political Science*, 39, 2, pp. 413–448.

Hinton, R.W.K. (1960), *The Prime Minister as an Elected Monarch*, in *Parliamentary Affairs*, 13, pp. 297–303.

Hobolt, S.B. (2016), *The Brexit vote: a divided nation, a divided continent*, in *Journal of European Public Policy*, 23, 9, pp. 1259–1277.

Holcombe, R.G. (2005), *Government Growth in the Twenty-First Century*, in *Public Choice*, 124, 1/2, Policy Challenges and Political Responses: Public Choice Perspectives on the Post-9/11 World, pp. 95–114.

Howell, G.W. (2005), *Unilateral Powers: A Brief Overview*, in *Presidential Studies Quarterly*, 35, 3, pp. 417–439.

Howell, W. (2003), *Power without Persuasion: The Politics of Direct Presidential Action*, Princeton, Princeton University Press.

Hutter, S., Krise, H. (2019), *European Party Politics in Times of Crisis*, Cambridge, Cambridge University Press.

Ie, K.W. (2020), *Tweeting power: The communication of leadership roles on prime ministers' twitter*, in *Politics and Governance*, 8, 1, pp. 158–170.

Ignazi, P. (1996), *The crisis of parties and the rise of new political parties*, in *Party Politics*, 2, 4, pp. 549–566.

Ilonszki, G. (2002), *Az elnöki parlamentarizmus és a parlament*, in *Századvég*, 2, pp. 109–133.

Iyengar, S., Westwood, S.W. (2015), *Fear and loathing across party lines. New evidence on group polarization*, in *American Journal of Political Science*, 59, 3, pp. 690–707.

Jacobs, L.R., Shapiro, R.Y. (1995), *The Rise of Presidential Polling The Nixon White House in Historical Perspective*, in *Public Opinion Quarterly*, 59, 2, pp. 163–195.

Janda, K. (2009), *Laws against Party Switching, Defecting, or Floor-Crossing in National Parliaments: The Legal Regulation of Political Parties*, Working Paper 2, August. Available at: www. partylaw. leidenuniv. nl/uploads/wp0209.pdf

Johnson, L. (2018), *Democracy Dies a Slow Death*, in *Yale Journal of International Affairs*, 13, pp. 19–24.

Jones, G.W. (1985), *The prime minister's power*, in *The British Prime Minister*, London, Palgrave, pp. 195–220.

Jones, M.P. (1995), *Electoral Laws and the Survival of Presidential Democracies*, Notre Dame, Notre Dame University Press.

Jordan, S., Bowling, C.J. (2016), *Introduction: the state of polarization in the states*, in *State and Local Government Review*, 48, 4, pp. 220–226.

Kane, J., Patapan, H. (2012), *The Democratic Leader: How Democracy Defines, Empowers and Limits Its Leaders*, Oxford, Oxford University Press.

Karpen, U. (2012), *Comparative law: perspectives of legisla*tion, in *Legisprudence*, 6, 2, pp. 149–189.

Karpf, D. (2017), *Digital politics after Trump*, in *Annals of the International Communication Association*, 41, 2, pp. 198–207.

Karvonen, L. (2010), *The Personalisation of Politics: A Study of Parliamentary Democracies*, Colchester, European Consortium for Political Research.

Kasińska-Metryka, A., Gajewski, T. (2020), (eds.), *The Future of Political Leadership in the Digital Age: Neo-Leadership, Image and Influence*, Arbingdon, Routledge.

Katz, J., Barris, M., Jain, A. (2013), *The social media president: Barack Obama and the politics of digital engagement*, New York, Springer.

Katz, R.S. (1986), *Party government: a rationalistic conception*, in G.G. Castles, R. Wildenmann (eds.), *Visions and realities of party government*, Berlin, de Gruyter, pp. 31–71.

Katz, R.S., Crotty, W.J., (eds.), (2005), *Handbook of Party Politics*, London, Sage.

Katz, R.S., Mair, P. (1993), *The evolution of party organizations in Europe: the three faces of party organization*, in *American Review of Politics*, 14, pp. 593–617.

Katz, R.S., Mair, P. (1994), *How Parties Organize: Change and Adaptation in Party Organizations in Western Democracies*, London, Sage.

Katz, R.S., Mair, P. (2009), *The Cartel Party Thesis: A Restatement*, in *Perspectives on Politics*, 7, 4, pp. 753–766.

Katz, R.S., Mair, P. (2018), *Democracy and the cartelization of political parties*, Oxford, Oxford University Press.

Kazai, V.Z. (2019), *The Illiberal Challenge to the Rule of Law Principle: The Neglected Procedural Aspect* (With Special Focus on Hungary), in 2019 ESIL Annual Research Forum, Goettingen, April.

Keeler, J.T. (1993), *Executive power and policy-making patterns in France: Gauging the impact of fifth republic institutions*, in *West European Politics*, 16, 4, pp. 518–544.

Kefford, G., McDonnell, D. (2018), *Inside the personal party: Leader-owners, light organizations and limited lifespans*, in *The British Journal of Politics and International Relations*, 20, 2, pp. 379–394.

Kelsen, H. (1967), *Willensbildung in der modernen Demokratie*, in K. Lenk, F. Neumann (eds.), *Theorie und Soziologie der politischen Parteien/Theory and Sociology of political parties*. Neuwied am Rhein, Hermann Luchterhand Verlag.

Kendall-Taylor, A., Frantz, E., Wright, J. (2017), *The global rise of personalized politics: It's not just dictators anymore*, in *The Washington Quarterly*, 40, 1, pp. 7–19.

Kenski, K., Hardy, B.W., Jamieson, K.H. (2010), *The Obama Victory: How Media, Money, and Message Shaped the 2008 Election*, Oxford, Oxford University Press.

Kerrouche, E. (2006), *The French Assemblée nationale: The case of a weak legislature?*, in *The Journal of Legislative Studies*, 12, 3–4, pp. 336–365.

Khakee, A. (2009), *Securing democracy: a comparative analysis of emergency powers in Europe*, Geneva, Centre for the Democratic Control of Armed Forces.

Kingdon, J.W. (1999), *America the Unusual*, New York, Worth Publishers.

Kirchheimer, O. (1966), *The Transformation of the Western European Party Systems*, in J. La Palombara, M. Weiner (eds.), *Political Parties and Political Development*, Princeton, Princeton University Press, pp. 177–200.

Kirton-Darling, E., Carr, H., Varnava, T. (2020), *Legislating for a pandemic: exposing the stateless State. Journal of law and Society*, 47, pp. 302–320.

Klar, S., Krupnikov, Y. (2016), *Independent politics*, Cambridge, Cambridge University Press.

Klein E. (2018), *The personal vote and legislative party switching*, in *Party Politics*, 24, 5, pp. 501–510.

Klein, E. (2021), *Explaining legislative party switching in advanced and new democracies*, in *Party Politics*, 27, 2, pp. 329–340.

Klieman, A.S. (1979), *Preparing for the Hour of Need: The National Emergencies Act*, in *Presidential Studies Quarterly*, 9, 1, pp. 47–65.

Kölln, A.K. (2015), *The effects of membership decline on party organisations in Europe*, in *European Journal of Political Research*, 54, 4, pp. 707–725.

Kopecký, P. (2004), *Power to the executive! The changing executive-legislative relations in eastern Europe*, in *The Journal of Legislative Studies*, 10, 2–3, pp. 142–153.

Körösényi, A. (2001), *Government and Politics in Hungary*, Budapest, Central European University Press.

Körösényi, A. (2001), *Parlamentáris vagy elnöki kormányzás? Az Orbàn kormány összehasonlító perspektívából*, in *Századvég*, 20, pp. 3–38.

Korosényi, A. (2005), *Political Representation in Leader Democracy*, in *Government and Opposition*, 40, 3, pp. 358–378.

Körösényi, A. (2013), *Political polarization and its consequences on democratic accountability*, in *Corvinus Journal of Sociology and Social Policy*, 4, 2, pp. 3–30.

Körösényi, A., Illés, G., Gyulai, A. (2020), *The Orbán Regime: Plebiscitary Leader Democracy in the Making*, London, Routledge.

Kostadinov, B. (2016), *President of the Republic. Croatian constitution's mimicry of the French constitutional model*, in *Revus. Journal for Constitutional Theory and Philosophy of Law/ Revija za ustavno teorijo in filozofijo prava*, 28, pp. 79–96.

Kostadinova, T., Levitt, B. (2014), *Toward a theory of personalist parties: Concept formation and theory building*, in *Politics & Policy*, 42, 4, pp. 490–512.

Krause, G.A., Cohen, D.B. (1997), *Presidential use of executive orders, 1953–1994*, in *American Politics Quarterly*, 25, 4, pp. 458–481.

Kreiss, D. (2016), *Prototype politics: Technology-intensive campaigning and the data of democracy*, Oxford, Oxford University Press.

Kreiss, D., Jasinski, C. (2016), *The Tech Industry Meets Presidential Politics: Explaining the Democratic Party's Technological Advantage in Electoral Campaigning, 2004–2012*, in *Political Communication*, 33, 4, pp. 544–562.

Kubiček, P. (1994), *Delegative Democracy in Russia and Ukraine*, in *Communist and Post-Communist Studies*, 27, 4, pp. 423–441.

Kundnani, H. (2020), *Europe after the Coronavirus: A "Return of the State"?*, in *IAI Papers*, 20, 32.

Kyle, D. (2004), *The Return of the American Voter? Party Polarization and Voting Behavior, 1988 to 2004*, in *Sociological Perspectives*, 53, 3, pp. 443–449.

Laakso, M., Taagepera, R. (1979), *Effective Number of Parties: A Measure with Application to West Europe*, in *Comparative Political Studies*, 12, 1, pp. 3–27.

Larkey, P.D., Chandler, S., Winer, M. (1981), *Theorizing about the growth of government: A research assessment*, in *Journal of Public Policy*, 1, 2, pp. 157–220.

Lasch, C. (1979), *The Culture of Narcissism: American Life in an Age of Diminishing Expectations*, New York, Norton.

Lavigne, M. (2020), *Strengthening ties: The influence of microtargeting on partisan attitudes and the vote*, in *Party Politics*, first Published April 23, 2020.

Lazar, N.C. (2009), *States of emergency in liberal democracies*, Cambridge, Cambridge University Press.

Lee, F.E. (2015a), *How Party Polarization Affects Governance*, in *Annual Review of Political Science*, 18, pp. 261–282.

Lee, J.M. (2015b), *Assessing Mass Opinion Polarization in the US Using Relative Distribution Method*, in *Social Indicators Research*, 124, 2, pp. 571–598

Leibholtz, G. (1958), *Strukturprobleme der modernen Demokratie*, Müller, Karlsruhe.

Levinson, S., Balkin, J.M. (2010), *Constitutional dictatorship: Its dangers and its design*, in *Minnesota Law Review*, 94, pp. 1789–1866.

Levitsky, S., Way, L.A. (2002), *Elections without democracy: The rise of competitive authoritarianism*, in *Journal of Democracy*, 13, 2, 2002, pp. 51–65.

Levitsky, S., Way, L.A. (2010), *Competitive authoritarianism: Hybrid regimes after the Cold War*, Cambridge, Cambridge University Press.

Levitsky, S., Ziblatt, D. (2018), *How Democracies Die*, New York, Crown Publishers.

Levy, J.D. (2017), *The return of the state? France's response to the financial and economic crisis*, in *Comparative European Politics*, 15, 4, 2017, pp. 604–627.

Levy, J.T. (2021), *The Separation of Powers and the Challenge to Constitutional Democracy*, in *Review of Constitutional Studies*, Vol. 25, n.1. pp. 1–18.

Lieberman, R.C., Mettler, S., Pepinsky, T.B., Roberts, K.M., Valelly, R. (2019), *The Trump presidency and American democracy: a historical and comparative analysis*, in *Perspectives on Politics*, 17, 2, pp. 470–479.

Lijphart, A. (1968), *The politics of accommodation: Pluralism and democracy in the Netherlands*, Berkeley, University of California Press.

Lijphart, A. (1977), *Democracy in Plural Societies*, New Haven, Yale University Press.

Lijphart, A. (1984), *Democracies: Patterns of Majoritarian and Consensus Government in Twenty-One Countries*, New Haven, Yale University Press.

Lijphart, A. (1999), *Patterns of Democracy: Government Forms and Performance in Thirty-Six Countries*, New Haven, Yale University Press.

Lilleker, D., Coman, I.A., Gregor, M., Novelli, E., (eds.), (2021), *Political Communication and COVID-19: Governance and Rhetoric in Times of Crisis*, London, Routledge.

Linder, W., Mueller, S. (2021), *Swiss democracy: Possible solutions to conflict in multicultural societies*, Cham, Palgrave.

Linz, J.J., Valenzuela, A. (1994), *The Failure of Presidential democracy. Comparative Perspectives*, Baltimore, John Hopkins University Press.

Lipset, S.M. (1963), *The first new nation: The United States in historical and comparative perspective*, New York, Basic Books.

Lipset, S.M., Rokkan, S. (1967), *Party Systems and Voter Alignments*, New York, Free Press.

Loft, P., Apostolova, V. (2017), *Acts and Statutory Instruments: the volume of UK legislation 1950 to 2016*, available at https://commonslibrary.parliament.uk/research-briefings/cbp-7438/.

López Guerra, L.M., Blanco Valdés, R.L., Pérez Francesch, J.L., Monreal Ferrer, A.L. (2000), *División de poderes: el gobierno*, Barcellona, Institut de Ciències Polítiques i Socials.

Loughlin, M. (2019), *The Contemporary Crisis of Constitutional Democracy*, in *Oxford Journal of Legal Studies*, 39, 2, pp. 435–454.

Lowi, T.J. (1979), *The End of Liberalism: The Second Republic of the US*, New York, W.W. Norton and Co.

Lowi, T.J. (1985), *The Personal President. Power Invested, Promise Unfulfilled*, Ithaca, Cornell University Press.

Lowi, T.J. (2009), *A New American State, and Four Different Roosevelts*, in T.J. Lowi and N.K. Nicholson (eds.), *Arenas of Power*, Boulder, Paradigm, pp. 111–125.

Lowi, T.J., Ginsberg, B., Shepsle, K.A., Ansolabehere, S. (2017), *American government: Power and purpose*, New York, Norton.

Lucardie, P. (2000), *Prophets, purifiers and prolocutors: Towards a theory on the emergence of new parties*, in *Party Politics*, 6, 2, pp. 175–185.

Lupo, N. (2006), *Emendamenti, maxi-emendamenti e questione di fiducia nelle legislature del maggioritario*, in E. Gianfrancesco and N. Lupo (eds.), *Le regole del diritto parlamentare nella dialettica tra maggioranza e opposizione. Atti del convegno, 17 marzo 2006*, Roma, Luiss University Press.

Lupu, N. (2015), *Party Polarization and Mass Partisanship: A Comparative Perspective*, in *Political Behavior*, 37, 2, pp. 331–356.

Maccanico, A. (2018), *Il tramonto della repubblica dei partiti. Diari 1985–1989*, Bologna, Il Mulino.

Mackintosh, J.P. (1970), *The Government and Politics of Britain*, London, Hutchinson.

Maeda, K. (2010), *Two modes of democratic breakdown: A competing risks analysis of democratic durability*, in *The Journal of Politics*, 72, 4, pp. 1129–1143.

Mainwaring, S., Gervasoni, C., España-Najera, A. (2017), *Extra-and within-system electoral volatility*, in *Party Politics*, 23, 6, pp. 623–635.

Mainwaring, S., Shugart, M.S., Matthew S. (1997), *Juan Linz, presidentialism, and democracy: a critical appraisal*, in *Comparative Politics*, 29, 4, pp. 449–471.

Mainwaring, S., Zoco, E. (2007), *Political Sequences and the Stabilization of Interparty Competition: Electoral Volatility in Old and New Democracies*, in *Party Politics*, 13, 2, pp. 155–178.

Mair, P. (1984), *Party Politics in Contemporary Europe: A Challenge to Party*, in *West European Politics* 7, 4, pp. 170–183.

Mair, P. (1997), *On the Freezing of Party Systems*, in P. Mair, *Party System Change: Approaches and Interpretations*, Oxford, Oxford University Press, pp. 3–16.

Mair, P. (2005), *Democracy Beyond Parties*, in *Center for the Study of Democracy*, eScholarship Repository, University of California, available at http://repositories.cdlib.org/csd/05–06.

Mair, P. (2013), *Ruling the void: The hollowing of Western democracy*, New York, Verso Trade.

Mandák, F. (2015), *Signs of Presidentialization in Hungarian Government Reforms – Changes After the New Fundamental Law*, in S. Zoltán, F. Mandáka and Z. Fejes (eds.), *Challenges and Pitfalls in the Recent Hungarian Constitutional Development. Discussing the New Fundamental Law of Hungary*, Paris, L'Harmattan, pp. 148–168.

Manin, B. (1997), *The principles of representative government*, Cambridge, Cambridge University Press.

Mansfield, H.C. (1989), *Taming the Prince: the Ambivalence of Modern Executive Power*, New York, The Free Press.

Marangoni, F. (2012), *Technocrats in government: The composition and legislative initiatives of the Monti government eight months into its term of office*, in *Bulletin of Italian politics*, 4, 1, pp. 135–149.

Margetts, H. (2006), *Cyber Parties*, in R.S. Katz and W.J. Crotty (eds.), *Handbook of Party Politics*, London, Sage, pp. 528–535.

Marsh, M. (2007), *Candidates or Parties?: Objects of Electoral Choice in Ireland*, in *Party Politics*, 13, 4, pp. 500–527.

Mayer, K.R. (1999), *Executive Orders and Presidential Power*, in *Journal of Politics*, 61, 2, pp. 445–466.

Mayer, K.R. (2001), *With the Stroke of a Pen*, Princeton, Princeton University Press.

Mayer, K.R., Price, K. (2002), *Unilateral Presidential Powers: Significant Executive Orders, 1949–1999*, in *Presidential Studies Quarterly*, 32, pp. 367–386.

McAllister, I. (2007), *The Personalization of Politics*, in R.J. Dalton, H.D. Klingemann (eds.), *The Oxford Handbook of Political Behavior*, Oxford, Oxford University Press, New York, pp. 571–588.

McCormick, R., Tollison, R. (1981), *Politicians, Legislation, and the Economy: An Inquiry into the Interest Group Theory of Government*, Boston, Martinus Nijhoff.

McCoy, J., Rahman, T., Somer, M. (2018), *Polarization and the Global Crisis of Democracy: Common Patterns, Dynamics, and Pernicious Consequences for Democratic Polities*, in *American Behavioral Scientist*, 62, 1, pp. 16–42.

McCoy, K.W. (2018), *Lawmaking by Decree?: Executive Orders and the Growth of Legislative Power*, in *Modern Presidential Administrations*, Arizona State University, 5, pp. 1–41.

McKechnie, D.B. (2017), *@potus: Rethinking presidential immunity in the time of twitter*, in *University of Miami Law Review*, 72, 1, pp. 1–33.

Metcalf, L.K. (2000), *Measuring Presidential Power*, in *Comparative Political Studies*, 33, 5, pp. 660–685.

Metz, M., Kruikemeier, S., Lecheler, S. (2020), *Personalization of politics on Facebook: Examining the content and effects of professional, emotional and private self-personalization*, in *Information, Communication & Society*, 23, 10, pp. 1481–1498.

Michels, R. (1962 [1911]), *Political Parties. A Sociological Study of the Oligarchical Tendencies of Modern Democracy*, New York, Collier Books.

Miglio, G. (1984), *Le contraddizioni interne del sistema parlamentare-integrale*, in *Italian Political Science Review/Rivista Italiana di Scienza Politica*, 14, 2, pp. 209–222.

Mikuli, P. (2021), *Separation of Powers*, in *Max Planck Encyclopedia of Comparative Constitutional Law*, Oxford, Oxford University Press.

Milewicz, K.M. (2020), *Constitutionalizing World Politics: The Logic of Democratic Power and the Unintended Consequences of International Treaty Making*, Cambridge, Cambridge University Press.

Milkis, S. (1993), *The president and the parties: The transformation of the American party system since the New Deal*, New York, Oxford University Press.

Milkis, S. (2011), *The American Presidency: Origins and Development*, Washington, CQ Press.

Modugno, F. (1996), *Riflessioni interlocutorie sulle conseguenze della trasformazione del decreto-legge*, in *Scritti in memoria di A. Piras*, Milano, Giuffrè.

Morlino, L. (1998), *Democracy Between Consolidation and Crisis. Parties, Groups, and Citizens in Southern Europe*, Oxford, Oxford University Press.

Morlino, L., Sorice, M. (eds.), (2021), *L'illusione della scelta. Come si manipola l'opinione pubblica in Italia*, Roma, Luiss University Press.

Mortati, C. (1973), *Brevi note sul rapporto fra costituzione e politica nel pensiero di Carl Schmitt*, in *Quaderni fiorentini per la storia del pensiero giuridico moderno*, 2, 1, pp. 511–532.

Mortati, C. (1973), *Le forme di governo. Lezioni*, Padova, Cedam.

Mortati, C. (1998 [1940]), *La Costituzione in senso materiale*, Milano, Giuffrè.

Mounk, Y. (2018), *Popolo vs Democrazia. Dalla cittadinanza alla dittatura elettorale*, Milano, Feltrinelli.

Mughan, A. (2000), *Media and the Presidentialization of Parliamentary Elections*, London, Palgrave.

Müller-Rommel, F. (2000), M*anagement of Politics in the German Chancellor's Office*, in B.P. Guy, R.A.W. Rhodes, V. Wright (eds.), *Administering the Summit. Administration of the Core Executive in Developed Countries*, Basingstoke, Palgrave, pp. 81–100.

Musella, F. (2012a), *Il Premier diviso. Italia tra parlamentarismo e presidenzialismo*, Milano, Bocconi.

Musella, F. (2012b), *Governare senza il Parlamento? L'uso dei decreti-legge nella lunga transizione italiana (1996–2012)*, in *Rivista Italiana di Scienza Politica*, 3, 2012, pp. 457–478.

Musella, F. (2014), *How personal parties change: party organisation and (in) discipline in Italy (1994–2013)*, in *Contemporary Italian Politics*, 6, 3, pp. 222–237.

Musella, F. (2018), *Political Leaders beyond Party Politics*, Cham, Palgrave.

Musella, F. (2019), *Constitutional Change in Presidentialised Regimes. Paths of Reform in Hungary and Italy*, in *DPCE Online*, 39, 2, http://www.dpceonline.it/index.php/dpceonline/article/view/740.

Musella, F. (ed.) (2019), *Il governo in Italia. Profili costituzionali e dinamiche politiche*, Bologna, Il Mulino.

Musella, F. (2020a), *I poteri d'emergenza nella Repubblica dei Presidenti*, in S. Staiano (ed.), *Nel Ventesimo anno del terzo millennio, Sistemi politici, istituzioni economiche e produzione del diritto al cospetto della pandemia da Covid-19*, Napoli, Editoriale Scientifica, pp. 701–721.

Musella, F. (2020b), *I poteri di emergenza nella Repubblica dei Presidenti*, in *Diritti regionali*, 2, 107–139.

Musella, F. (ed.) (2020c), *L'emergenza democratica. Presidenti, decreti, crisi pandemica*, Napoli, Editoriale Scientifica.

Musella, F. (2020d), *The Personalization of Italian Political Parties in Three Acts*, in *Contemporary Italian Politics*, 12, 4, pp. 411–424.

Musella, F., Vercesi, M. (2019), *Definitions and measures of party institutionalization in new personal politics: The case of the 5 star movement*, in *Zeitschrift für Vergleichende Politikwissenschaft*, 13, 2, pp. 225–247.

Musella, F., Webb, P. (2015), *The revolution of personal leaders*, in *Italian Political Science Review/Rivista Italania di Scienza Politi*ca, 45, 3, pp. 223–226.

Musella, F., Webb, P., (eds.), (2015), *The Personal Leader in Contemporary Party Politics*, special issue of *Rivista Italiana di Scienza Politica/Italian Political Science Review*, 45, 3.

Mushaben, J.M. (2016), *The Best of Times, the Worst of Times: Angela Merkel, the Grand Coalition, and "Majority Rule" in Germany*, in *German Politics and Society*, 34, 1, pp. 1–25.

Negrine, R., Lilleker, D.G. (2002), *The Professionalization of Political Communication: Continuities and Change in Media Practices*, in *European Journal of Communication*, 17, 3, pp. 305–23.

Neocleous, M. (2006), *The problem with normality: Taking exception to "permanent emergency*, in *Alternatives*, 31, 2, pp. 191–213.

Neumann, S. (1956), *Modern Political Parties. Approaches to Comparative Politics*, Chicago, University of Chicago Press.

Neustadt, R.E. (1990 [1960]), *Presidential power: The politics of leadership*, New York, Free Press.

Newell, J.L. (2018), *Silvio Berlusconi: A study in failure*, Manchester, Manchester University Press.

Niskanen, W. (1971), *Bureaucracy and Representative Government*, Chicago, Aldine-Atherton.

Norris, P. (2001), *Digital Divide: Civic Engagement, Information Poverty, and the Internet Worldwide*, Cambridge, Cambridge University Press.

North, D.C. (1985), *The growth of government in the United States: an economic historian's perspective*, in *Journal of Public Economics*, 28, 3, pp. 383–399.

Nunziata, F. (2021), *Il platform leader*, in *Rivista di Digital Politics*, 1, 1, pp. 127–146.

O'Brien, D.Z., Shomer, Y. (2013), *A Cross-National Analysis of Party Switching*, in *Legislative Studies Quarterly*, 38, 1, pp. 111–141.

O'Donnell, G.A. (1999), *Delegative Democracy*, in *Counterpoints: Selected Essays on Authoritarianism and Democratization*, Notre Dame, University of Notre Dame Press.

Ollier, M.M. (2011), *Centralidad Presidencial y Debilidad Institucional en las Democracias Delegativas*, in G. O'Donnell, O. Iazzetta, H. Quiroga (eds.), *Democracia Delegativa*, Buenos Aires, Prometeo, pp. 115–136.

Olson, W.J., Woll, A. (1999), *Executive Orders and National Emergencies: How Presidents Have Come to "Run the Country" by Usurping Legislative Power*, Cato Institute.

Onida, V. (2004), *Il mito delle riforme costituzionali*, in *Il Mulino*, 53, 1, pp. 15–29.

Ortega y Gasset, J. (1960), *The Revolt of the Masses*, New York, Norton.

Ostrogorskij, M.J. (1964), *Democracy and the Organization of Political Parties: The United States*, New Jersey, Transaction Publishers.

Ouyang, Y., Waterman, R.W. (2015), *How Legislative (In)Activity Impacts Executive Unilateralism: A Supply and Demand Theory of Presidential Unilateralism*, in *Congress & the Presidency*, 42, pp. 317–341

Padgett, S. (ed.), (1994), *Adenauer to Kohl. The Development of the German Chancellorship*, London, Hurst.

Pakulski, J., Körösényi, A. (2012), *Toward leader democracy*, London, Anthem Press.

Palanza, V. (2018), *Checking presidential power: executive decrees and the legislative process in new democracies*, Cambridge, Cambridge University Press.

Panebianco, A. (1988), *Political Parties: Organization and Power*, Cambridge, Cambridge University Press.

Papakyriakopoulos, O., Hegelich, S., Shahrezaye, J.C.M Serrano (2018), *Social media and microtargeting: Political data processing and the consequences for Germany*, in *Big Data & Society*, 5, 2, pp. 1–15.

Parmelee, J.H., Bichard, S.L. (2011), *Politics and the Twitter revolution: How tweets influence the relationship between political leaders and the public*, Rowman and Littlefield, Lexington.

Pasquino, G. (1997), *Semi-presidentialism. A Political Model at Work*, in *European Journal of Political Research*, 31, 1, pp. 128–137.

Pasquino, G. (2001), *Teorie della transizione e analisi del sistema politico: il caso italiano*, in *Italian Political Science Review/Rivista Italiana di Scienza Politica*, 31, 2, 2001, pp. 313–327.

Pasquino, G. (2014), *Italy: The Triumph of Personalist Parties*, in *Politics & Policy*, 42, 4, pp. 548–566.

Paye, J.C. (2006), *From the state of emergency to the permanent state of exception*, in *Telos*, 136, pp. 154–166.

Pedersen, M.N. (1979), *The dynamics of European party systems: changing patterns of electoral volatility*, in *European journal of political research*, 7, 1, pp. 1–26.

Peltzman, S. (1980), *The growth of government*, in *The Journal of Law and Economics*, 23, 2, pp. 209–287.

Pennings, P. (1997), *The politics of problem-solving in postwar democracies*, in *Consensus democracy and institutional change*, London, Palgrave Macmillan, pp. 21–42.

Pérez Sola, N. (2020), *El uso del decreto-ley por parte del gobierno español:¿ se ha roto el equilibrio entre legislativo y ejecutivo?*, in *Diritto Pubblico Europeo-Rassegna online*, 1, pp. 1–20, available at https://doi.org/10.6092/2421–0528/6719.

Pfiffner, J.P. (2017), *The unusual presidency of Donald Trump*, in *Political Insight*, 8, 2, pp. 9–11.

Pfiffner, J.P. (2018), *The contemporary presidency: Organizing the Trump presidency*, in *Presidential Studies Quarterly*, 48, 1, pp. 153–167.

Piccione, D. (2018), *Il Comitato per la legislazione e la cangiante natura dei decreti del Presidente del Consiglio dei Ministri*, in *federalismi.it*, 3, pp.1–14.

Pildes, R.H. (2014), *Romanticizing Democracy, Political Fragmentation, and the Decline of American Government*, in *Yale Law Journal*, 124, pp. 804–851.

Pinelli, C. (2009), *Un sistema parallelo. Decreti-legge e ordinanze d'urgenza nell'esperienza italiana*, in *Diritto pubblico*, 15, 2, pp. 317 – 338.

Pious, R.M. (1979), *The American Presidency*, New York, Basic Books.

Pious, R.M. (2007), *Inherent war and executive powers and prerogative politics*, in *Presidential Studies Quarterly*, 37, 1, pp. 66 – 84.

Pious, R.M. (2009), *Prerogative Power and Presidential Politics*, in *The Oxford Handbook of the American Presidency*, Oxford, Oxford University Press.

Pistone, S. (2004), *Ragion di Stato*, in N. Bobbio, N. Matteucci e G. Pasquino, *Dizionario di Politica*, Torino, Utet, pp. 793 – 800.

Poguntke, T. (2002), *Party Organizational Linkage: Parties without Firm Social Roots?*, in K.R. Luther, F. Müller-Rommel (eds.), *Political Parties in the New Europe*, Oxford, Oxford University Press, pp. 43 – 62.

Poguntke, T., Webb, P. (eds.), (2005), *The Presidentialization of Politics: A Comparative Study of Modern Democracies*, Oxford, Oxford University Press.

Polsby, N.W. (1983), *Some Landmarks in Modern Presidential-Congressional Relations*, in A. King (ed.), *Both Ends of the Avenue*, Washington, American Enterprise Institute, pp. 1 – 25.

Polsby, N.W. (1978), *Presidential cabinet making: Lessons for the political system*, in *Political Science Quarterly*, 93, 1, pp. 15 – 25.

Pomper, G.M. (1978), *The impact of the American voter on political science*, in *Political Science Quarterly*, 93, 4, pp. 617 – 628.

Poole, K.T., Rosenthal, H. (1984), *The Polarization of American Polities*, in *Journal of Politics*, 46, 4, pp. 1061 – 1079.

Posner, E.A., Vermeule, A. (2009), *Crisis governance in the administrative state: 9/11 and the financial meltdown of 2008*, in *The University of Chicago Law Review*, 76, 4, pp. 1613 – 1682.

Posner, E.A. (2015), *Presidential Leadership and the Separation of Powers*, in *University of Chicago Public Law & Legal Theory*, Working Paper No. 545.

Posner, E.A., Vermeule, A. (2011), *The Executive Unbound: after the Madisonian Republic*, Oxford, Oxford University Press.

Powell, G.B. (1982), *Contemporary Democracies: Participation, Stability, and Violence*, Cambridge, Harvard University Press.

Powell, G.B. (2010), *Party system polarization and ideological congruence: Causal mechanisms*, in *APSA 2010 Annual Meeting Paper*, available at SSRN: https://ssrn.com/abstract=1642786.

Prezorwski, A. (2019), *Crises of Democracy*, Cambridge, Cambridge University Press.

Protsyk, O. (2004), *Ruling with decrees: presidential decree making in Russia and Ukraine*, in *Europe-Asia Studies*, 56, 5, pp. 637 – 660.

Pryce, S. (1997), *Presidentializing the Premiership: The Prime Ministerial Advisory System and the Constitution*, New York, Springer.

Puddington, A. (2017), *Breaking Down Democracy: Goals, Strategies, and Methods of Modern Authoritarians*, (Freedom House, June 2017), archived at http://perma.cc/DCK4-VVLL.

Pünder, H. (2009), *Democratic Legitimation of Delegated Legislation – A Comparative View on the American, British and German Law*, in *International & Comparative Law Quarterly*, 58, 2, pp. 353 – 378.

Quiroga, H. (2011), *Parecidos de Familia. La Democracia Delegativa y el Decisionismo Democrático*, in G. O'Donnell, O. Iazzetta, H. Quiroga (eds.), *Democracia Delegativa*, Buenos Aires, Prometeo, pp. 35–52

Raffiotta, E.C. (2020), *Norme d'ordinanza. Contributo alla teoria delle ordinanze emergenziali come fonti normative*, Bologna, Il Mulino,

Ragsdale, L., Theis, J.J. (1997), *The Institutionalization of the American Presidency, 1924–1992*, in *American Journal of Political Science*, 41, 4, pp. 1280–1318.

Rahat, G., Kenig, O. (2018), *From party politics to personalized politics? Party change and political personalization in democracies*, Oxford, Oxford University Press.

Rayment, E., Vanden Beukel, J. (2020), *Pandemic Parliaments: Canadian Legislatures in a Time of Crisis*, in *Canadian Journal of Political Science/Revue canadienne de science politique*, 53, 2, pp. 379–384.

Reda, V. (2011), *I sondaggi dei presidenti. Governi e umori dell'opinione pubblica*, Milano, Bocconi.

Regalia, M. (2018), *Electoral reform as an engine of party system change in Italy*, in *South European Society and Politics*, 23, 1, pp. 81–96.

Rhodes-Purdy, M., Madrid, R.L. (2020), *The perils of personalism*, in *Democratization*, 27, 2, pp. 321–339.

Rhodes, R.A.W. (2006), *Executives in parliamentary government*, in S.A. Binder, R.A.W. Rhodes and B.A. Rockman (eds.), *The Oxford Handbook of Political Institutions*, Oxford, Oxford University Press, pp. 323–343.

Riggs, F.W. (1997), *Presidentialism versus parliamentarism: Implications for representativeness and legitimacy*, in *International Political Science Review*, 18, 3, pp. 253–278.

Robinson, J.A., Acemoglu, D. (2012), *Why nations fail: The origins of power, prosperity and poverty*, London, Profile.

Robinson, N. (2003), *The Politics of Russia's Partial Democracy*, in *Political Studies Review*, 1, 2, pp. 149–166.

Rodon, T., Hierro, M.J. (2016), *Podemos and Ciudadanos shake up the Spanish party system: The 2015 local and regional elections*, in *South European Society and Politics*, 21, 3, pp. 339–357.

Rodríguez Gutiérrez, F.J. (2011), *El Decreto-Ley como instrumento ordinario de gobierno en Andalucía*, in *Revista general de derecho constitucional*, 11, pp. 8–38.

Rodríguez-Teruel, J. (2020), *Executive Politics in Spain*, in D. Muro and I. Lago (eds.), *The Oxford Handbook of Spanish Politics*, Oxford, Oxford University Press, pp. 190–209.

Rodríguez-Teruel, J., Barberà, O., Barrio, A., Casal-Bértoa, F. (2018), *From stability to change? The evolution of the party system in Spain*, in M. Lisi (ed.), *Party System Change, the European Crisis and the State of Democracy*, Basingstoke, Routledge, pp. 248–270.

Rolla, G. (2015), *Profili costituzionali dell'emergenza*, in *Rivista AIC*, 2, pp. 1–26.

Ronga, U. (2020), *Il Governo nell'emergenza "permanente": le modalità della produzione normativa*, in S. Staiano (ed.), *Nel ventesimo anno del terzo millennio. Sistemi politici, istituzioni economiche e produzione del diritto al cospetto della pandemia da Covid-19*, Napoli, Editoriale Scientifica, pp. 45–92.

Rottinghaus, B., Warber, A.L. (2015), *Unilateral Orders as Constituency Outreach: Executive Orders, Proclamations, and the Public Presidency*, in *Presidential Studies Quarterly*, 45, pp. 289–309.

Roots, R.I. (2000), *Government by Permanent Emergency: The Forgotten History of the New Deal Constitution*, in *Suffolk University Law Review*, 33, 2, pp. 259–292.

Rossiter, C. (1948), *Constitutional dictatorship: crisis government in the modern democracies*, Princeton, Princeton University Press.

Roth, G. (1987), *Politische Herrschaft und persönliche Freiheit. Heidelberger Max Weber-Vorlesungen 1983*, Part I: Charisma und Patrimonialismus, Frankfurt, Suhrkamp Verlag.

Rudalevige, A. (2012), *The contemporary presidency: Executive orders and presidential unilateralism*, in Presidential Studies Quarterly, 42, 1, pp. 138–160.

Rudalevige, A. (2016), *The contemporary Presidency: The Obama administrative presidency: Some late-term patterns*, in *Presidential Studies Quarterly*, 46, 4, pp. 868–890.

Rufai, S.R., Catey, B. (2020), *World leaders' usage of Twitter in response to the COVID-19 pandemic: a content analysis*, in *Journal of Public Health*, 42, 3, pp. 510–516.

Rullo, L. (2021), *The COVID-19 pandemic crisis and the personalization of the government in Italy*, in *International Journal of Public Leadership*, 17, 2, pp. 196–207.

Rullo, L., Nunziata, F. (2021), *Sometimes the Crisis Makes the Leader? A Comparison of Giuseppe Conte digital communication before and during the COVID-19 pandemic*, in *Comunicazione Politica*, forthcoming.

Ruscio, K.P. (2004), *The Leadership Dilemma in Modern Democracy*, London, Edward Elgar Publishing.

Russell, M., Serban, R. (2020), *The muddle of the 'Westminster Model': a concept stretched beyond repair*, in *Government and Opposition*, pp. 1–21, published online 27 July.

Rutledge, P.E. (2020), *Trump, COVID-19, and the War on Expertise*, in *The American Review of Public Administration*, 50, 6–7, pp. 505–511.

Ryfe, D.M. (1999), *Franklin Roosevelt and The Fireside Chats*, in *Journal of Communication*, 49, 4, pp. 80–103.

Sabine, G.H. (1961 [1937]), *A History of Political Theory*, New York, Holt, Rinehart and Winston.

Sadecki, A. (2014), *In a state of necessity. How has Orbàn changed Hungary*, Ośrodek Studiów Wschodnich im Marka Karpia, Centre for Eastern Studies.

Saiegh, S.M. (2009), *Political prowess or "Lady Luck"? Evaluating chief executives' legislative success rates*, in *The Journal of Politics*, 71, 4, pp. 1342–1356.

Samuels, D.J., Shugart, M.S. (2010). *Presidents, Parties, and Prime Ministers: How the Separation of Powers Affects Party Organization and Behavior*, Cambridge, Cambridge University Press.

Sànchez-Pomed, L. (2020), *Las elecciones del 28 de abril (y 26 de mayo): reflexiones sobre la forma de gobierno y sobre el sistema de partidos*, in *Diritto Pubblico Europeo Rassegna online*, 1.

Sartori, G. (1966), *European Political Parties: The Case of Polarized Pluralism*, in J. LaPalombara and M. Weiner (eds.), *Political Parties and Political Development*, Princeton, Princeton University Press, pp. 137–176

Sartori, G. (1968), *Representational Systems*, in D.L. Sills (ed.), *International Encyclopedia of the Social Sciences*, New York, Macmillan Free Press, Vol. 13, pp. 470–475.

Sartori, G. (1972), *Appunti per una teoria generale della dittatura*, in K. von Beyme (ed.), *Theorie und Politik*, Den Haag, Martinus Nijhoff, pp. 456–485.

Sartori, G. (1976), *Parties and party system*, Cambridge, Cambridge University Press.

Sartori, G. (1979), *Opinione Pubblica*, in *Enciclopedia del Novecento*, Roma, Treccani.

Sartori, G. (1987), *Democracy Theory Revisited*, Chatham, Chatham House.

Sartori, G. (1991), *Comparing and miscomparing*, in *Journal of theoretical politics*, 3, 3, pp. 243–257.

Sartori, G. (1994), *Ingegneria costituzionale comparata*, Bologna, Il Mulino.

Sartori, G. (1997), *Comparative Constitutional Engineering: An Inquiry Into Structures, Incentives and Outcomes*, New York, New York University Press.

Sata, R., Karolewski, I.P. (2020), *Caesarean politics in Hungary and Poland*, in *East European Politics*, 36, 2, pp. 206–225.

Schattschneider, E.E. (1942), *Party Government*, New Brunswick, Transaction Publisher.

Schedler, A., (ed.), (2006), *Electoral Authoritarianism: The Dynamics of Unfree Competition*, Boulder, Lynne Rienner.

Schenkaan, N., Repucci, S. (2019), *The Freedom House Survey for 2018: Democracy in Retreat*, in *Journal of Democracy*, 30, 2, pp. 100–114.

Scheppele, K.L. (2005), *Small emergencies*, in *Georgia Law Review*, 40, pp. 835–862.

Scheppele, K.L. (2006), *North American emergencies: The use of emergency powers in Canada and the United States*, in *International Journal of Constitutional Law*, 4, 2, pp. 213–243.

Scheppele, K.L. (2008), *Legal and extralegal emergencies*, in K.E. Whittington, R.D. Kelemen, G.A. Caldeira, (eds.), *The Oxford handbook of law and politics*, Oxford, Oxford University Press, pp. 165–184.

Scheppele, K.L. (2018), *Autocratic legalism*, in *The University of Chicago Law Review*, 85, 2, pp. 545–584.

Scheuerman, W.E. (2012), *Emergencies, Executive Power, and the Uncertain Future of US Presidential Democracy*, in *Law & Social Inquiry*, 37, 3, pp. 743–767.

Schlesinger, A.M. (1973), *The Imperial Presidency*, Boston, Houghton Mifflin.

Schmitt, C. (1972), *Le categorie del politico: saggi di teoria politica*, Bologna, Il Mulino.

Schmitt, C. (2014), *Die Diktatur. Von den Anfängen des modernen Souveränitätsgedankens bis zum proletarischen Klassenkampf*, Berlin, Duncker & Humblot, 1921; translated in C. Schmitt, *Dictatorship*, New York, John Wiley & Sons.

Schmitt, H. (2014), *Partisanship in nine western democracies*, in Bartle, J., Bellucci, P. (eds.), *Political Parties and Partisanship: Social Identity and Individual Attitudes*, New York, Routledge, pp. 97–109.

Schumpeter, J.A. (1942), *Capitalism, Socialism and Democracy*, New York, Harper & Row.

Schurmann, F. (2002), *Emergency Powers. The New Paradigm in Democratic America*, in *New California Media*, 23.

Segal, J.A., Spaeth, H.J., Benesh, S.C. (2005), *The Supreme Court in the American legal system*, Cambridge, Cambridge University Press.

Shane, P.M. (2009), *Madison's nightmare: How executive power threatens American democracy*, Chicago, University of Chicago Press.

Shanto, I., Westwood, S.J. (2015), *Fear and Loathing across Party Lines: New Evidence on Group Polarization*, in *American Journal of Political Science*, 59, 3, pp. 690–707.

Shevtsova, L. (2000), *The Problem of Executive Power in Russia*, in *Journal of Democracy*, 11, 1, pp. 32–39.

Shugart, M.S., Carey, J.M. (1992), *Presidents and assemblies: Constitutional design and electoral dynamics*, Cambridge, Cambridge University Press.

Siegel, S.N. (2018), *Political Norms, Constitutional Conventions, and President Donald Trump*, in *Indiana Law Journal*, 93, pp. 177–205.

Siewert, M.B., Wurster, S., Messerschmidt, L., Cheng, C., Büthe, T. (2020), *A German Miracle? Crisis Management During The COVID-19 Pandemic In A Multi-Level System*, in *Executives, presidents and cabinet politics (PEX)*, https://pex-network.com/, June 25.

Sikk, A. (2005), *How unstable? Volatility and the genuinely new parties in Eastern Europe*, in *European Journal of Political Research*, 44, 3, 391–412

Simoncini, A. (2006), *L'emergenza infinita: la decretazione d'urgenza in Italia*, Macerata, EUM.

Smolka, T. (2021), *Decline of democracy – the European Union at a crossroad*, in *Zeitschrift für Vergleichende Politikwissenschaft*, 1, 25, pp. 81–105.

Soren, J., Bowling, C.J. (2017), *Introduction: The State of Polarization in the States*, in *State & Local Government Review*, 48, 4, pp. 220–226.

Spitzer, R. (1988), *The Presidential Veto: Touchstone of the American Presidency*, Albany, State University of New York Press.

Staffan L., (ed.), (2009), *Democratization by Elections: A New Mode of Transition*, Baltimore, Johns Hopkins University Press.

Staiano, S. (2005), *Brevi note su un ossimoro: l'emergenza stabilizzata*, in *Giurisprudenza costituzionale e principi fondamentali: alla ricerca del nucleo duro delle costituzioni*, Atti del Convegno annuale del Gruppo di Pisa, Capri 3–4 giugno 2005, Torino, Giappichelli, pp. 649–661.

Staiano, S. (2019), *La forma di governo nella Costituzione come norma e come processo*, in F. Musella (ed.), *Il governo in Italia. Profili costituzionali e dinamiche politiche*, Bologna, Il Mulino, pp. 29–70.

Stanyer, J. (2013), *Intimate politics: Publicity, privacy and the personal lives of politicians in media saturated democracies*, New York, John Wiley & Sons.

Steel, R.W. (1981), *Il polso del popolo. Franklin D. Roosevelt e la misurazione dell'opinione pubblica americana*, in M. Vaudagna, *Il New Deal*, Bologna, il Mulino, pp. 237–247.

Stepan, A., Skach, C. (1993), *Constitutional Frameworks and Democratic Consolidation: Parliamentarianism versus Presidentialism*, in *World Politics*, 46, 1, pp. 1–22.

Steven, E.S. (2017), *The Trump presidency: Outsider in the oval office*, Lanham, Rowman & Littlefield.

Stoppino, M. (2004), *Dittatura*, in N. Bobbio, N. Matteucci e G. Pasquino, *Dizionario di Politica*, Torino, Utet, pp. 288–297.

Stromer-Galley, J. (2020), *Presidential campaigning in the Internet age*, Oxford, Oxford University Press.

Sunstein, C. (2018), *Can It Happen Here? Authoritarianism in America*, New York, HarperCollins.

Suphan, A., Veverka, J. (1963), *The growth of government expenditure in Germany since the unification*, in *FinanzArchiv/Public Finance Analysis*, 23, 2, pp. 169–278.

Szente, Z. Mandák, F., Fejes, Z. (2015), *Challenges and Pitfalls in the Recent Hungarian Constitutional Development*, Paris, Éditions L'Harmattan.

Taras, D., Davis, R., (eds.), (2019), *Power Shift? Political Leadership and Social Media: Case Studies in Political Communication*, London, Routledge.

Tatalovich, R., Schiern, S.E. (eds.), (2014), *The Presidency and Political Science. Paradigms of presidential power from the founding fathers to the present*, London, Routledge.

Teodoldi, L. (ed.), (2019), *Il Presidente del Consiglio dei ministri dallo Stato liberale all'Unione Europea*, Milano, Biblion.

Thies, M.F. (2000), *On the primacy of party in government: Why legislative parties can survive party decline in the electorate*, in R.J. Dalton and M.P. Wattenberg (eds.), *Parties Without Partisans?: Political Change in Advanced Industrial Democracies*, Oxford, Oxford University Press, pp. 238–257.

Thomas, P. (2020), *Parliament Under Pressure: Evaluating Parliament's Performance in Response to COVID-19*, in *The Samara Centre for Democracy*, 2 April, https://www.samar acanada.com/democracy-monitor/parliament-under-pressure.

Thomassen, J. (ed.), (2005), *The European voter: a comparative study of modern democracies*, Oxford, Oxford University Press.

Thrower, S. (2018), *Calling the Shots: The President, Executive Orders, and Public Policy*, in *Political Science Quarterly*, 133, 4, pp. 781–784.

Triepel, H. (1927), *Die Staatsverfassung und die politischen Parteien*, Berlin, Humboldt-Universität zu Berlin.

Triepel, H. (1967), *Verfassungsrecht und Verfassungswirklichkeit*, in K. Lenk and F. Neumann (eds.), *Theorie und Soziologie der politischen Parteien/Theory andSociology of political parties*, Neuwied am Rhein, Hermann Luchterhand Verlag.

Tripodina, C. (2020), *La Costituzione al tempo di Coronavirus*, in *Costituzionalismo.it*, 1, www.costituzionalismo.it

Troisi, M. (2019), *Il governo nelle decisioni della Corte costituzionale*, in F. Musella (ed.), *Il governo in Italia. Profili costituzionali e dinamiche politiche*, Bologna, Il Mulino, pp. 95–122.

Tsebelis, G., Rasch, B.E. (2011), *Governments and legislative agenda setting: an introduction.The Role of Governments in Legislative Agenda setting*, London, Routledge, pp. 1–20.

Tulis, J.K. (1987), *The Rethorical Presidency*, Princeton, Princeton University Press.

Turner, B.S. (2001), *Charisma and Charismatic*, in N.J. Smelser, P.B. Baltes (eds.), *International encyclopedia of the social & behavioral sciences*, 11, Amsterdam, Elsevier, pp. 1651–1653.

Tuttnauer, O. (2020), *Government-opposition relations in a fragmented, personalized, and multidimensional setting: The case of Israel*, in *Party Politics*, 26, 2, pp. 203–214.

Uitz, R. (2015), *Can you tell when an illiberal democracy is in the making? An appeal to comparative constitutional scholarship from Hungary*, in *I-CON*, 13, 1, 279–300.

Urbinati, N. (2019), *Me the people: How populism transforms democracy*, Cambridge, Harvard University Press.

Valbruzzi, M. (2020), *Regno Unito: un premierato personalizzato alla prova della pandemia*, in F. Musella, *L'emergenza democratica. Presidenti, decreti, crisi pandemica*, Napoli, Editoriale Scientifica, pp. 199–260.

Valenzuela, A., Linz, J. (eds.), (1994), *The Failure of Presidential Democracy*, Baltimore, Johns Hopkins University Press.

Van Aelst, P., Sheafer, T., Stanyer, J. (2011), *The personalization of mediated political communication: A review of concepts, operationalizations and key findings*, in *Journalism*, 13, 2, pp. 203–220.

Van Biezen, I., Mair, P., Poguntke, T. (2012), *Going, Going, … Gone? The Decline of Party Membership in Contemporary Europe*, in *European Journal of Political Research*, 51, 1, pp. 24–56.

Van Dijck, J., Poell, T., De Waal, M. (2018), *The platform society: Public values in a connective world*, Oxford, Oxford University Press.

Van Haute, E. (2011), *Party membership: and under-studied mode of political participation*, in E. Van Haute (ed.), *Party Membership in Europe: Explorations into the Anthills of Party Politics*, Bruxelles, Université de Bruxelles, pp. 7–22.

Van Haute, E., Paulis, E., Sierens, V. (2018), *Assessing party membership figures: the MAPP dataset*, in *European political science*, 17, 3, pp. 366–377.

Vanoni, L.P., Baraggia, A. (2017), *Dividing Powers. A Theory of the Separation of Powers*, Padova, Wolters Kluwer.

Várnagy, R., Ilonszki, G. (2018), *Opposition Parties in European Legislatures: Conflict or Consensus?*, London, Routledge.

Vedaschi, A., (2020), *Il Covid-19, l'ultimo stress test per gli ordinamenti democratici: uno sguardo comparato*, in *DPCE online*, 2, 2020, pp. 1453–1489.

Ventura, S. (2009), *Nicolas Sarkozy: l'"iperpresidenza" e la riforma delle istituzioni*, in *Quaderni costituzionali*, 29, 1, pp. 143–163.

Vercesi, M. (2020), *L'autonomia decisionale del cancelliere tedesco tra resistenza istituzionale e gestione della crisi*, in F. Musella (ed.), *L'emergenza democratica. Presidenti, decreti, crisi pandemica*, Napoli, Editoriale Scientifica, pp. 89–131.

Verzichelli, L. (1996a), *I gruppi parlamentari dopo il 1994: fluidità e riaggregazioni*, in *Rivista Italiana di Scienza Politica*, 26, 2, pp. 391–413.

Verzichelli, L. (1996b), *La classe politica della transizione*, in *Italian Political Science Review/ Rivista Italiana di Scienza Politica*, 26, 3, pp. 727–768.

Vile, M.J.C. (1967), *Constitutionalism and the Separation of Powers*, Oxford, Oxford University Press.

Vittoria, A. (2020), *Il Presidente francese: ancora un "monarque républicain"?*, in F. Musella (ed.), *L'emergenza democratica. Presidenti, decreti, crisi pandemica*, Napoli, Editoriale Scientifica, pp. 261–302.

Vittoria, A. (2021), *La presidenza Macron. Tra populismo e tecnocrazia*, Milano, Mimesis.

Volcansek, M. (1999), *Constitutional politics in Italy*, London, Palgrave.

Volpi, M. (1997), *Le forme di governo contemporanee tra modelli teorici ed esperienze reali*, in *Quaderni costituzionali*, 17, 2, 1997, pp. 247–282.

von Beyme, K. (2011), *Government*, in B. Badie, D. Berg-Schlosser, L. Morlino (eds.), *International Encyclopedia of Political Science*, London, Sage, pp. 1036–1042.

Waldron, J. (2012), *Separation of Powers or Division of Power?*, in *NYU School of Law, Public Law Research Paper*, 12, 20, pp. 1–33.

Wang C.H. (2014), *The effects of party fractionalization and party polarization on democracy*, in *Party Politics*, 20, 5, pp. 687–699.

Warber, A.L. (2006), *Executive orders and the modern presidency: Legislating from the oval office*, Boulder, Lynne Rienner Publishers.

Warber, A.L. (2014), *Public Outreach, Executive Orders, and the Unilateral Presidency*, in *Congress & the Presidency*, 41, pp. 269–288.

Warber, A.L., Ouyang, Y., Waterman, R.W. (2018), *Landmark executive orders: Presidential leadership through unilateral action*, in *Presidential Studies Quarterly*, 48, 1, pp. 110–126.

Waslin, M. (2020), *The use of executive orders and proclamations to create immigration policy: Trump in historical perspective*, in *Journal on Migration and Human Security*, 8, 1, pp. 54–67.

Wattenberg, M.P. (1984), *The decline of American political parties, 1952–1984*, Cambridge, Harvard University Press.

Wattenberg, M.P. (2009). *The decline of American political parties, 1952–1996*, Cambridge, Harvard University Press.

Wauters, B., Bouteca, N., de Vet, B. (2021), *Personalization of parliamentary behaviour: conceptualization and empirical evidence from Belgium (1995–2014)*, in *Party Politics*, 27, 2, pp. 246–257.

Webb, P. (2005), *Political parties and democracy: The ambiguous crisis*, in *Democratization*, 12, 5, pp. 633–650.

Webb, P., Poguntke, T. (2013), *The presidentialisation of politics thesis defended*, in *Parliamentary Affairs*, 66, 3, 2013, pp. 646–654.

Webb, P., Poguntke, T., Kolodny, R. (2012), *The presidentialization of party leadership? Evaluating party leadership and party government in the democratic world*, in *Comparative political leadership*, London, Palgrave Macmillan, pp. 77–98.

Weber, M. (1947 [1922]), *Theory of Social and Economic Organization*, Trans. A.R. Anderson, P. Talcott, London/New York, Oxford University Press.

Whiteley, P.F. (2011), *Is the party over? The decline of party activism and membership across the democratic world*, in *Party Politics*, 17, 1, pp. 21–44.

Wilson, W. (1908), *Constitutional Government in the United States*, New York, Columbia University Press.

Wodak, R. (2020), *Crisis communication and crisis management during COVID-19*, in *Global Discourse: An interdisciplinary journal of current affairs*, published online, February 15.

Wood, B.D. (2009), *The Myth of Presidential Representation*, Cambridge, Cambridge University Press.

Woolley, S.C., Howard, P.N. (eds.), (2018), *Computational propaganda: political parties, politicians, and political manipulation on social media*, Oxford, Oxford University Press.

Zeno-Zencovich, V. (2020), *Introduction*, in A. Baraggia, C. Fasone, P.L. Vanoni, (eds.), *New challenges to the separation of powers: dividing power*, Cheltenham, Edward Elgar Publishing, pp. 1–5.

Zucco, C., Power, T.J. (2020), *Fragmentation Without Cleavages? Endogenous Fractionalization in the Brazilian Party System*, in *Comparative Politics*, first online 4th August.

Index

https://doi.org/10.1515/9783110721720-010

www.ingramcontent.com/pod-product-compliance
Lightning Source LLC
Chambersburg PA
CBHW070345270326
41926CB00017B/3987